ENGLISH GRAMMAR DIGEST

Trudy Aronson
Cambria English Institute

Prentice-Hall, Inc., Englewood Cliffs, New Jersey 07632

Library of Congress Cataloging in Publication Data

Aronson, Trudy.
   English grammar digest.

   Includes index.
   1.   English language—Text-books for foreign speakers.
   2.   English language—Grammar—1950-   I.   Title.
PE1128.A68 1984   428.2′4   83-13952
ISBN 0-13-281014-X

Editorial/production supervision and
   interior design: Kate Kelly
Cover design: 20/20 Services, Inc., Mark Berghash
Manufacturing buyer: Harry Baisley

Printed in the United States of America

10   9   8   7   6   5   4   3   2   1

ISBN 0-13-281014-X

PRENTICE-HALL INTERNATIONAL, INC., *London*
PRENTICE-HALL OF AUSTRALIA PTY. LIMITED, *Sydney*
EDITORA PRENTICE-HALL DO BRASIL, LTDA., *Rio de Janeiro*
Prentice-Hall Canada Inc., *Toronto*
Prentice-Hall of India Private Limited, *New Delhi*
Prentice-Hall of Japan, Inc., *Tokyo*
Prentice-Hall of Southeast Asia Pte. Ltd., *Singapore*
Whitehall Books Limited, *Wellington, New Zealand*

TO SYDNEY, CAROL, RICHARD, JANET, ZOBI, AND LUKE

CONTENTS

Seven
PARTS OF SPEECH   82

PREFACE

The English Grammar Digest is an intensive review course in grammar and in writing structure for intermediate and advanced students of English as a Second Language. The book has been designed to promote good sentence construction and writing habits and to prepare students for the "Structure and Written Expressions" section of the TOEFL, a college or university qualifying English test which measures knowledge of standard English.

The text progresses developmentally from grammatical structures to proper forms in sentence writing. Included are succinct, easily understood explanations; numerous examples that serve as models and reinforcement; firm reminders to avoid typical errors; contrasts and comparisons of structures; oral and writing reinforcement; and a variety of exercises including progressively-complex TOEFL-type tests plus five full simulated TOEFL tests on "Structure and Written Expression."

In the Supplement of the book are the principal parts of irregular verbs; common errors in word usage; and a considerable number of popular idioms and two-word verbs illustrated by examples.

The book is intended for class and independent study and may be used in either short-term or long-term courses. Answers to the tests and references to the explanations are on perforated pages in the back of the book.

TO THE TEACHER

There is no single approach or absolute chronology in the use of this book. The procedure will inevitably vary, depending on the time allowed for the course, the course itself, and the nature of the class. Since both aural and visual approaches are effective, we recommend, after the initial presentation, reading selected material aloud as the students follow, emphasizing points and answering questions as they arise. Students may then be assigned to review the material and to prepare for the exercises and tests. Teachers of short-term courses can cover a relatively large number of grammar points at each class session and can assign large portions for independent study and review. The graphic nature of the explanations and examples facilitates home reinforcement. Section tests, too, may be assigned as homework wherein the need for specific areas of review will become quickly apparent to the student.

Any exercise may be oral, written, or both; omitted or included; executed and corrected at home or in class. It must be emphasized that all of the grammar and writing points in the book, including those dealing with less common forms, are important in preparation for the TOEFL. Questions on the simulated TOEFL tests are deliberately complex in preparation for the actual tests.

Teachers, particularly those of longer-term courses, may choose to have their students remove either all or a part of the perforated answer pages, returning them to the students at a later date. For writing improvement we suggest that teachers require their students to do all of the written exercises, to write complete answers to the oral exercises, and to initiate sentences of their own, patterning them after the modeled examples. For the oral exercises, "Practice Asking and Answering Questions Such as the Following," teachers may wish to pair students for classroom practice in order to promote correct usage in speaking as well as in writing.

The pretest, given initially to apprise students of the kind of knowledge they will need, should be given again at the end of the course with the four other simulated TOEFL tests.

TO THE STUDENT

Carefully study each section of the book, including the Supplement, until you thoroughly understand and become familiar with the material presented. Make use of the index and the table of contents to find specific subject matter. The goal to strive for is, of course, to apply what you have learned. It is advisable to examine the sentence examples in the book for their construction, vocabulary, idioms, and expressions as well as for their grammatical structures. Any words that you don't understand should be looked up in a dictionary.

We hope that you will retain the English Grammar Digest as a reference book, referring to it freely and repeatedly, and that the book will continue to benefit you in your pursuit of good English usage.

ACKNOWLEDGMENTS

I wish to thank Dean de La Peña and Director Fimbres of the Cambria English Institute in Los Angeles for the opportunity to develop an intensive review course in grammar and writing structure preparatory to college and university classes and preparatory to taking the TOEFL and other qualifying English tests.

Trudy Aronson

PRETEST

STRUCTURE AND WRITTEN EXPRESSION

Time—25 minutes

Directions: In sentences 1–15 select the word or phrase that best completes the sentence and, with your pencil, fill in the circle marked A, B, C, or D, as in the example below.

Peter's jacket cost _____ Jack's.   Ⓐ Ⓑ Ⓒ Ⓓ
(A) twice more than
(B) two times more as
(C) twice as much as
(D) twice more as
The correct answer above is (C).

1. None of the clocks in the old section of the city work anymore, but they _____
   perfectly.   Ⓐ Ⓑ Ⓒ Ⓓ
   (A) were used to work
   (B) were used to working
   (C) use to work
   (D) used to work

2. Some waterspouts _____ begin over the water and, with great speed, move
   towards the shore.   Ⓐ Ⓑ Ⓒ Ⓓ
   (A) alike some hurricanes
   (B) like some hurricanes
   (C) are like some hurricanes
   (D) which they are like some hurricanes

3. In the zoo there was _____ .   Ⓐ Ⓑ Ⓒ Ⓓ
   (A) a hundred-years-old elephant
   (B) hundred-year-old elephant
   (C) a hundred-years-aged elephant
   (D) a hundred-year-old elephant

4. The governor has repeatedly stated that, before he leaves office, he _____ balance the budget.   Ⓐ Ⓑ Ⓒ Ⓓ
   (A) would like
   (B) had wanted to
   (C) would like to
   (D) likes to

5. Behavioral scientists say that it is essential that an infant _____ loving attention.   Ⓐ Ⓑ Ⓒ Ⓓ
   (A) be given
   (B) is given
   (C) should be given
   (D) receives

6. The microphone went dead while the narrator _____ the cast.   Ⓐ Ⓑ Ⓒ Ⓓ
   (A) was introduced
   (B) was introducing
   (C) has been introducing
   (D) had introduced

7. _____ , the students placed their pencils on their desks and left the room.
   (A) Being finished the test   Ⓐ Ⓑ Ⓒ Ⓓ
   (B) All the test now being over
   (C) Before the bell's ringing
   (D) Having completed the test

8. In the morning the streets were flooded. There _____ a cloudburst during the night.   Ⓐ Ⓑ Ⓒ Ⓓ
   (A) must have been
   (B) has been
   (C) must be
   (D) must to been

9. Although the city is small, its library is as complete _____ .   Ⓐ Ⓑ Ⓒ Ⓓ
   (A) as a large city
   (B) like a large city
   (C) as that of a large city
   (D) like larger cities

10. The transportation director favors repairing existing highway systems _____ new highways.   Ⓐ Ⓑ Ⓒ Ⓓ
    (A) rather than to build
    (B) instead of to build
    (C) instead to build
    (D) rather than building

11. Before Matisse, the famous French artist, _____ his own style of painting, he had painted in the classical style.   Ⓐ Ⓑ Ⓒ Ⓓ
    (A) developed
    (B) had developed
    (C) was develop
    (D) will have developed

12. Daniel Webster, _____ for his brilliant oratory, made his most famous speech in the Senate in 1830. Ⓐ Ⓑ Ⓒ Ⓓ
    (A) who was knowing
    (B) known
    (C) was known
    (D) having known

13. Can you tell me _____ ? Ⓐ Ⓑ Ⓒ Ⓓ
    (A) who Babe Ruth was
    (B) who was Babe Ruth
    (C) whom Babe Ruth was
    (D) whom was Babe Ruth

14. North America produces a great deal more wheat _____ . Ⓐ Ⓑ Ⓒ Ⓓ
    (A) as South America
    (B) than does South America
    (C) like South America does
    (D) than like South America

15. Most doctors agree that exercise improves the circulation of the blood; _____ there are doctors who believe that excessive exercise may do some damage. Ⓐ Ⓑ Ⓒ Ⓓ
    (A) on the contrary
    (B) otherwise
    (C) on the other hand
    (D) therefore

Directions: In questions 16–40 select the underlined word or phrase that is _not_ acceptable in standard written English and fill in the circle marked A, B, C, or D, as in the example below.

Keeping clean is surely one of the most important rule of good hygiene. Ⓐ Ⓑ Ⓒ Ⓓ
  A   B   C   D
The correct answer above is (D).

16. Nobody had the opportunity during the course of several meetings to express
                                   A
    their opinion on the subject of increased taxes. Ⓐ Ⓑ Ⓒ Ⓓ
      B   C   D

17. Some art connoisseurs have remarked that Picasso was more versatile than
                  A   B   C
    any artist. Ⓐ Ⓑ Ⓒ Ⓓ
      D

18. Rarely are animals products, such as meat, milk, or eggs, sold directly to
          A   B   C
    the consumer. Ⓐ Ⓑ Ⓒ Ⓓ
        D

19. The traffic's noise is becoming a problem to the Smiths, accustomed as they
          A   B   C   D
    are to the peacefulness of country life. Ⓐ Ⓑ Ⓒ Ⓓ

20. The article stating the state Supreme Court had overturned the decision made
          A   B   C
    by the lower court on the issue of high-rise construction.   Ⓐ Ⓑ Ⓒ Ⓓ
    D

21. The winner had indeed demonstrated remarkable reserves of energy, which
                  A
    was apparently available to him at the crucial time.   Ⓐ Ⓑ Ⓒ Ⓓ
      B   C   D

22. A diamond, used not only in jewelry but in industrial cutting devices, is one of
             A   B   C
    nature's hardest substances.   Ⓐ Ⓑ Ⓒ Ⓓ
    D

23. In a corporation it is usual the chairman who presides over meetings.
               A B   C   D   Ⓐ Ⓑ Ⓒ Ⓓ

24. Having worked with the elderly for several years, Mrs. Jones knows how impor-
             A   B
    tant it is to behave kindly and with thoughtfulness towards them.   Ⓐ Ⓑ Ⓒ Ⓓ
    C   D

25. The photosynthesis process, which plants absorb carbon dioxide and release
                             A   B
    oxygen, is just the opposite of that of man.   Ⓐ Ⓑ Ⓒ Ⓓ
                        C   D

26. Although Ponce de Leon didn't find the "Fountain of Youth" which he
    had sought but he did discover a beautiful area of land named Florida.
         A   B   C   D   Ⓐ Ⓑ Ⓒ Ⓓ

27. Those who shop regularly for food and clothing generally they are aware of
        A   B   C   D
    quality and prices.   Ⓐ Ⓑ Ⓒ Ⓓ

28. It was King Louis XIV who had the magnificent Palace of Versailles build;
                                                                A
    however, the cost was so great that the people of France were angered.
        B   C   D
                                                           Ⓐ Ⓑ Ⓒ Ⓓ

29. The people of Pakistan, which land is quite mountainous, are nevertheless pri-
                            A   B   C   D
    marily farmers.   Ⓐ Ⓑ Ⓒ Ⓓ

30. Much of the forest, along with the farmland, near the Mount Saint Helens vol-
       A   B
    cano, appears to be destroyed at the time of the eruption.   Ⓐ Ⓑ Ⓒ Ⓓ
         C   D

31. Of the two suspension bridges in Northern California, the Bay Bridge, not the
         A
    Golden Gate bridge, is the largest.   Ⓐ Ⓑ Ⓒ Ⓓ
        B   C   D

32. The man avoided, by turning suddenly into a driveway, to hit the child riding a
                          A   B   C
    tricycle across the street.   Ⓐ Ⓑ Ⓒ Ⓓ
        D

33. The inventor found himself laying awake at night in an effort to understand the
            A   B   C   D
    error in his design.   Ⓐ Ⓑ Ⓒ Ⓓ

34. Naturally, one would not suspect that people like ourselves would neglect
     A   B   C

    to vote in an election.   Ⓐ ⒷＣ Ⓓ
     D

35. Vaslav Nijinsky was the Polish ballet dancer leaped remarkable heights into the
                      A   B   C   D

    air.   Ⓐ Ⓑ Ｃ Ⓓ

36. Predicting a shortage of young workers in the near future, unemployment and
           A   B   C

    low wages are expected to decrease, researchers say.   Ⓐ Ⓑ Ⓒ Ⓓ
                 D

37. The reason that the building industry declined was because the interest rate on
               A   B   C

    loans was so high.   Ⓐ Ⓑ Ⓒ Ⓓ
         D

38. Children should be given immunizing injections in order to prevent them catch-
             A   B   C

    ing some of the serious diseases.   Ⓐ Ⓑ Ⓒ Ⓓ
           D

39. If Keats didn't die at the young age of 26, he might have become England's
            A   B   C   D

    greatest lyric poet.   Ⓐ Ⓑ Ⓒ Ⓓ

40. We found the food in the Thai restaurant to be quite different than that in the
       A   B   C   D

    Vietnamese restaurant.   Ⓐ Ⓑ Ⓒ Ⓓ

One
TENSES

Present Tense

The *present tense* is used to express a general truth or fact. The action often occurs **regularly or habitually**. Generally the present tense verb conveys a sense of permanence. (Notice, in the following examples, that the verb agrees with the subject.)

1. The X.X. Company *employs* a staff of forty engineers.
2. As in other languages, changes in English *continue* to occur.
3. Four times a year, the department heads *attend* a conference.
4. Homonyms *sound* alike buy they *don't have* the same meaning.
5. A gothic arch *is* one which *rises* to a point.
6. Kenji and Alain never *miss* their weekly bridge game.
7. The Chans *aren't* home today. They're at their studio.
8. I *understand* that there *are* about 16,000 kinds of butterflies in the world.
9. Whenever the science class students *have* time, they *like* to look at the slides of earlier field trips.
10. If (or: when) one travels to other countries, one learns about other cultures. (or: one will learn about other cultures).

NOTE: Sometimes *will* plus the root verb is used to describe an expected customary result. Compare:
When one listens, one learns a lot.
When one listens, one will learn a lot.

Present tense is also used for direct commands, requests, and suggestions.

(You) *Open* your books and turn to page 81.
　　　　Willie, (you) *read* your essay please.
(You) *Try* to swim with your eyes open.

Frequency Adverbs With Present Tense

Some frequency adverbs are: *frequently, usually, sometimes, generally, always, occasionally, often, never, seldom, rarely*. Notice the placement in the following sentences. These adverbs are usually before the "action" verb but after the "be" verb.

1. Students *often have* difficulty deciding on a major.

2. Many of the club members *are seldom* at the meetings.
3. A shrewd politician *generally understands* psychological distinctions.

NOTE: The following adverbs are already negative in sense, so you do not use a negative
form with them: never, seldom, rarely, scarcely, hardly, barely.
(wrong):   (He doesn't seldom smile.)
RIGHT: He *seldom smiles.*

Do not confuse adverbs of measure with adverbs of frequency. Adverbs of measure refer to
"how much" and express an insufficiency or some difficulty (scarcely, hardly, barely, all
similar in meaning). Frequency adverbs refer to "how often" (never, seldom, rarely).

(wrong):   (He scarcely attends class.)
RIGHT: He *rarely* attends class.
RIGHT: Because of his hearing loss, he *scarcely* hears me when I speak.

The following sentences illustrate the use and placement of frequency adverbs with negative
constructions. Notice that the frequency adverbs are placed before the contraction, with the
exception of *always.*

The history lectures in Room 22 *sometimes aren't* interesting.
They *generally don't retire* before midnight.
He *doesn't always leave* before six o'clock. Sometimes he works until seven o'clock.

Avoid the following kinds of errors:
(wrong):   (She complains that he doesn't sometimes listen to her.)
RIGHT: She complains that he *sometimes doesn't listen* to her.
(wrong):   (Mr. Moto often go on business trips.)
RIGHT: Mr. Moto often *goes* on business trips.
(wrong):   Although Rhode Island is the smallest state in the United States, it don't have
the fewest number of people.)
RIGHT: Although Rhode Island is the smallest state in the United States, it *doesn't have*
the fewest number of people.
(wrong):   (Kevin is never forgetting to send birthday cards to his friends.)
RIGHT: Kevin *never forgets* to send birthday cards to his friends.
(wrong):   (Mrs. Rossi has thirty years.)
RIGHT: Mrs. Rossi *is thirty.* Mrs. Rossi is *thirty years old.* Mrs. Rossi is *thirty years of age.* Mrs.
Rossi is *a thirty-year-old woman.*
(wrong):   (There is still people in California who searches for gold.)
RIGHT: There *are* still people in California who *search* for gold.
(wrong):   (The poor man isn't hardly able to walk.)
RIGHT: The poor man *is hardly* able to walk.

Modals and Other Expressions in Present Time

Modals are auxiliaries which add meaning to the verb. Frequently they are used in a present tense sense; that is, they are used to express statements of general truth and habitual

action. The headings below classify the modals and *expressions* according to their general meaning. Modals are: *can, could, may, might, shall, should, will, would, must, need.*

Necessity and Requirement

1. One *must obey* the laws of the country in which he or she resides.
2. Every night the performers *must be* in the theater by 7:00 P.M.
3. At most public swimming pools people *have to take* a shower before entering the pool.
4. For good nutrition, one *needs* a balanced diet.

No Necessity

1. People *don't need* a lot of money in order to be happy.
2. Gretchen *doesn't have to work* Saturdays.

Assumption: "Probably True"

Must and *must not* are frequently used to mean that one logically assumes or concludes something.

1. Mrs. Lindbloom is absent today; she *must be* ill.
2. Shuo always gets excellent grades. He *must study* hard every night.
3. I no longer see Miss Prinz in the reception room. She *must not work* there anymore.

Expectation or Advisability

1. People *should return* things that they borrow.
2. Joe *shouldn't practice* his drums after 10:00 P.M.
3. News announcers *ought to be* objective when they report the news.
4. He *is supposed to remain* in bed for at least one week.
5. If one doesn't want to gain weight, one *had better eat* low-calorie food.

Possibility: "Perhaps" or "Perhaps Not"

1. The doctor *may not be* in; he *may not work* on Wednesdays.
2. That store *may* or *may not sell* stamps; I'm not sure.
3. Ginny seems quiet today. She *might (or: may) be* worried about something.

Permission: No Permission

1. In this park people *may (or: can) cook* food if they want to.
2. According to health regulations, individuals *can't take* pets into markets.
3. State laws say that hunters *must not kill* deer out of season.

Ability; Inability

"Know How To" "Not Know How To"; "Be Able To" "Not Be Able To"; "Can" "Cannot"

1. Eli *knows how to* play bridge but his brother *doesn't know how to* play bridge.
2. A rhinoceros *isn't able* to see well but it *is able* to run fast.
3. Minoru *can write* English well but he *can't* speak it well.

Avoid the following kinds of errors:

(wrong):   (Clarissa should think her mother is wise because she frequently asks her mother
            xxxxxxxxxxxxxxxxx
            for advice.)

RIGHT: Clarissa *must think* her mother is wise because she frequently asks her mother for advice.

(wrong):   (Every day Mrs. Tuch must to examine the receipts.)
            xxxxxxxxxxxxxxxxxxxxxxxxx

RIGHT: Every day Mrs. Tuch *must examine* the receipts.

(wrong):   (Everyone suppose to put the book on the shelf when he is through.
            xxxxxxxxxxxxx

RIGHT: Everyone *is supposed to* put the book on the shelf when he is through.

Present Continuous

The *present continuous tense* is used to express action that the subject is currently in the process of or in the middle of doing. The present continuous conveys **a temporary sense;** the action is expected to cease within a few minutes, a few hours, a week, a month, a period, a term, a semester, etc.

auxiliary *be* **+** *-ing* form of the verb (present participle)

Compare:

Present Tense: Dr. Newsom *teaches* physics.
Present Continuous Tense: Dr. Newsom *is teaching* physics this period.

Clues such as the following are often used with the present continuous: *Look! Listen! right now, this period, today, this week, at the present time, currently, at this moment, for the time being, temporarily.*

1. **Listen!** Won Yong *is singing* a folk song from his native land.
2. Please don't disturb her. She*'s sleeping.*
3. Tom*'s taking* a course in chemistry **this semester.**
4. **At the present time,** the flight attendants *are negotiating* a contract.
5. What program *are* you *watching?*
6. Is anyone *using* the telephone?
7. Ms. Mora *is* a ski instructor but **currently** she*'s selling* shoes.
8. The students who *are taking* the test right now *are being* very careful not to make any errors.

NOTE: Being, the present participle of *be,* is used in judging behavior:
      At this moment, she is being careful (silly; patient, careless, foolish, etc.).

---

9. Don't you think they*'re being* foolish to worry about it at this time?
10. I*'m not teaching* **this month.** I*'m working* on a special project.
11. She prefers a place of her own; **for the time being,** however, she *is staying* with her aunt.

NOTE: When the emphasis is on the subject's whereabouts, put the present participle (*-ing* form) after the place.

---

12. Richard *is* in the sound studio *recording* music.
13. Peter*'s* in the laboratory **at this time** *injecting* the mice with the new vaccine.
14. Some designers *are* in Paris **this month** *viewing* this year's collection.
15. Last term Veronica was in Mr. Vernon's class but **this term** she*'s* in Mr. Mack's class *learning* how to construct scenery.

EXCEPTION: The following verbs generally do *not* express an ongoing or continuous action. They express a state of mind, ownership, or the senses: *know, understand, believe, remember, think, love, hate, like, prefer, appreciate, need, want; own, have, possess, belong, cost, owe; see, notice, recognize, perceive, seem, appear (seem), look like, resemble, hear, smell, taste.*

The child resembles his father.
This soup that you made tastes delicious.
The red sweater belongs to Myrna.
Listen! I hear a train.

Avoid the following kinds of errors:

(wrong):   (Sammy can't come with us today because he completes his assignment.)

RIGHT: Sammy can't come with us today because he's *completing* his assignment.

(wrong):   (My sisters, Sylvia, Conny, and Bea, visit me this week.)

RIGHT: My sisters, Sylvia, Conny, and Bea, *are visiting* me this week.

(wrong):   (Mr. Stern is in his office dictate a letter.)

RIGHT: Mr Stern *is* in his office *dictating* a letter.

(wrong):   (Wisely, Patty isn't believing everything she reads in the newspaper.)

RIGHT: Wisely, Patty *doesn't believe* everything she reads in the newspaper.

(wrong):   (You may go into the baby's room. She doesn't sleep now.)

RIGHT: You may go into the baby's room. She *isn't sleeping now.*

Modals in Continuous Form

Modals (and other expressions) can be used in a continuous form to express the continuing, ongoing nature of the action.

modal **+** *be* **+** *-ing* form of the verb

1. Let's go see the wild flowers. They *should be blooming* now.
2. Ornithologists are careful not to disturb rare birds that *might be sitting* on their eggs.
3. Computers are so sophisticated today that people *must be wondering* what will come next.
4. The guard *is supposed to be* inside *protecting* the building.
5. I'd rather not visit them now; they *might* (or *may*) *be eating* dinner.
6. I'm not sure where Mrs. Ngoc is, but she *could be* in the film lab *developing* some photographs.

Avoid the following kinds of errors:

(wrong):   (Irma can't fall asleep. She may worry about the test tomorrow.)

RIGHT: Irma can't fall asleep. She *may be worrying* about the test tomorrow.

(wrong):   (Instead of spending his whole salary, he ought to saving some of it.)

RIGHT: Instead of spending his whole salary, he *ought to be saving* some of it.

EXERCISE I. 1.

The structure in the parentheses is incorrect. Write the correct form.

1. Todd (don't have) a car, so he (is taking) a train home on weekends.
2. Whenever Harry (have) free time, he (like) to work on model ships.
3. The chairman (prepares) a speech today for the company meeting.
4. Professor Pomerane (scarcely) misses a class, even though he (writes) a book this year.
5. The postman looks like a snowman. It (must snow) heavily outside.
6. I (can't hardly) see! The wind (blows) hard and the sand (gets) in my eyes.
7. In our class there (is) people from many different countries; therefore our teacher (is planning, usually) the lessons carefully.

8. Gemma (should ~~to~~ be) working on the project with John but she's in the recreation room (plays) ping-pong.
9. Ken (has) only (thirteen years) but he (is appearing) older.
10. Although Eli (don't know) to draw very well, he (is having) an excellent sense of color.

EXERCISE I. 2.

Practice asking and answering the following questions. Answer in complete sentences.

1. What do you usually do in the evenings?
2. What television programs do you watch on a regular basis?
3. What are you doing now?
4. What are you supposed to be doing?
5. What subjects are you taking this term?
6. What kind of sports do you know how to play?
7. What kind of a person do you admire?
8. Where are you staying this year?

Present Perfect

The *present perfect tense* refers to a time period from some point in the past to the present time.

have or *has* **+** *the past participle* of the verb.

There are **two** types of present perfect action:

1. Action that begins in the past and continues to the present.
    The Waltons *have owned* a toy store for seventeen years.
2. Action that is completed before the present.
    My niece Barbara *has bought* a new car.

Words often used to show continued action from the past to the present are: *since, for, up to the present, until now, so far, for the past hour, for the past few days, in a long time, for a short time, in quite a while, all day, all week, lately.*

NOTE: Use *for* to show duration of time. (Sometimes the word *for* is implied; that is, it is understood but not stated.)

She has lived in the United States *for* six years.
She has lived in the United States six years.

NOTE: Use *since* in a phrase or a clause to show when the action began.

He has studied English *since September.* (phrase)
He has studied English *since he arrived.* (The past tense is used in the "*since* clause.")

Below are examples of the *present perfect tense* describing *continued action* **from the past to the present.**

1. Marvin and Hal *have worked* together as partners **for twelve years.**
2. **How long have** you *taken* music lessons?
3. **Since he graduated from college,** he's (he has) *attended* every reunion.

4. **So far,** they*'ve enjoyed* the biology class very much.
5. **For the past few nights** he *has slept* on the floor.
6. Miss Arnoff *hasn't taught* the physics class **in a long time.**
7. **Lately,** the company *has had* financial problems.

(The above examples may also be in the present perfect continuous tense. See PRESENT PERFECT CONTINUOUS).

Avoid the following kinds of errors:

    (wrong):   (They are in the same class the past three years.)
                   xxxxx
    RIGHT: They *have been* in the same class the past three years.
    (wrong):   (Perhaps the animal is ill; it didn't eat anything since Monday.)
                             xxxxxxxxxxxxxx
    RIGHT: Perhaps the animal is ill; it *hasn't eaten* anything since Monday.

Below are examples of the *present perfect tense* describing **action completed at some point from the past to the present.** Unlike the past tense, the action has no association with the time it took place. We are not told (nor is it implied) when the action occurred; the time of the action is unimportant. The intention is simply to state that an action took place one or more times; often it is implied that the action may occur again in the future. (Although the action is actually past, this form is commonly used in affiliation with present time.) Words commonly used are: *many times, several times, once, twice, three times* etc., *ever, finally, just, already, recently.* The words *not, never, still,* and *yet* are used with the negative. Frequently we use present perfect with superlative degree adjectives (best, funniest, the most exciting etc.).

1. Claudia has the smallest camera I *have ever seen.*
2. The Smiths are fortunate because they *have* **already** *found* an apartment (*or*: they *have found* an apartment **already**).
3. Logan *has studied* music but he *has* **never** *been* inside of a concert hall.
4. Computers *have become* smaller and easier to use.
√5. They *have eaten* in that garden restaurant **many times.**
6. Engineers *have* **just** *repaired* one of the damaged bridges.
7. There are a number of national parks that we **still** *haven't visited.*
8. *Have* you *flown* on a plane only once?
9. I believe that Joel *has* **finally** *reached* a decision.
10. Mr. Yves *has* **just** *received* an offer for a job but he *hasn't decided* what to do about it **yet** (*or*: he *hasn't* **yet** *decided* what to do about it).

Avoid the following kinds of errors:

    (wrong):   (Cora was never in a foreign country.)
                     xxxxxxxxxxxxx
    RIGHT: Cora *has never been* in a foreign country.
    (wrong):   (She works there for a long time.)
                     xxxxxxxx
    RIGHT: She *has worked* there for a long time.
    (wrong):   (Mr. Moore has took a leave of absence.)
                        xxxxxx
    RIGHT: Mr. Moore has *taken* a leave of absence.
    (wrong):   (He has the most interesting collection of coins we ever saw.)
                                              xxxxxxxxxxxx
    RIGHT: He has the most interesting collection of coins we *have ever seen.*
    (wrong):   (Since he has joined the group, he performed as a soloist.)
                    xxxxxxxxxxxxxxx   xxxxxxxxxxxxxx
    RIGHT: Since he joined the group, he *has performed* as a soloist.
    (wrong):   (When have you been in Alaska?)
                    xxxxxxxxxxxxxxxxxxxx

RIGHT: When *were* you in Alaska?
(wrong):   (So far the girls didn't miss a single class.)
           xxxxxxxxxxxxxxx
RIGHT: So far the girls *haven't missed* a single class.
(wrong):   (In what year have you begun to study law?)
           xxxxxxxxxxxxxxxxxxxxxxxx
RIGHT: In what year *did you begin* to study law?

Present Perfect Continuous

The *present perfect continuous* **emphasizes the continuing sense of the action from an earlier time to the present.**

aux. *have been* or *has been* **+** *-ing* form of the verb
It *has been raining* in London since our arrival.

(Or: It has rained in London since our arrival.) (Either the present perfect or present perfect continuous may be used when the verb expresses continued action from the past to the present.)

Length of time is mentioned or implied with present perfect continuous.

1. The church bells *have been ringing* **all morning**.
2. The finance committee *has been working* on its budget **for nearly a month**.
3. Because of poor sales, corporate profit *has been decreasing* **lately**.
4. Dennis may change his major because of the problems he*'s been having* in mathematics.
5. Armando and Cedric *have been* in the music library *listening* to some tapes.
6. The girls *haven't been arguing*. They*'ve been discussing* politics.

Avoid the following kinds of errors:

(wrong):   (Mikhail has been repairing his car a number of times.) not a continuing action
           xxxxxxxxxxxxxxxxxxxxxxxxxxx
RIGHT: Mikhail *has repaired* his car a number of times.
RIGHT: Mikhail *has been repairing* his car since 6:00 A.M. this morning.

Below is a synopsis of present and past-to-present time forms:

Permanent fact:	Debby can dance beautifully. She dances in shows.
Past to present:	Debby has danced in a musical show for two years.
Temporary:	Debby is dancing in a show in Dallas this week.
Past to present:	Debby has been dancing in a musical show five nights a week since I met her.
Completed action at points from past to present:	Debby has danced in musical shows hundreds of times.
(Past tense:)	(Debby danced in an award-winning show a year ago.)

EXERCISE I. 3.

Complete the following sentences. Use the present perfect and when appropriate, the present perfect continuous, of the verb in the parentheses.

1. For eight months I (take) _____ *have taken* an exercise class.
2. The college (offer) *has been offering* parent-education classes since June.
3. Brian (see) *has seen* the Statue of Liberty twice.
4. He's hungry because he (eat, not) *hasn't eaten* in seven hours.
5. Hugh, the bus driver, (receive, just) *received* an award for safe driving.
6. The last few years they (grow) _____ *have grown* their own vegetables.

7. They (visit) _~~have~~ visited_ the Butchart Gardens several times.
8. (Register, you) _Have you registered_ for the course yet?
9. Lately environmentalists (express) _have been expressing_ concern about the rapid development close to the national park.
10. Although Vito (be) _was_ here for a long time, he (forget, never) _has never forgotten_ the beauty and traditions of his homeland.

EXERCISE I. 4.

Practice asking and answering questions such as the following.

1. What have you been doing since I saw you last year?
2. How long have you been studying English?
3. Have you visited any interesting places recently?
4. What courses have you been taking?
5. What subjects have you taken in the past?
6. What are some adventures that you haven't experienced as yet?
7. Has your friend come to visit you?
8. What are some things that you feel you have accomplished?

MIXED EXERCISE 1. PART A

(Mixed Exercises are Toefl-type questions. They include questions pertaining to material from the beginning to the present point of progress.)
Fill in the circled letter that represents the *correct* form, as in 1. Before you answer each question, think about: clues, sentence logic, subject-verb agreement, etc. Be able to give the reason for your selection! Be able to explain why the other three are incorrect!

1. Since seven o'clock this morning, Mr. Yokota _____ in his garden.
   A   worked
   B   is working
   C   has been working   Ⓐ Ⓑ Ⓒ Ⓓ
   D   works

2. The law requires employers to pay the wages that they _____ .   Ⓐ Ⓑ Ⓒ Ⓓ
   A   owes
   B   are owing
   C   have owned
   D   owe

3. There is a warning to stay away from the machinery while it _____ .
   A   spin
   B   is spinning
   C   has been spinning   Ⓐ Ⓑ Ⓒ Ⓓ
   D   is spin

4. After a month of rain, forecasters are predicting fine weather. People _____ relieved.
                                                                        Ⓐ Ⓑ Ⓒ Ⓓ
   A   may feeling
   B   must be feeling
   C   must to feel
   D   must feeling

5. The pilots must need a rest; they _____ from a long flight.   Ⓐ Ⓑ Ⓒ Ⓓ
   A   have just returned
   B   returned just
   C   have return
   D   have just been returning

6. Have you noticed that the planet Venus _____ exceptionally bright the past few nights?
                                                                        Ⓐ Ⓑ Ⓒ Ⓓ
   A   is being
   B   had
   C   has been
   D   is been

7. Our cactus plant _____ magnificent flowers once a year.   Ⓐ Ⓑ Ⓒ ⓓ
    A   is been producing   C   have produced
    B   producing   D   produces

8. Mr. Sims is in the newspaper room _____ to find a particular article.
    A   trying   C   tries   Ⓐ Ⓑ Ⓒ Ⓓ
    B   try   D   he's trying

9. The accountants are examining the new calculators but they _____ financial
    matters.   Ⓐ Ⓑ Ⓒ Ⓓ
    A   should to discuss   C   are supposed to be discussing
    B   supposed to discuss   D   must be discussing

10. Ever since Picasso's paintings went on exhibit, there _____ large crowds at
    the museum every day.   Ⓐ Ⓑ Ⓒ Ⓓ
    A   is   C   has been
    B   have been   D   are being

MIXED EXERCISE 1: PART B

Fill in the circled letter that represents the *incorrect* form, as in 1. Before you answer each question, think about: clues, sentence logic, subject–verb agreement, etc. Be able to explain why the word or phrase you have chosen is not acceptable and how you can correct it.

1. Although the tickets have just went on sale, the students are rushing to buy
                       A   B   C   D
    them.   Ⓐ Ⓑ Ⓒ Ⓓ
2. Emanuel being careful not to make grammatical errors while he's writing his
                A   B   C   D
    composition.   Ⓐ Ⓑ Ⓒ Ⓓ
3. His English is excellent because he has been speaking English since he has
                A   B   C
    been a boy of twelve.
     D   Ⓐ Ⓑ Ⓒ Ⓓ
4. The plants in their garden looks unhealthy because they haven't had enough
                  A   B   C
    sunlight.
     D   Ⓐ Ⓑ Ⓒ Ⓓ
5. Whenever the days are very warm, the animals in the wild animal zoo aren't
     A   B   C
    seldom active.
     D   Ⓐ Ⓑ Ⓒ Ⓓ
6. Jareonta, the student who makes a speech right now, is majoring in drama and
                                 A   B   C
    hopes some day to become a great actress.
          D   Ⓐ Ⓑ Ⓒ Ⓓ
7. Apparently the plant manager has left the country. He may be in Europe negoti-
                             A   B
    ate a contract.
     C D   Ⓐ Ⓑ Ⓒ Ⓓ
8. Even though the bankers are still arranging the loan, the architect prepares the
                             A   B   C
    building plans.
     D   Ⓐ Ⓑ Ⓒ Ⓓ

9. Although the doctor is <u>usually</u> available <u>for office visits</u>, he <u>isn't sometimes</u> <u>able</u>
                          A   B   C   D

    to make house calls.   Ⓐ Ⓑ Ⓒ Ⓓ

10. When disasters <u>occur</u> in local communities, it <u>is</u> the students who <u>have been</u>
                     A   B

    <u>agreeing</u> to help <u>again and again.</u>
       C   D   Ⓐ Ⓑ Ⓒ Ⓓ

PAST TIME FORMS

Past Tense

The *past tense* is used to express a completed action which took place at a specified time in the past. The specified time is either stated or implied.

Stated: Our friends *were* late for the concert last night.

Implied: Our friends were late for the concert. (*The concert* refers to a special event. A special event is understood to be held at a specific time.)

NOTE: More than one past tense may be used in a sentence when the actions occurred in the past at the same time.

---

1. When Alice *lost* her puppy, she *cried.*
2. The Wymans *attended* the art auction but they *didn't buy* any of the paintings.
3. Historians believe that the Chinese *invented* glasses about 2,400 years ago.
4. As soon as the actress *began* to speak, everyone *applauded.*
5. When the institution *ran* daily counseling sessions, absenteeism *decreased* significantly.
6. Last week the commissioner *had to attend* five meetings which *took place* consecutively.
7. At the conclusion of the exhibition, the scientist *indicated* that the dolphins *were able to distinguish* certain commands.
8. When my father was a young man, he *could ride* a horse as expertly as a cowboy.
9. Mrs. Siegel *knew how to speak* Chinese years ago but she has forgotten how.

NOTE: In the case of achieving a goal, use "be able to," *not* "could."
         Steve applied everywhere and finally he *was able to get* a good job.
         (wrong): (Steve applied everywhere and finally he could get a good job.)
                                          xxxxxxxxxxxxx

Used to and *would* are used to refer to **frequently repeated action in the past.** *Used to* implies "not anymore."

    When I was a child, I *used to ice skate.*
    When Kuang saw a beautiful sunset, he *would watch* it until it disappeared.
    There *used to be* bluebirds in the northeast region but they disappeared some years ago.
    Every time Elsie heard a particular song, she *would become* sad.

NOTE: Don't confuse <u>used to</u> with <u>be used to</u>, <u>become used to</u>, or <u>get used to.</u> The last three expressions refer to activity to which one has become accustomed, that is, a customary, comfortable activity. Any tense may be used.

Ted doesn't mind getting up at 4:00 a.m. because he *is used to* it.

At first Betty was afraid of driving on the freeways but she finally *has become used to* it (*or: has gotten used to it*).

Use past tense when referring to the deceased.

Unfortunately, their dog Peppy, which *was* a cocker spaniel, was killed last week.

Present and past auxiliary verbs *do, does,* and *did* are sometimes used in statements for emphasis.

I agree with you. You *do* have a good reason for being angry.

Judy thinks that Donald doesn't like her, but he *does* like her.

She certainly *did* persist in presenting her opinion.

Avoid the following kinds of errors:

(wrong):   (The earliest immigrants have come to America for religious freedom.)

RIGHT: The earliest immigrants *came* to America for religious freedom.

(wrong):   (She didn't go out last night because she has a headache.)

RIGHT: She didn't go out last night because she *had* a headache.

(wrong):   (Although she is no longer living, we think of her as a woman who has great courage and kindness.)

RIGHT: Although she is no longer living, we think of her as a woman who *had* great courage and kindness.

(wrong):   (Scott rung the doorbell four times before Ann opened the door.)

RIGHT: Scott *rang* the doorbell four times before Ann opened the door.

(wrong):   (She was used to live in Ohio but now she lives in Maryland.)

RIGHT: She *used to live* in Ohio but now she lives in Maryland.

(wrong):   (Jesse told me that you was interested in studying sculpture.)

RIGHT: Jesse told me that you *were* interested in studying sculpture.

(wrong):   (One of the shipping clerks confirmed the fact that the plane did had a capacity load.)

RIGHT: One of the shipping clerks confirmed the fact that the plane *did have* a capacity load.

Past Continuous

The *past continuous tense* is used in sentences with two past actions to show that, while one action was going on, another action occurred.

aux. *was* or *were* **+** *-ing* form of the verb

While I *was taking* a bath, the telephone *rang.*

The **past continuous** describes the **longer action;** the **past tense** describes the **shorter action.** (*While* and *as* are often used with the past continuous form.)

1. While the farmers *were planting* crops, a windstorm *struck*.
2. Steve *was working* on his income tax form when his friends *invited* him to go to a baseball game.
3. As people *were beginning* to leave their seats, the violinist *announced* an encore.
4. Girard *thought* that his friend Luis *was being* reckless when he *didn't stop* for a red traffic light.
5. Traffic *resumed* while city workers *were* still *removing* debris from the street.
6. The president and his party *were* on a helicopter *returning* from an inspection of the area when they *heard* the news.

The **past continuous** is often used **following a preceding sentence** and also **in response to a question.**

7. She didn't want to interrupt him. He *was counting* the receipts.
8. "Where were you last night?" "I *was* in the library *reading.*"

Sometimes the **past continuous** is used to **emphasize the continuing sense of one of the two past actions** even though the actions occurred during the same time span.

Miguel *memorized* the new words while he *was eating* breakfast.

The **past continuous** is sometimes used to **stress two continuing actions.**

While Lynn *was sewing,* Esther *was painting.*

Avoid the following kinds of errors:

(wrong):   (He cut himself as he shaved.)
            xxxxxxxxxx
RIGHT: He cut himself as he *was shaving.*
(wrong):   (The maintenance man was replacing the broken window.)
            xxxxxxxxxxxxxxxxxxxx
RIGHT: While the maintenance man *was replacing* the broken window, two birds *flew* into the room.
(wrong):   (While we were in the den watch television, we heard a noise.)
            xxxxxxxxx
RIGHT: While we *were* in the den *watching* television, we heard a noise.

EXERCISE I. 5.

Fill in the blanks with the appropriate verb form, past tense or past continuous.

1. A young fellow (deliver) _____ a telegram to Shiraz while the latter (entertain) _____ friends.
2. When I (walk) _____ in the rain, I suddenly (see) _____ a beautiful rainbow.
3. While we (watch) _____ the play, an usher (came over) _____ to us to check our tickets.
4. The engineer (hear, not) _____ the warning bell because he (be) _____ in the engine room (check) _____ the gauges.
5. When the inspector (hear) _____ the noise, he immediately (investigate) _____ .
6. While the racing car (turn) _____ the corner, one of the rear wheels (come) _____ loose.
7. Leah (demonstrate) _____ a dance step when she (trip) _____ on a rug and (fall) _____ .

8. Sean (can play, not) _____ hockey this morning because he (have to work) _____ in his brother's store.
9. Unfortunately, the brothers (move) _____ the furniture in an uncovered truck when it (start) _____ to rain.
10. The firm (do) _____ business when fire inspectors (order) _____ management to stop.

EXERCISE I. 6.

Practice asking and answering questions such as the following. Answer in complete sentences.

1. What did you do last weekend?
2. What was the class doing when the bell rang?
3. What things were you looking for when I saw you in the department store?
4. What were some of the funny, happy, or interesting incidents in your life and approximately when did they occur?
5. What did you see when you were walking through the park yesterday?
6. What were some of the salient events in the news today or yesterday?
7. What were you doing when I called you last night?

Past Perfect

The *past perfect tense* is used in sentences with two past actions to show <u>that one of the actions was completed before the other action.</u>

aux. *had* **+** *past participle* of the verb

Vincent suddenly *realized* that he *had seen* the film.

Use the past perfect tense for the *first* completed action, and use the past tense for the *second* completed action.

NOTE: In the examples below, notice the use of the following words: *many times, several times, once, twice, ever, already, just, by the time, still, yet.*

---

1. After Arman *had revised* the essay twice, he *handed* it *in.*
2. The play *had already begun* by the time they *arrived.*
3. The ship *couldn't leave* because the dock workers *hadn't yet loaded* the cargo.
4. He *had* just *reported* the accident when a policeman *arrived.*
5. Although the lamp *had fallen* on the floor, it *appeared* undamaged.
6. Before America *gained* independence, it *had been* a British colony.

NOTE: The past perfect tense is frequently used with past reporting verbs, that is, verbs that are used to "report" speech and thoughts, such as: *said, told, knew, thought, asked, believed.* <u>Use the past perfect tense when the action had occurred *before* it was reported.</u> (The past tense is used if the action took place at the time it was reported.) (See Section IV for more on reporting verbs.)

---

7. Roberto *said* that he *had taken* the test twice.
8. She *told* him he *looked* familiar and that she *had* probably *met* him at the pharmacy convention. (*Told* and *looked* took place at the same time.)
9. The nurse *thought* that the patient still *hadn't taken* his medicine.
10. The report *stated* that people *had demonstrated* because they *were* concerned about nuclear weapons. (*Stated* and *were* took place at the same time.)
11. She *told* him that she *had had* the best time that she'*d* ever *had.*

Avoid the following kinds of errors:

    (wrong):   (By the time the floodwaters subsided, the dam collapsed.)

    RIGHT: By the time the floodwaters subsided, the dam *had collapsed.*

    (wrong):   (She had gone to the post office yesterday.)

    RIGHT: She *went* to the post office yesterday.

    RIGHT: She didn't need to buy stamps. She *had gone* to the post office the day before. (Use past perfect in relation to past tense.)

    (wrong):   (Since she didn't bring the proper lens for her camera, she wasn't able to photograph the unusual scene.)

    RIGHT: Since she *hadn't brought* the proper lens for her camera, she wasn't able to photograph the unusual scene.

NOTE: The past tense is sometimes implied.

By evening (by the time it *was* evening) Tovah *had finished* the assignment.

NOTE: The words *before* and *after* clearly designate the sequence of events. Consequently, the past tense, instead of the past perfect, is generally used when the two actions or events have taken place in rapid succession.

After he *mailed* his letter, he *bought* some stamps.
Vahik *wiped* the windows before he *started* the car.
Before the composer *started* to write, he *sharpened* several pencils.

Past Perfect Continuous

The *past perfect continuous tense* is used in sentences with two past actions to emphasize the fact that the first action had been continuous *before* the second action took place.

    aux. *had been* **+** *-ing* form of the verb

We *had been waiting* for the plane an hour before it *landed.*

Compare meanings and tenses in the following continuous forms:

Present perfect continuous:	Billy isn't hungry; he *has been snacking* all afternoon. In fact, he*'s been snacking* since he got home.
Past continuous:	Billy *was snacking* on potato chips and candy when we saw him.
Past perfect continuous:	Billy didn't want any dinner. He wasn't hungry because he *had been snacking* on candy and potato chips.

NOTE: **Length of time** is mentioned or implied with past perfect continuous tense.

---

1. Miss Yeager *had been working* in the institute **for three years** when she *declared* herself a candidate for political office.
2. They *had been talking* on the telephone **for several minutes** when they *were* suddenly *cut off.*
3. He said he *had been looking* for his notebook **since ten o'clock.**
4. Her eyes were red when I saw her. It was apparent that she *had been crying.*
5. By the time construction on the annex *began,* the service club *had been raising* funds **for seven years.**
6. The warning light *had been flashing* for **quite a while** when the explosion *occurred.*

Avoid the following kinds of errors:

(wrong):   (Bobby came home with a black eye; he was fighting with a schoolmate.)
            xxxxxxxxxxxxxxxx

RIGHT: Bobby came home with a black eye; he *had been fighting* with a schoolmate.

(wrong):   (The men were working for four hours when the noon whistle blew.) Past contin-
            xxxxxxxxxxxxxxxxxxxxxxxxxxxxxxxxxxxxxxx
            uous is *not* used with length of time.

RIGHT: The men *were working* when the noon whistle blew.

RIGHT: The men *had been working for four hours* when the noon whistle blew.

EXERCISE I. 7.

Complete the following sentences. Use the past perfect and when appropriate, the past perfect continuous form, of the verb in the parentheses.

1. By the time I got to her place, she (go) _____ .
2. Ingemar (compete) _____ for a number of years when he won the riding championship.
3. When the experiment failed, Dr. Jones realized that he (mix) _____ the chemicals incorrectly.
4. Many people (be) _____ out of a job for a long period before the recovery took place.
5. The Civil War (go on) _____ for four years when the armistice was declared in 1865.
6. Clara was too tired to join us. She explained that she (clean) _____ house all day.

EXERCISE I. 8.

Underline the correct structure in the following sentences. Look for any existing clues including the tense in other clauses of the sentences.

1. Kim decided not to water the garden because it (has been raining) (was raining) (had been raining) all night.
2. Since the company went out of business, Gerard (hasn't been working) (wasn't working) (hadn't been working).
3. John thinks that he (has lost) (lost) (had lost) his history book last Tuesday when he (stops) (stopped) (had been stopping) at the gymnasium on his way home.
4. The account was higher than expected because it (had been accruing) (was accruing) (has been accrued) interest for some time.
5. Abraham Lincoln was assassinated as he (was watched) (had been watching) (was watching) a play.
6. A federal grand jury began an investigation to determine whether anyone (have been violating) (had been violate) (had violated) the law.
7. By the time Cortez arrived in Mexico, the Aztec Indians (were developed) (had developed) (developed) a remarkably advanced technology.

EXERCISE I. 9.

Practice asking and answering questions such as the following. Answer in complete sentences.

1. Had the class already begun when you walked in this morning?
2. Were you disappointed that you hadn't received a better grade?
3. How long had you been living there when you moved?
4. How long had you been studying when your roommate returned?
5. Did you explain why you hadn't written earlier?
6. Had the job market improved by the time you graduated high school?

Past Modal

>   *modal* **+** *have* **+** *past participle* of the verb

>   Yuri *should have paid* his rent yesterday but he forgot.

Past Continuous Modal

>   *modal* **+** *have* **+** *been* **+** *-ing* form of the verb

>   The man *may have been telling* the truth but the police weren't sure.

Below are examples of the use of modals and common expressions in the past. The headings classify the modals and expressions according to their general meaning.

Past Intentions:

>   Actions that had been thought of or planned but that were *not* accomplished

1. The salesman *would have sold* his products but he was late for his appointment.
2. They *were going to go* to the ball game last Saturday but it rained.
3. The company *was going to manufacture* computers but it was unable to raise the necessary capital.
4. They *would have been* here yesterday but they were delayed by the weather.
5. She *was supposed to leave* for New York last night but she put off the trip until next week.
6. Joshua *had been intending to study* medicine but he decided to enter law school.
7. He *had planned to take* a vacation but he bought a car instead.

Past Actions Not Intended:

>   Actions that occurred unexpectedly or after a sudden change of plans

1. The guest *wouldn't have stayed* for dinner but the host insisted.
2. Adriana *wasn't going to take* the art class but her friend persuaded her to.
3. Yan *hadn't intended to stay* late but he became interested in the subject everyone was talking about.
4. She *hadn't planned to attend* the conference but she changed her mind.
5. They *weren't supposed to enter* the building by the back door; however, the front door was locked.

Regrettable Past Actions:

>   Actions accomplished or not accomplished, but later regretted

1. I *should have studied* additional languages when I attended college.
2. The judge *shouldn't have ordered* the release of the prisoner.
3. When he heard the noise, the mechanic *should have suspected* a faulty transmission.
4. The contractor *should have been supervising* his men as they worked.
5. They *ought to have called* the fire department as soon as they saw the smoke. They *ought not to have waited*. OR: They *shouldn't have waited*.
6. When they saw the crowd, they *regretted* that they hadn't made a reservation.
7. The witness said that she *was sorry* that she had given false testimony.

Past Modals Expressing Probability, Possibility, and Opportunity

1. I can't find my pen. I *must have left* it on my desk. (probability)

2. The driver *may have taken* an alternate route. (possibility)
3. We *could have seen* the eclipse last night but we went to bed early. (opportunity)
4. Sue didn't call back. She *may not have known* my number. (possibly not)
5. It's too bad that Polly wasn't here last night; she *could have met* the guest speaker. (opportunity)
6. Russ slept until noon. He *must have been working* late last night. (probability)
7. He *might have chosen* another career but, at the time, he didn't have enough money to attend graduate school. (possibility)
8. Girgis has just left. Perhaps you can catch him; he *couldn't have gone* far. (probably not)

Past Modals Expressing Inability
1. He *couldn't have done* the job without the assistance of others.
2. Without a mortgage, the couple *wouldn't have been able* to purchase the house.

Avoid the following kinds of errors:

(wrong):	(There was no estimate on the form. The assessor may have forget to include it.)
RIGHT:	There was no estimate on the form. The assessor *may have forgotten* to include it.
(wrong):	(Akbar would help you yesterday but he had to work.)
RIGHT:	Akbar *would have helped* you yesterday but he had to work.
(wrong):	(They would be ready on time last night but their car wouldn't start.)
RIGHT:	They *would have been* ready on time last night but their car wouldn't start.
(wrong):	(She must of been embarrassed when she didn't recognize him.)
RIGHT:	She *must have* been embarrassed when she didn't recognize him.

Below is a synopsis of past time forms:

(Completed action unassociated with specific time:)	(Adrian *has broken* his glasses.)
Completed action at a specific time, stated or implied:	Adrian *broke* his glasses this morning.
Action in process when second action occurred:	Adrian *broke* his glasses while he *was fixing* his car.
Action completed before the second action:	Adrian wasn't able to see well because he *had broken* his glasses.
Action in process before second action occurred:	Adrian *had been repairing* his car for an hour when he broke his glasses.
Action showing past intention:	Adrian *was going to change* the oil but he didn't.
Action showing past regret:	Adrian said that he *shouldn't have broken* his glasses.
Repetitive action of the past:	Adrian *used to be* a mechanic but now he's an electronic technician.
	Whenever Adrian had time, he *would fix* his friends' cars.

EXERCISE I. 10.

Write logical responses for each question or statement as in number 1. Use the correct past form of the modal or the expression in parentheses. Add *but* clauses when it is logical to do so.

1. Did you go to the meeting last night? (I would go)

I would have gone to the meeting but I had to study.

2. Did you do your homework? (I should do)
3. Where did you leave your book? (I must leave)
4. I thought Bob had planned to sing in the chorus last night. (He ''be'' going to)
5. Why didn't your roommate answer the phone? (He may sleep)
6. Were you able to go to the rock concert last week? (I could go)
7. I was surprised to learn that you had watched the horror film. (I ''be'' going to, not)
8. Did Sue return the books yesterday? (She would return)
9. Did the policeman give Sami a speeding ticket? (Yes. He should drive, not)
10. When the lion roared, the child started to cry. (The child must be)

EXERCISE I. 11.

Practice asking and answering questions such as the following. Answer in complete sentences.

1. What were you going to do when you got home yesterday?
2. Do you think you should have told her about the situation?
3. Couldn't he have bought a car instead of a motorcycle?
4. Why do you think you should have apologized?
5. Do you think she may not have understood you?
6. What makes you think he must have heard the bad news?
7. Why weren't you supposed to go out last night?

MIXED EXERCISE 2: PART A

Fill in the circled letter that represents the *correct* form. Be able to give the reason for your selection.

1. We _____ you a ride this morning but the car was full. Ⓐ Ⓑ Ⓒ Ⓓ
   - A. will give
   - B. would give
   - C. would have given
   - D. would be giving

2. By the time they entered the concert hall, the musicians _____ the introduction to the opera. Ⓐ Ⓑ Ⓒ Ⓓ
   - A. was playing
   - B. had played
   - C. played
   - D. have played

3. The baker ran out of sugar while he _____ . Ⓐ Ⓑ Ⓒ Ⓓ
   - A. had been baking
   - B. was baking
   - C. baked
   - D. had baked

4. In spite of the fact that Johanna has many personal problems, she _____ present every day since the first day of class. Ⓐ Ⓑ Ⓒ Ⓓ
   - A. has been
   - B. had been
   - C. is
   - D. was

5. Can you tell me when she _____ ? Ⓐ Ⓑ Ⓒ Ⓓ
   - A. has moved
   - B. had moved
   - C. moved
   - D. was moving

6. The jury is still out. The members _____ the case. Ⓐ Ⓑ Ⓒ Ⓓ
   - A. must still be discussing
   - B. must discuss
   - C. could still discuss
   - D. maybe discussing

7. Esperanza hasn't been able to attend the last few nights. She _____ do some work for her father.   Ⓐ Ⓑ Ⓒ Ⓓ
   A. must   C. had had to
   B. must to   D. has had to

8. Whenever the safety commission _____ its regulations, there are complaints.
   A. is enforcing   C. enforce   Ⓐ Ⓑ Ⓒ Ⓓ
   B. enforces   D. enforced

9. When he decorated the cake, he _____ roses around each candle.
   A. puts   C. has put   Ⓐ Ⓑ Ⓒ Ⓓ
   B. had put   D. put

10. They _____ for seven hours when they spotted a sign that said "Guests."
    A. were driving   C. had been driving   Ⓐ Ⓑ Ⓒ Ⓓ
    B. drove   D. had drove

MIXED EXERCISE 2: PART B

Fill in the circled letter that represents the *incorrect* form. Be able to explain why the word or phrase you have chosen is not acceptable and how you can correct it.

1. Paul <u>shouldn't</u> <u>to be talking</u> at the same time that the teacher <u>is giving</u> instruc-
        A   B   C
   tions <u>to the class</u>.   Ⓐ Ⓑ Ⓒ Ⓓ
        D

2. <u>Over the past years</u>, Marco <u>had had</u> the opportunity <u>to travel</u> to many remote
        A   B   C
   areas <u>of the earth</u>.   Ⓐ Ⓑ Ⓒ Ⓓ
        D

3. While his wife is away, Mr. Quinn <u>is trying</u> to be both mother and father to his
                                        A
   children, but he <u>admits</u>, he <u>don't</u> <u>always succeed</u>.   Ⓐ Ⓑ Ⓒ Ⓓ
                 B   C   D

4. Mr. Farraj, a reliable man, <u>would certainly keep</u> his appointment yesterday but
                                    A
   his car <u>wouldn't start</u> and he <u>was unable</u> <u>to get</u> a taxi.   Ⓐ Ⓑ Ⓒ Ⓓ
           B   C   D

5. <u>Years ago</u>, when they <u>lived</u> <u>on a farm</u>, they <u>were used to</u> get up at five o'clock
       A   B   C   D
   every morning.   Ⓐ Ⓑ Ⓒ Ⓓ

6. It was <u>a bitterly cold day</u> and Fred <u>hadn't barely</u> <u>started</u> the car when <u>one of the</u>
           A   B   C
   <u>tires</u> became flat.   Ⓐ Ⓑ Ⓒ Ⓓ
    D

7. Dr. Malin <u>is</u> a <u>capable, dedicated</u> doctor and his patients <u>have missed</u> him ever
            A   B   C
   <u>since</u> his death.   Ⓐ Ⓑ Ⓒ Ⓓ
    D

8. <u>Since three weeks</u>, bankers <u>have been protesting</u> the new law because they
         A   B
   <u>feel</u> that it <u>is</u> unfair to depositors.   Ⓐ Ⓑ Ⓒ Ⓓ
    C   D

9. It's <u>a good thing</u> that they <u>had been wearing</u> their seat belts when the accident
   A   B   C

<u>occurred</u>.   Ⓐ Ⓑ Ⓒ Ⓓ
 D

10. Gregorio <u>told us</u> that he <u>was</u> in New Zealand <u>on business</u> several times.
           A   B   C   D   Ⓐ Ⓑ Ⓒ Ⓓ

FUTURE TIME FORMS

Future Tense

The *future tense* is used to express an action that will occur at some time in the future.

> Paul *will enter* college next fall.

Will and *Be going to* are commonly used in the future tense. Although they have a similar meaning, they are usually used for slightly different functions.
    Compare:

To make an announcement:	The Teppermans *will celebrate* their fiftieth anniversary in October.
	I'*ll wash* the dishes and Syd *will dry* them.
To describe a plan:	Tom and Stu *are going to play* tennis after school.
	We'*re going to have* a picnic Sunday.

Shall is used **in questions** but is seldom used in statements except in formal documents and in some literature and poetry.

Shall I come with you? (Would you like me to come with you?)

Sentences in future time often contain *time clauses*, beginning with such words as *when, after, before, as soon as, until,* and *while*. Future time sentences also sometimes contain a conditional clause beginning with *if* or *unless*. Use the *present tense* in time clauses and conditional clauses.

1. **When he arrives at the airport**, his partner *will be* there to meet him.
2. We *are going to* play golf on Saturday **if it doesn't rain.**
3. **As soon as classes are over**, Mandy *is going to board* a train for Kentucky.
4. The marketing agent *will consult* the designer **before he proceeds.**
5. *Shall I buy* you some stamps **while I'm at the post office?**
6. **Unless scientists and government leaders find solutions**, starvation *will continue* to plague the very poor of the world.

NOTE: Occasionally the present perfect, instead of the present tense, is used in the time or conditional clause in order to emphasize the fact that the action is to be completed.

> When Mr. Jones *has finished (or: finishes)* the survey, he'll confer with the city planner.
> As soon as we *have changed (or: change)* into our bathing suits, we're going to go swimming.

Avoid the following kinds of errors:

(wrong):   (If her designs will be acceptable, the fashion house will buy them.)
                              xxxxxxxxx
RIGHT: If her designs *are* acceptable, the fashion house will buy them.

(wrong):   (We're going to have choral practice as soon as Nabil and Belen will return.)
                                                                        xxxxxxxxxxxxxx
RIGHT: We're going to have choral practice as soon as Nabil and Belen *return (or: have
             returned.)*

The present continuous is sometimes used as a less formal way of expressing coming events. Compare:

The football season *will begin* next Saturday.
The football season *is beginning* next Saturday.

He won't be here tomorrow. He's *going to drive* to Arizona.
He won't be here tomorrow. He*'s driving* to Arizona.

They *will arrive* on Saturday.
They *are arriving* on Saturday.

The word *would* is used in polite forms. Compare:

Will you get me a glass of water?
Would you (would you be willing to) get me a glass of water?

Use *would* (not *will*) with *like* and *care*.

I *would like* to see that play.
(wrong):   (I will like to see that play.)
                  xxxxxxxxxxxx
Would you like to go for a walk?
(wrong):   (Will you like to go for a walk?)
                  xxxxxxxxxxxxxxxxxx
Would you care to have some coffee?
Also: Would you care for some coffee?
Also: Do you care for some coffee?
(wrong):   (Will you care for some coffee?)
                  xxxxxxxxxxxxxxxxxxx

Don't use *like* with *do* for a specific occasion. *Like* means to enjoy in a general sense.

Would you like some coffee?
(wrong):   (Do you like some coffee?)
                  xxxxxxxxxxxxxxxx
(Do you like coffee or do you usually drink something else?)
Would your roommate like to go to *the movie* with us?
(wrong):   (Does your roommate like to go to a movie with us?)
                  xxxxxx

Modals in Future Time

Modals and other expressions are used to project future time. The headings below classify their use. Reminder! Use present tense in time and conditional clauses.

Necessity

1. The students *must* take a placement test after they register (*or:* have registered) next week.
2. Mr. Moretti *has to* go to Washington on a business trip unless his associate volunteers to go.
3. Before the two women expand their business, they *need to* calculate their increased overhead.
4. Mr. Techapanichgul *is required to* renew his driver's license if he wants to continue to drive.

No Necessity

1. They *don't have to* report for duty until next month.
2. We *don't need to* make a reservation before we go to the show.
3. Paul *isn't required to* repeat the class if he makes up the final test.

Recommendation or Expectation

1. She *should* be here soon.
2. Consumers *should* demand products of good quality.
3. He *had better* read the instructions before he proceeds.
4. If Paula wants to be certified, she *had better not* fail the examination tomorrow.
5. Wilson *shouldn't* notify them until he confirms the news.
6. The weather bureau *is supposed to* issue both short- and long-range predictions.
7. We *are not supposed to* use Room 2 until the paint dries.
8. She *ought to know* basic grammar before she takes Mr. Renfrew's writing class.
9. He *ought not to* (*shouldn't*) apply unless he is qualified.

Permission

1. Lim, who has advanced rapidly, *may* take an advanced class if she wishes. (or: is permitted to take an advanced class if she wishes.)
2. If we're quiet, we *can* watch the rehearsal tonight. (or: are allowed to watch the rehearsal tonight.)

No Permission

1. The Robinsons told their children that, in the future, they *must not* swim in areas that have no lifeguard. (or: are forbidden to swim in areas that have no lifeguard.)
2. Uka *may not* take the reference book home unless she gets permission. (or: is not permitted to take the reference book home unless she gets permission.)
3. Mr. Palmeretti says that Luigi *can't* use the car until he washes it. (or: is not permitted to use the car until he washes it.)

Possibility

1. Mr. Paillard *may* move to the United States if he obtains a good position.
2. If the weather doesn't clear up, we *might not* (*may not*) go out.

Ability

1. Dr. Wang *can* see you today if he has no emergencies.
2. When the noise ceases, the musicians *will be able* to resume playing.

The following sentences contain some **additional expressions used to project future plans.** Remember that **present tense** is used **in time and conditional clauses.** Note that in some cases either the present tense or the present continuous may be used.

1. Jory *expects/is expecting* to take a trip to Alaska when school is out.
2. They *plan/are planning* to purchase a video game if they find one that they like.
3. I *hope/am hoping* to see them when they come to California.
4. Sarah *intends/is intending* to enter the Olympics if she qualifies.

5. She *would like to* (*or wants to*) travel when she has the time and the money.

Avoid the following kinds of errors:

(wrong):	Mr. Bernardi can give you the information as soon as he will get the new schedule.)
	xxxxxxxxxx
RIGHT:	Mr. Bernardi can give you the information as soon as he *gets* (*or: has gotten*) the new schedule.
(wrong):	(When he comes next week, she will hope to see him.)
	xxxxxxxxxxxx
RIGHT:	When he comes next week, she *hopes/is hoping* to see him.
(wrong):	(He has better to come soon or else the dinner will get cold.)
	xxxxxxxxxxxxxxxxx
RIGHT:	He *had better* come soon or else the dinner will get cold.
(wrong):	(When will I come to see you?) Wrong, if meaning is as below.
	xxxxx
RIGHT:	When would you like me to come to see you?
RIGHT:	When shall I come to see you?
RIGHT:	When should I come to see you?

NOTE: The present tense of *be* plus an infinitive is sometimes used to emphasize duty or obligation. Compare:

Betty will report for duty next week.
Betty *is to report* for duty next week.
You have to be on time for your appointment.
You *are to be* on time for your appointment.
John must appear in court on March 2.
John *is to appear* in court on March 2.

EXERCISE I. 12.

Give complete answers to the following questions using the same future form as in the question. Add time and conditional clauses using: if, when, unless, before, as soon as, while, after.

1. Do you plan to go to the game Friday?
   Yes, I plan to go to the game unless my boss asks me to work overtime.
2. Can you go with us to the theater?
3. Where are you going to travel next summer?
4. When will the new department store open?
5. What are we supposed to with our books?
6. Where would you like to go tonight?
7. Is the prime minister arriving tonight?
8. When shall I tell you about the course?
9. What are you going to do tonight?
10. Is the drama department going to present a play?

EXERCISE I. 13.

Practice asking and answering the following kinds of questions. Add time and conditional clauses. Answer in complete sentences.

1. Do you have to write a report?
2. Can you go away next weekend?
3. Must you leave early?

4. Shouldn't you let them know that you are going to be late?
5. When are you supposed to return?
6. Will you help me?
7. Are you going to work tomorrow?
8. Would you like to go shopping tonight?

Future Continuous

The *future continuous* is used to describe an action that will be in process at a particular time in the future, often in relation to another action.

aux. *will be* + *-ing* form of the verb

When Mr. Lin returns from his meeting, his wife *will be sleeping*. Compare:

Present continuous: He can't play golf today because he *is working*.
Future continuous: He can't play golf next Sunday because he *will be working*.

NOTE: Modals other than *will*, as well as other expressions, are also used in future continuous form. Notice present tense in time and conditional clauses in the sentences below.

---

1. According to the schedule, their plane *should be arriving* soon.
2. The Burtons *hope to be sailing* to Canada this time next month.
3. If you go there now, he *will* probably *be practicing* his cello.
4. Tomorrow at this time, he'*ll be flying* to Paris.
5. The Vanderviver brothers *expect to be working* on their grandfather's farm next summer while their parents are in Europe.
6. Although she's not attending this month's class, she *will be attending* next month's class. They *won't be staying* with us when they come; they'*ll be staying* at a hotel.

Avoid the following kinds of errors:

(wrong):   (Wait until seven o'clock so that they won't still eat.)
                                              xxxxxxxxxxxxxxxxxxx
RIGHT: Wait until seven o'clock so that they *won't still be eating*.
(wrong):   (If we don't hurry, the musicians will play by the time we arrive.)
                                              xxxxxxxxxxxxx
RIGHT: If we don't hurry, the musicians *will be playing* by the time we arrive.

EXERCISE I. 14.

Fill in the blanks with the correct form, present tense or the future continuous tense.

1. Lucho probably (watch) _____ television when Ali (get) _____ there.
2. When Mrs. Hidalgo (go) _____ to school tomorrow, Anna and Keeko (work) _____ in the office.
3. We must not disturb him after 2:00 P.M. because he (prepare) _____ his income tax form at that time.
4. By the time Earl (drive) _____ home from the airport, his friend Bradley (fly) _____ to Brazil.
5. What _____ you (do) _____ while your husband (attend) _____ business meetings?
6. Your employer would like to talk to you at four o'clock because he (confer, still, not) _____ with his attorneys at that time.

EXERCISE I. 15.

Practice asking and answering the following questions. Answer in complete sentences.

1. What do you think you'll be doing a year from now?
2. What do you think she'll be doing when we get there?
3. Are you hoping to be working by next fall?
4. Is your friend expecting to be staying with you when he comes?
5. How long will you be using the telephone?
6. Will your friends be waiting for you at the airport when you arrive?
7. What are you going to be doing tonight?

Future Perfect

The *future perfect tense* is used to describe an action that will have been completed by a certain time in the future, often in relation to another action. It is formed with the auxiliary *will have* plus the *past participle of the verb*.

Compare:

Present perfect: Elba *has given* the teacher her test paper.
Future perfect: Lorraine hasn't given the teacher her test paper yet, but she *will have given* the teacher her test paper by the end of the period.

Notice the use of present tense in the time and conditional clauses of the examples below. Notice also other future perfect expressions with *expect, plan, hope, intend, may.*

1. By the time you **arrive**, Sidney and Perle *will have left*.
2. When we **see** Luke again, he *will have grown* tall.
3. They *will have completed* the English course by January.
4. Yoji *expects to have graduated* before he **returns** to his country.
5. Mr. Lee *plans to have visited* every national park by next September.
6. The presidential advisors *hope to have* resolved the problem by the time they **return**.
7. Although the incident **is** disturbing to you now, in a few months you *may have forgotten* all about it.
8. A year from now my nephew *will have begun* to practice medicine.
9. Because of illness, he *will not have been able* to get his degree by the end of the year.

Avoid the following kinds of errors:

(wrong):   (By the time Christmas is over, Betty will spend all the money she has saved.)
                      xxxxxxxxxxxxxx
RIGHT: By the time Christmas is over, Betty *will have spent* all the money she has saved.
(wrong):   (When the prisoner is released, he will be in prison for seven years.)
                      xxxxxxxxxx
RIGHT: When the prisoner is released, he *will have been* in prison for seven years.

NOTE: Some past participles, such as *finished, done, gone,* and *repaired,* are more commonly used as past participle adjectives and used in causative passive forms. (See Adjectives—Past Participles as Adjectives and see Causative Passive Forms.) Compare:

When her guests arrive, Jean will have finished the preparations. (future perfect)
When her guests arrive, Jean will have the preparations finished. (causative passive)
When her guests arrive, Jean will be finished with the preparations. (past participle adjective)

If we don't hurry, they will have gone.
If we don't hurry, they will be gone.

Before he leaves town, he will have done the report.
Before he leaves on his trip, he will have the report done.
Before he leaves on his trip, he will be done with the report.

By the time you need your car, the mechanic will have repaired it.
By the time you need your car, the mechanic will have it repaired.

NOTE: Use the active future perfect when a passive form can't be used.

(wrong):   (By next week, Irina will be seen all the fine cathedrals in Rome.)
xxxxxxxxxxxxxxxx

(wrong):   (By next week, Irina will have all the fine cathedrals in Rome seen.)
xxxxxxxxxxxxxxxxxxxxxxxxxxxxxxxxxxxxxxxxxxxxxxxxxxxxxxxx

RIGHT: By next week, Irina *will have seen* all the fine cathedrals in Rome.

Future Perfect Continuous

The *future perfect continuous tense* is used to describe an action in the future which will have been going on up to a certain designated time or in relation to another action.

aux. *will have been* **+** *-ing* form of the verb.

The next time I see her, she *will have been living* in her new apartment for one month.

NOTE: The length of time is often mentioned with future perfect continuous action.

By ten o'clock, I *will have been typing* **for three hours**.
Yervan *will have been doing* homework **several hours** when his friend comes to pick him up.
By the night of the play, the cast *will have been rehearsing* a month.

Avoid the following kinds of errors:

(wrong):   (By the time the project is finished, Carol and her colleagues will be working on
xxxxxxxxxxxxxxxxxxxxxx
it a full year.)

RIGHT: By the time the project is finished, Carol and her colleagues *will have been working* on it a full year.

Below is a synopsis of future time forms:

Action to occur in the future:	Bill *is going to write* to his friend Ed.
	Bill *will tell* his friend about his trip.
	Bill *may write* to Lou also if he has time.
Future action in progress:	Bill *will be writing* to Ed while his wife is at the library.
Action completed by a certain future time:	Bill *will probably have written* two letters by the time his wife returns.
Continuous future action up to a certain time or event:	Bill *will have been writing* letters for a few hours when his wife returns.

EXERCISE I. 16.

Fill in the blanks with the future perfect or when correct to do so, the future perfect continuous.

1. When Ken arrives in Arizona, the interior decorator (redecorate) _____ his new office.

2. By the end of fall, Joe (replace) _____ Bob as chief operating officer.
3. Next Tuesday, Dorothy (be) _____ here for a full month.
4. In ten minutes they (talked) _____ on the telephone for an hour.
5. When the clock strikes twelve, they (discuss) _____ the proposal since 9 a.m.
6. By the time the rainy weather begins, Mr. Erlich and his son Barry hope to (build) _____ a new roof on their house.

EXERCISE I. 17.

Practice asking and answering questions such as the following. Answer in complete sentences.

1. What will you have learned by the time the course is over?
2. How many years will you have been in school when you graduate?
3. What do you expect to have achieved five years from now?
4. By what year will you have completed your education?
5. What are possible ways in which the world may have improved by the end of the century?

EXERCISE I. 18.

The following words and groups of words are a mixture of "clues" to the various tenses. Complete the sentences using appropriate forms of tenses and modals.

1. Look out!
2. Since this morning,
3. A short time ago,
4. The dog bit the postman while the postman
5. As soon as class begins, ten minutes from now, the instructor
6. Mr. Oliver _____ but he was busy.
7. Up to now, Roy
8. Don't call them between 6:00 and 7:00 P.M. because probably they
9. By the end of next week, Henry
10. We're going to go to the show tonight if
11. Her bathing suit was still wet; apparently she
12. Everyone is praising last night's performance. I didn't see it but it _____ excellent.
13. By the time we reached the airport, the plane
14. At this time next week my lucky friend expects _____ to Hawaii.
15. Patricio _____ to the basketball game last night but he was too tired.
16. I'm not sure where he is, but he _____ in the laboratory.
17. From 1976 to 1982
18. While Bu's at football practice later today, Jia Ming
19. They _____ the opera "Tosca" many times.
20. Next weekend, we _____ after

MIXED EXERCISE 3: PART A

Fill in the circled letter that represents the *correct* form. Check clues and sentence logic. Be able to give a reason for your selection and to explain why the others are incorrect.

1. Michiko couldn't come to the telephone when Mrs. Sakuda called her because she _____ in the laboratory.   Ⓐ Ⓑ Ⓒ Ⓓ
   A. had been working   C. was working
   B. has been working   D. worked

2. For some time, Jack _____ his paintings to the Perlson Art Gallery.
   A. is selling
   B. has been selling
   C. has selled
   D. was sold
   Ⓐ Ⓑ Ⓒ Ⓓ

3. By this time next week, the winners _____ their awards.
   Ⓐ Ⓑ Ⓒ Ⓓ
   A. will have receive
   B. will have received
   C. will be received
   D. will have been receiving

4. We walked in the opposite direction as soon as we realized that we _____ the wrong path.
   Ⓐ Ⓑ Ⓒ Ⓓ
   A. had taken
   B. were taken
   C. took
   D. have taken

5. If they _____ , everyone can have a chance to speak.
   Ⓐ Ⓑ Ⓒ Ⓓ
   A. took turns answering
   B. would take turns answering
   C. are take turns answering
   D. take turns answering

6. Last month I read a book about the ethics of a primitive society. This month _____ a recently published historical novel.
   Ⓐ Ⓑ Ⓒ Ⓓ
   A. I've reading
   B. I'd been reading
   C. I'm reading
   D. I was reading

7. By next October that couple _____ together for 25 years.
   Ⓐ Ⓑ Ⓒ Ⓓ
   A. have performed
   B. will be performing
   C. will have been performing
   D. will perform

8. What a lovely night! The moon _____ brightly.
   Ⓐ Ⓑ Ⓒ Ⓓ
   A. shines
   B. is shining
   C. shined
   D. was shining

9. The deficit _____ so large, we will probably have to pay additional taxes.
   A. is growing
   B. grows
   C. has growed
   D. was growing
   Ⓐ Ⓑ Ⓒ Ⓓ

10. Charles _____ her but he changed his mind.
    A. would call
    B. was planned to
    C. would have call
    D. was going to call
    Ⓐ Ⓑ Ⓒ Ⓓ

MIXED EXERCISE 3: PART B

Fill in the circled letter that represents the *incorrect* form.

1. While Mary was in the library <u>doing</u> research, she <u>was finding</u> a book which
                                        A   B

   <u>contained</u> letters the author <u>had written</u> to a son.
     C   D
   Ⓐ Ⓑ Ⓒ Ⓓ

2. Even though Lucy and Sadie <u>have walked</u> <u>many miles</u> today, they <u>will like</u> to
                                            A   B   C

   visit the place <u>where</u> Mozart was born.
                      D
   Ⓐ Ⓑ Ⓒ Ⓓ

3. It's fortunate that he <u>hasn't never forgotten</u> <u>how to speak</u> his native language
   A   B   C
as he was very young when he <u>left</u> his country.   Ⓐ Ⓑ Ⓒ Ⓓ
                           D

4. The gallery owner <u>told us</u> that he already returned the works of last <u>month's</u>
                A   B   C
exhibition to the <u>various</u> artists.   Ⓐ Ⓑ Ⓒ Ⓓ
                D

5. Last week the court <u>has ruled</u> that the law <u>pertaining</u> to school financing <u>was</u>
                     A   B   C
<u>unconstitutional</u>.   Ⓐ Ⓑ Ⓒ Ⓓ
     D

6. While the candidate <u>will speak</u> <u>at</u> the public meeting tonight, his campaign man-
                      A   B
ager <u>will arrange</u> the location for his <u>next appearance</u>.   Ⓐ Ⓑ Ⓒ Ⓓ
        C   D

7. <u>Since seven months</u> the ranchers haven't had <u>any</u> rain and they <u>are worried</u>
             A   B   C
that their cattle <u>won't have</u> sufficient grazing land.   Ⓐ Ⓑ Ⓒ Ⓓ
             D

8. <u>Do you think</u> that Ollie <u>should borrow</u> his friend's car last night when he
      A   B
<u>hadn't asked</u> his friend <u>for permission</u>?   Ⓐ Ⓑ Ⓒ Ⓓ
    C   D

9. <u>Once a year</u> the Lombardos, who <u>lives</u> across the street <u>from us</u>, <u>return</u> to Italy
     A   B   C   D
for a visit with their parents and relatives.   Ⓐ Ⓑ Ⓒ Ⓓ

10. The animals that <u>had been bought</u> for the zoo <u>were</u> so weak from <u>their</u> long
                A   B   C
journey across the ocean that they <u>couldn't</u> scarcely walk.   Ⓐ Ⓑ Ⓒ Ⓓ
                              D

Two

PASSIVE VOICE
AND
CAUSATIVE PASSIVE VOICE

THE PASSIVE VOICE

When the subject does the action, as is the case in most sentences, the verb action is in the *active voice.*

Next term the college *will offer* a course in printing.

When the action is done to the subject *by someone* or is caused *by an outside influence,* the verb action is in the *passive voice.* (*Passive* means "not active.")

Next term, a *course* in printing *will be offered* by the university. (Obviously, a course cannot offer; it has to *be offered.*)

All tenses of the *be* auxiliary are used in the passive voice.

appropriate form of aux. *be* **+** past participle of the verb

These vegetables *have been grown* by local farmers.
She looks happy; she *must have been told* the good news.

(In the first sentence above, "local farmers" are the agents who perform the action. In the second sentence, no agent is mentioned. It isn't necessary to name the agent unless it's important to the meaning of the sentence.)

In the following sentences, the **object** of the active-voiced sentence becomes the **subject** of the passive-voiced sentence. Only transitive verbs, that is, verbs followed by a direct object, may be changed to passive voice.

Compare:

A professional photographer took the class **pictures.**
The class **pictures** *were taken* by a professional photographer.

Scientists were monitoring the **spacecraft** when some of the equipment ceased to function.
The **spacecraft** *was being monitored* when some of the equipment ceased to function.

The passive voice sentences below demonstrate various verb forms.

1. Present tense: Miss Nadell *is driven* to work by her friend each day.
2. Present modal: Children *should be taught* good behavior.
3. Present continuous: We can't cool the room because the air-conditioner *is being repaired.*
4. Present perfect: Pilot layoffs *have been caused* by the substantial reduction of flights.
5. Past tense: Last week some land near the lake *was surveyed* as a possible site for a bird sanctuary.
6. Past modal: Ordinarily the room *would have been cleaned* but the janitor was ill yesterday.
7. Past modal: The criminal *may not have been recognized* because of a disguise.
8. Past continuous: The new drapes *were being hung* when the visitors showed up.
9. Past perfect: The outcome of the election was announced before all of the votes *had been counted.*
10. Future: Many believe that one day the earth *will be destroyed* if people do not learn to live in peace.
11. Future modal: The teacher said the report *must be done* by Monday.
12. Future modal: Mr. Donat feels that he *should be given* a raise in pay.
13. Future expression: I *expect to be told* about the new publication soon.
14. Future perfect: The cable that Mrs. Rabin has sent *will have been received* by the time she boards the plane.

EXCEPTION: The passive infinitive, instead of the future passive, is sometimes used to make an announcement or to stress an obligation.

present tense of *be* + *to be* + past participle

Compare:

Amelia will be awarded a full scholarship.
Amelia *is to be awarded* a full scholarship.

The instructions must be followed precisely.
The instructions *are to be followed* precisely.

Avoid the following kinds of errors:

(wrong):   (The test which the students took yesterday had prepared by the Educational
           xxxxxxxxxxxxxxxxxxxx
           Testing Service.)
RIGHT: The test which the students took yesterday *had been prepared* by the Educational
           Testing Service.
(wrong):   (We can't make toast this morning because the toaster is repairing.)
                                                     xxxxxxxxxxxxxxxx
RIGHT: We can't make toast this morning because the toaster *is being repaired.*
(wrong):   (The water should be tested before people were permitted to drink it.)
           xxxxxxxxxxxxxxxxxxxxxx
RIGHT: The water *should have been tested* before people were permitted to drink it.
(wrong):   (Thomas Jefferson, who considered to be one of the greatest American patriots,
                               xxxxxxxxxxxxxx
           wrote the Declaration of Independence.)
RIGHT: Thomas Jefferson, who *was considered* to be one of the greatest patriots, wrote the
           Declaration of Independence.
(wrong):   (Corn used to make tortillas.)
                 xxxxxxxxxxxxxxxx
RIGHT: (Corn *is used to make* tortillas.)
(wrong):   (The building hopes to be finished by next month.)
           xxxxxxxxxxxxxxxxxxxxxxxxxxxxxxxxxxxxxxxxxxxxxx

NOTE: Only a person can hope, expect, plan, and intend.

RIGHT: The *contractor hopes that the building will be finished* next month.

NOTE: Don't use the passive voice when the subject does the action.

(wrong): (The graph was shown that there had been an increase in sales.)
                        xxxxxxxxxxxxxx
RIGHT: The graph *showed* that there had been an increase in sales.
(wrong): (Stella is agreed with Antony that a hearing should be held.)
                    xxxxxxxxxxxxx
RIGHT: Stella *agrees* with Antony that a hearing should be held.
RIGHT: Stella *is in agreement* with Antony that a hearing should be held.
(wrong): (Suddenly the book was fallen from the shelf.)
                            xxxxxxxxxxxxxxx
RIGHT: Suddenly the book *fell* from the shelf.

EXERCISE II. 1.

Change the following sentences to the passive voice, as demonstrated in number 1, with the object becoming the subject. The verb in the passive voice must be in the same tense as that in the active voice. Remember, the subject and verb must agree. (Don't add the agent or "*by* phrase" unless you think it is important.)

1. One of the senators made a stirring speech on the floor of the Senate yesterday.
   A stirring speech was made on the floor of the Senate yesterday.
2. The mayor of the city has just welcomed the foreign heads of state.
3. Yesterday the postman didn't deliver the mail until 5:00 P.M.
4. The publisher will publish the new textbook next May.
5. A cement mixer is causing the noise.
6. By dawn tomorrow the firefighters will have extinguished the forest fire.
7. Teachers need the cooperation of students in order to have a successful program.
8. As soon as the ambulance arrived, the attendants drove the wounded man to the hospital.
9. They can't install the washing machine until the tenant moves in.
10. A demolition team was tearing down an old building as we drove by.

EXERCISE II. 2.

Practice asking and answering questions such as the following. Answer in complete sentences.

1. What subjects are you being taught this term?
2. Have your classes been scheduled for days or for evenings?
3. Are the papers usually corrected by the instructor himself?
4. Do most of your compositions have to be rewritten?
5. Why must the essays be typed?
6. Were some of the students transferred to other rooms?
7. When will your car be repaired?
8. Why was the game cancelled yesterday?

THE CAUSATIVE PASSIVE VOICE

When a sentence is in the passive voice, we have learned that something has been done to the subject. When a sentence is in the causative passive, something has been done to the *object*. Verbs *have* or *get* are used in causative passive form to indicate that the subject asked someone to do something to a particular object.

Use a form of *have* or *get* **+** *object* **+** *past participle*

Sometimes the subject itself is responsible for the causative passive action (7, 11).

1. The Dean *will have* the welcoming **speech given** by a student.
2. Yakov *was getting* his **shoes shined** when he witnessed an accident.
3. After a year of toothaches, Warren *had* one of his **teeth pulled**.
4. Sydney *had* just *had* his **suit dry-cleaned** when a passing car sprayed mud all over him.
5. The editor *plans to have* the **material divided** into three sessions.
6. If you don't want to have an accident, you *had better have* your **brakes fixed**.
7. By two o'clock the secretary *will have* all of the **reports typed**.
8. By the next time I see Leonid, he *will have had* his **appendix removed**.
9. When the articles are compiled, she*'s going to have* **them sent** to me.
10. Jimmy *has* his **teeth checked** twice a year. (by a dentist)
11. Corky *got* his **composition finished** by eight o'clock.

NOTE: Sometimes the causative passive action has not been initiated by the subject and, in fact, may take place without the subject's approval.

---

12. That woman *will have* her **child taken away** from her if she doesn't take proper care of him.
13. Two of the men *might get* their **licenses revoked** by the court.
14. How did the dog *get* its **foot caught** in the trap?

Avoid the following kinds of errors:

(wrong):   (He must have the book report wrote by next week.)
~~~~~~~~

RIGHT: He must have the *book report written* by next week.

(wrong):   (The owner is going to have installed a shower when he builds the house.)
~~~~~~~~~~~~~~~~~~~~~~~~~~~~

RIGHT: The owner is going to have *a shower installed* when he builds the house.

(wrong):   (The reception room looked different. The doctor must have the room
~~~~~~~~~~~~~~~~~

redecorate.)
~~~~~~~~~~~~~~~~

RIGHT: The reception room looked different. The doctor *must have had* the room *redecorated.*

EXERCISE II. 3.

Using the correct form of *have* or *get*, complete each sentence with a causative passive form. The first sentence is done for you.

1. Next month we <u>are going to have</u> a chestnut tree <u>planted</u> in the garden.
2. Right now, Jane _____ her hair _____ .
3. She was going to _____ a coat _____ by a tailor but she couldn't afford it.
4. Unfortunately, Mrs. Larsen _____ just _____ her purse _____ .
5. Twenty years from now, they _____ their mortgage _____ .

6. I can't wear this dress to the party because it's dirty. I should _____ it _____ last week.
7. Yesterday the teacher _____ the papers _____ by the students.
8. He must _____ his watch _____ before next week.

EXERCISE II. 4.

Practice asking and answering the following kinds of questions. Answer in complete sentences.

1. Did you get your schedule changed yesterday?
2. Are you going to have your apartment painted?
3. When will you have your work completed?
4. Have you ever had anything stolen?
5. Do you have to have your test answers written in ink?
6. Has your friend had his bicycle repaired?
7. Is your roommate having a desk moved in?
8. Were you getting your hair done when your boyfriend walked in?
9. What have you (or someone else) had done recently?
10. What do you want done to certain things in the future?

MIXED EXERCISE 4: PART A

Fill in the circled letter that represents the *correct* form. Be able to give a reason for your selection.

1. Since the first space mission, many communication satellites _____ .
   A. was launched
   B. have been launched
   C. are launched
   D. had been launch
   Ⓐ Ⓑ Ⓒ Ⓓ

2. Yesterday Pete _____ a ticket for speeding.
   A. was gave
   B. had been given
   C. was given
   D. gave
   Ⓐ Ⓑ Ⓒ Ⓓ

3. Before leaving camp, the Boy Scouts _____ the fire.
   A. put out
   B. had putted out
   C. had put
   D. were putting out
   Ⓐ Ⓑ Ⓒ Ⓓ

4. By the time the applicant makes up his mind, the offer _____ .
   A. will cancel
   B. will be cancelling
   C. will have been cancelled
   D. will have been cancel
   Ⓐ Ⓑ Ⓒ Ⓓ

5. Doug has recently had his poetry _____ .
   A. publish
   B. to publish
   C. be publish
   D. published
   Ⓐ Ⓑ Ⓒ Ⓓ

6. In a few months, the firm _____ its production.
   A. will be increasing
   B. will increased
   C. is increased
   D. has increase
   Ⓐ Ⓑ Ⓒ Ⓓ

7. The day before yesterday we _____ a very bad storm.
   A. had had
   B. had
   C. were having
   D. have had
   Ⓐ Ⓑ Ⓒ Ⓓ

8. She complains that she _____ headaches.   Ⓐ Ⓑ Ⓒ Ⓓ
   A. has frequently   C. frequently has
   B. has had frequently   D. have frequent

9. New officers _____ by our club when we hold our next meeting.   Ⓐ Ⓑ Ⓒ Ⓓ
   A. elected   C. expect to elect
   B. will elect   D. will be elected

10. Brigette thinks her dress is a little too long, so she plans to get it _____ .
    A. shortened   C. shorten   Ⓐ Ⓑ Ⓒ Ⓓ
    B. be shortened   D. to have shortened

MIXED EXERCISE 4: PART B

Fill in the circled letter that represents the *incorrect* form. Be able to explain why the word or phrase you have chosen is not acceptable and how you can correct it.

1. On the days that he's not busy, he liked to write poetry, or paint with watercol-
       A   B   C
   ors, or cook an unusual dish.   Ⓐ Ⓑ Ⓒ Ⓓ
                 D

2. My brakes had not been tested yet when I came to pick up my car; in fact, the
                  A   B   C
   brakes were testing as I walked into the service station.   Ⓐ Ⓑ Ⓒ Ⓓ
        D

3. When we next see Alice and Max, who are presently parents of two children,
           A   B
   they will had had a new baby in their family.   Ⓐ Ⓑ Ⓒ Ⓓ
       C   D

4. As an editor, Ms. Zeitland must do a voluminous amount of reading, but she
                       A   B
   says that the fact that she has to read a great deal doesn't bother her because
                           C
   she used to it.   Ⓐ Ⓑ Ⓒ Ⓓ
      D

5. The music for the opera, which will perform next month, has been written by
                       A   B
   one of the students in the music department.   Ⓐ Ⓑ Ⓒ Ⓓ
         C   D

6. Pedro must not be very adventurous. He claims that he never ate Chinese food,
         A   B   C   D
   Japanese food, or German food.   Ⓐ Ⓑ Ⓒ Ⓓ

7. When the dealer sold the appliance to the customer, he should give him an
                          A   B   C
   instruction book to be sure the appliance would be operated properly.
                                   D
                        Ⓐ Ⓑ Ⓒ Ⓓ

8. We can begin the meeting when Josephina brings the report that she has pre-
       A   B   C
   pared last week.   Ⓐ Ⓑ Ⓒ Ⓓ
     D

9. Chef Orlando is in the kitchen <u>at this time</u> <u>prepared</u> the feast that <u>is sponsored</u>
                                                A   B   C

    <u>annually</u> by the restaurant association.   Ⓐ Ⓑ Ⓒ Ⓓ
      D

10. When heavy rains <u>are threatened</u> to flood the fields, the farmers <u>must have</u> their
                                  A   B

    crops <u>picked</u> earlier than they <u>had intended.</u>   Ⓐ Ⓑ Ⓒ Ⓓ
        C   D

Three

FORMATION OF QUESTIONS, TAG ENDINGS, AND NEGATIVE QUESTIONS

FORMATION OF QUESTIONS

Present and Past Tense With Yes/No Questions

present aux. *do, does*	past aux. *did*
Statement: Jorge plays bridge. Does Jorge play bridge? Do you/we/they play bridge?	Jorge played bridge last night. Did Jorge play bridge last night? Did you/we/they play bridge last night?
present	past
Statement: Emily is busy. Is Emily busy? Am I busy? Are you/we/they busy?	Emily was busy yesterday. Was Emily busy yesterday? Was I busy yesterday? Were you/we/they busy yesterday?

Question Formation of Other Tenses

Use the same auxiliary in the question as in the statement.
Statement: He should ask for an appointment.
            Should he ask for an appointment?

When there is more than one auxiliary, place *only the first auxiliary* before the subject.
Statement: He should have asked for an appointment last week.
            Should he have asked for an appointment last week?
(wrong):   (Should have he asked for an appointment last week?)
            xxxxxxxxxxxxxxxxxxxxxxxxxxxx

Information Question Words: *Who, Whom, Whose, Where, When, Why, Which, How, What*

When using information question words, *maintain the basic question order.*
              Will Luke be five in July?
         When will Luke be five?
In what month will Luke be five?
On what date will Luke be five?
       How old will Luke be in July?
(wrong):   (How old Luke will be in July?)
            xxxxxxxxxxxxxx

Using *Who, Whom, Whose*

Who is used as a subject.
Who saw him?
(wrong):   (Who did see him?)
                  xxxx

Whom is used as the object of a verb.
Whom did he see? (The word *he* is the subject: He saw whom.)
Conversational: (Who did he see?)

Whom is also used as the object of a preposition.
With whom did he speak? (*or:*) Whom did he speak with?
(wrong): (With who did he speak?) Use *whom*, in both formal English and conversation when preceded by a preposition.
              xxxxxx
Conversational: Who did he speak with? (*Who* may be used in conversation, but not in formal English, when the preposition is at the end of the sentence or the clause.)

Whose refers to possession.
Whose birthday did you celebrate?
Whose book are you reading?

Using Prepositions with Question Words

When a preposition occurs in a statement or in a response, the question must also contain the preposition. Compare:
In whose home was the party held?
or: Whose home was the party held in? (less formal)
The party was held *in* Jory's home.
From which college did she graduate?
or: Which college did she graduate from?
She graduated *from* Britt College.
To what subject was he attracted?
or: What subject was he attracted to?
He was attracted *to* the subject of politics.
(wrong):   (Whose home was the party held?)
                  xxxxxxxxxxxxxxxxxxxxxxxxxxxxxxxxxxxxxxxxx
(wrong):   (Which college did she graduate?)
                  xxxxxxxxxxxxxxxxxxxxxxxxxxxxxxxxxxxxxxxxx
(wrong):   (What subject was he attracted?)
                  xxxxxxxxxxxxxxxxxxxxxxxxxxxxxxxxxxxxxxxx

EXERCISE III. 1.

Change the following statements to questions, as demonstrated in number 1.

1. By the time classes begin, he will have completed the required reading.
   Will he have completed the required reading by the time classes begin?
2. The concert was attended by the majority of the student body.
3. She has decided to take a course in shorthand before she applies for a job.
4. If they finish their work early, they're going to go for a long walk.
5. When the candidate gave his speech, he was being careful not to offend any political group.

EXERCISE III. 2.

Make up questions with the words indicated in the parentheses, as demonstrated in number 1. (Use the same verb form as that in the statement.)

1. Stuart saw a bullfight in Mexico? (What?) (Where?)

What did Stuart see in Mexico?
Where did Stuart see a bullfight?
2. Katsumi has won this year's debating contest. (Who?) (What kind of contest?)
3. Zobi's cat was found yesterday by Jack, a next-door neighbor. (Whose?) (Who?)
4. Karen should have lent her bicycle to George so that he wouldn't have been late. (Why?) (To whom?)
5. Mr. and Mrs. Perry will be staying at the Logan Hotel all next week. (At which hotel?) (How long?)

TAG ENDINGS

Tag endings are used in both questions and statements in order to avoid repetition.
Compare:

Kate works full time. Doesn't she work full time?
Kate works full time, *doesn't she?*

John can play the piano and Mary can play the piano also.
John can play the piano and *so can Mary.*

The tense in the tag ending **must agree with the tense in the preceding clause.**

Those flowers *are* fragrant, *aren't* they?
He *played* tennis yesterday but she *didn't.*

Use the same auxiliaries in the tag ending as are in the preceding clause, but change them to negative or positive when necessary.

Myra *should have* come on time and Damian *should have* too.
Bea *can* play the flute but Celia *can't.*

Notice, in each section below, whether the tag ending is positive or negative. Compare the tag ending verb structure with the verb structure in the preceding clause.

Tag Endings with "Be"

Endings with Yes/No Questions
He is busy, isn't he? They were busy last period, weren't they?
She isn't busy, is she? They weren't busy last period, were they?

Tag Endings of Agreement
He was absent yesterday and so was she.
He was absent yesterday and she was too.

Tag Endings of a Contrary Position
The classrooms aren't open but the library is.
The library is open but the classrooms aren't.

Tag Endings of Agreement with "Either" and "Neither"
Her sons weren't home but her daughter was.

Her daughter was home but her sons weren't.

Tag Endings with Present and Past Tense Action Verbs

Tag Endings with Yes/No Questions
> He speaks French, doesn't he?
> She doesn't speak French, does she?

Tag Endings of Agreement
> Dean went to Oklahoma last year and so did Debby.
> Dean went to Oklahoma last year and Debby did too.

Tag Endings of a Contrary Position
> The apple tree produced fruit but the peach tree didn't.
> The peach tree didn't produce fruit but the apple tree did.

Tag Endings of Agreement with "Either" and "Neither"
> The food didn't contain any sugar and neither did the beverage.
> The food didn't contain any sugar and the beverage didn't either.

Tag Endings with Other Auxiliaries

Tag Endings with Yes/No Questions
> I have met you before, haven't I?
> He hasn't met you before, has he?

Tag Endings of Agreement
> He may come tonight and she may too.
> He may come tonight and so may she.

Tag Endings of a Contrary Position
> The piano will be moved but the stereo set won't be.
> The stereo set won't be moved but the piano will be.

Tag Endings of Agreement with "Either" and "Neither"
> He shouldn't have disturbed them and neither should she have.
> He shouldn't have disturbed them and she shouldn't have either.

NOTE: Only one auxiliary is used before the subject in the tag ending.

> (wrong):   (They could have come last week, couldn't have they?)
>   xxxxxxxxxxxxxxxxxxxx
> RIGHT: They could have come last week, *couldn't they have*?

NOTE: When you are in agreement with a negative remark, respond with *no, not yes.*

> (wrong):   ("He doesn't speak English, does he?") ("Yes, he doesn't.")
>   xxxxx
> RIGHT: "He doesn't speak English, does he?" "*No*, he doesn't."
> RIGHT: "The Senate hasn't approved the measure." "*No*, it hasn't."

Special Tag Endings
> I'm being silly, *am I not*? (*Aren't I* is commonly used in conversation.)

Let's go to the show, *shall we*? (*Let's* proposes a plan for "you and me.")
Sondra ought to buy a dictionary, *shouldn't she?*
The earth revolves around the sun, *as do other planets.* (See Literary Variations in Section VIII.)

NEGATIVE QUESTIONS

Negative questions are asked to obtain confirmation. They are similar to yes/no questions with tag endings. Contractions are used in negative questions. Like tag endings, negative questions are sometimes used simply to pursue conversation. Compare the first two questions below.

She's the woman whom you met last night, *isn't she?*
Isn't she the woman whom you met last night?
Aren't those flowers lovely?
Haven't they moved to Alabama yet?
Won't he be at the dance tonight?
Hadn't he had any experience when he started his job?
Weren't you photographing the birds when I walked by?

EXERCISE III. 3.
Practice asking and answering questions such as the following.

1. You're a new student, aren't you?
2. You haven't been here very long, have you?
3. He plays the trumpet very well, doesn't he?
4. These photographs were taken on the campus, weren't they?
5. Didn't your friend call you yesterday?
6. Isn't he attending school this term?
7. Haven't we met before?

EXERCISE III. 4.
Complete the following with a tag question.

1. The wind blew some of the trees down last night, _____ ?
2. James hasn't told you about the assignment yet, _____ ?
3. Ruth and Jordan dislike big parties, _____ ?
4. She'll be taking a music lesson tonight, _____ ?
5. These shirts were made in Korea, _____ ?

EXERCISE III. 5.
Fill in the blanks with a subject, and add a tag ending as designated in the parentheses.

1. _____ likes to write poetry and _____ (so)
2. _____ weren't able to finish the text and _____ (either)
3. _____ is still sleeping _____ (but)
4. _____ won't be shown until next week and _____ (neither)
5. _____ voted against the proposal and _____ (too)

MIXED EXERCISE 5: PART A

Fill in the circled letter that represents the *correct* form. Be able to give a reason for your selection.

1. Mr. Caulfield went to bed as soon as he got home. He _____ for ten straight hours.
   Ⓐ Ⓑ Ⓒ Ⓓ
   A. had been working
   B. was working
   C. worked
   D. had been worked

2. If the alarm doesn't work on your clock, why don't you _____ ? Ⓐ Ⓑ Ⓒ Ⓓ
   A. have repaired it
   B. repaired it
   C. to repair it
   D. have it repaired

3. Howard _____ to speak with them but they appeared to be in a hurry.
   A. would stop
   B. would of stopped
   C. would have stopped Ⓐ Ⓑ Ⓒ Ⓓ
   D. will stop

4. By the end of this month she expects to _____ six chapters. Ⓐ Ⓑ Ⓒ Ⓓ
   A. be written
   B. have written
   C. have wrote
   D. have been written

5. When _____ ?
   Ⓐ Ⓑ Ⓒ Ⓓ
   A. will be the package delivered
   B. will the package be deliver
   C. will the package deliver
   D. will the package be delivered

6. The couple are looking for an apartment, _____ ?
   Ⓐ Ⓑ Ⓒ Ⓓ
   A. don't they
   B. aren't they
   C. didn't they
   D. are they

7. _____ did you buy the gift?
   Ⓐ Ⓑ Ⓒ Ⓓ
   A. For whom
   B. Who
   C. For who
   D. Whom for

8. _____ just before the entertainment was presented? Ⓐ Ⓑ Ⓒ Ⓓ
   A. Why they left
   B. Why they did leave
   C. Why did they leave
   D. Why they had left

9. The moment he mailed the letter, he was sorry that he _____ . Ⓐ Ⓑ Ⓒ Ⓓ
   A. wrote it
   B. had written it
   C. had been writing it
   D. was writing it

10. The customer complained that the lamps had not been delivered yet, _____ .
    A. and neither the chairs had been
    B. and the chairs too
    C. and the chairs weren't either
    D. and neither had the chairs
    Ⓐ Ⓑ Ⓒ Ⓓ

MIXED EXERCISE 5: PART B

Fill in the circled letter that represents the *incorrect* form. Be able to correct it.

1. If the storms continue, the sand on the beaches <u>maybe</u> <u>completely</u> <u>eroded</u>.
  A   B   C   D

   Ⓐ Ⓑ Ⓒ Ⓓ

2. Wei Yee and Lien <u>were going</u> to stay home from school today because they <u>had</u>
                        A

   <u>gone</u> to bed late, but Wei Yee <u>didn't want</u> to miss the test and <u>neither didn't</u>
     B   C   D
   Lien.   Ⓐ Ⓑ Ⓒ Ⓓ

3. Malcolm <u>had lost</u> the archery championship on three different occasions, but in
             A

   the event which <u>was held</u> last week, he <u>could win</u> the trophy <u>at last</u>.
                     B   C   D Ⓐ Ⓑ Ⓒ Ⓓ

4. There <u>was</u> a brightly decorated package in the office but <u>no one</u> seemed to
          A   B

   know to <u>whom</u> it <u>belong</u>.   Ⓐ Ⓑ Ⓒ Ⓓ
            C   D

5. When construction was <u>about</u> to <u>begin</u> on the site <u>near the woods</u>, some of the
                             A   B   C

   beautiful trees had to <u>cut down</u>.   Ⓐ Ⓑ Ⓒ Ⓓ
                        D

6. Since room 7 <u>is</u> too small to accommodate everyone, the class <u>is meet</u> in Room
                 A   B

   12 for the <u>time being</u>, and later it <u>will meet</u> in Room 14.   Ⓐ Ⓑ Ⓒ Ⓓ
             C   D

7. Why <u>has been</u> the annual meeting of stockholders <u>postponed</u> when <u>most</u>
           A   B

   people <u>have already made</u> plans to attend?   Ⓐ Ⓑ Ⓒ Ⓓ
         C   D

8. <u>Haven't</u> Henry and Simon <u>decide</u> <u>not to</u> give up their jobs until they <u>get</u> new
     A   B   C   D
   ones?   Ⓐ Ⓑ Ⓒ Ⓓ

9. Just as I was <u>about to mail</u> my letters, the mail <u>was loading</u> <u>onto</u> the mail trucks.
       A   B   C   D   Ⓐ Ⓑ Ⓒ Ⓓ

10. Aaron <u>is going to remain</u> at the warehouse until he <u>will be notified</u> that his serv-
                  A   B

    ices <u>are</u> <u>no longer</u> needed.   Ⓐ Ⓑ Ⓒ Ⓓ
        C   D

Four

INDIRECT SPEECH

Myron *said* that he would attend the meeting.
He *realized* that everyone was expecting him.

Direct speech is used to express ideas and thoughts directly to the other person or persons. **Indirect speech is used to report what someone has said or thought.** Compare the following sentences:

Direct speech: He said, "I'm very happy to see you."
Indirect speech: He said that he was very happy to see me.

REPORTING VERBS

The most common "reporting verbs" in indirect speech are *say, tell,* and *ask*. Other reporting verbs are *explain, state, declare, remark, mention, inform, report, announce, respond, reply, promise, indicate, point out, worry, admit, complain, confess, claim, remind, notify*. "Thought" reporting verbs are: *think, notice, know, believe, wonder, demonstrate, recall, remember, forget, show, realize*.

A *reporting verb* is usually followed by a *noun clause*. A noun clause contains a subject and a verb and, like a noun, it is used as a subject or an object. Noun clauses often begin with *that*. The word *that* can be stated or implied.

Mr. Njorge *mentioned* **that he had been educated in England.**
Mr. Njorge *mentioned* **he had been educated in England.**

Most reporting verbs may not be followed directly by a personal noun or a pronoun before the noun clause.

Mrs. Marsh explained (or: *explained to Roger*) that she needed a computer.
(wrong):   (Mrs. Marsh explained Roger that she needed a computer.)
           xxxxxxxxxxxxxxxxxxxxxx

The exceptions to the above rule are *tell, ask, inform, notify, show, remind, promise*.

She *showed the teacher* that she had understood the problem.
He *told us* that he had seven sisters and one brother.

SEQUENCE OF TENSES

Sometimes reporting verbs are in the present tense, but those that report what someone has said are **usually in the past tense.** Compare:

He *tells* me that he *is* in the Intermediate Level.
He *told* me that he *was* in the Intermediate Level.

In formal English, the verb in the noun clause that follows a past tense reporting verb must be in a past time form.

Aristotle *said* that Denise *was* in her class. (at the present time)
Aristotle *said* that Denise *had been* in her class. (at an earlier time)

In less formal, popular usage today, the verb in the noun clause is often in a present time form *if the fact or the event is still true.* Popular usage is usually used in newspapers, periodicals, and the like. Compare:

Formal:	The artist *said* that he usually *used* watercolors.
Informal:	The artist *said* that he usually *uses* watercolors.
Formal:	Ruth *said* that she *was* busy and she *couldn't* go out tonight.
Informal:	Ruth *said* that she *is* busy and she *can't* go out tonight.
Formal:	A bank official *reported* that the escrow *hadn't been* completed yet.
Informal:	A bank official *reported* that the escrow *hasn't been* completed yet.
Formal:	A federal judge *declared* last week that the railroad between the two cities *had to* resume service next month.
Informal:	A federal judge *declared* last week that the railroad between the two cities *has to* resume service next month.

In the list below, **formal changes from direct speech to indirect speech** are described. Study the differences in punctuation, pronouns, and tenses.

1. "Yervan swims every day."
   Yervan remarked that he *swam* every day.
2. "Sarkis is working on his research paper."
   Sarkis informed us that he *was working* on his research paper.
3. "Jill Markham has received a scholarship."
   Mrs. Markham wanted us to know that Jill *had received* a scholarship.
4. "Bea has been practicing the flute since noon."
   Mark replied that Bea *had been practicing* the flute since noon.
5. "Janet visited her friend Lynn last month."
   Janet declared that she *had visited* her friend Lynn last month.
6. "The men were fishing when their boat capsized."
   She observed that the men *had been fishing* when their boat capsized.
7. "She's going to leave at 8:00 P.M."
   He reminded them that she *was going to leave* at 8:00 P.M.
8. "The Rooneys are planning to travel before they return to Ireland."
   The Rooneys' friends knew that the Rooneys *were planning to travel* before they *returned* to Ireland.
9. "He can speak to you tomorrow."
   Your counselor stated that he *could speak* to you tomorrow.

10. "Cindy may help you."
    Margaret indicated that Cindy *might help* us.
11. "Richard will conduct the chorus."
    Brian thought that Richard *would conduct* the chorus.
12. "An expert has to assess the value."
    The young woman explained that an expert *had to assess* the value.

NOTE: *Must, should, ought to,* and *had better* remain the same.

---

13. "Ted should assist Bob."
    Betty pointed out that Ted should assist Bob.

OTHER INDIRECT SPEECH FORMS

Orders and requests are followed by infinitives.

1. The sergeant commanded, "Fire!"
   The sergeant commanded the soldiers *to fire*.
2. My friend said, "Please call me tonight."
   My friend asked me *to call* her tonight.
3. "Everyone must stop writing," ordered the proctor.
   The proctor ordered everyone *to stop* writing.
4. "Simone, you ought to get more exercise."
   The doctor has advised Simone *to get* more exercise.

For yes/no responses, use *if, whether,* or *whether or not* in the noun clause.

1. "Are you going to the party, Hideaki?" she asked.
   She wondered *if* Hideaki was going to the party.
2. "Have you filled in the application?"
   The clerk asked her *whether* she had filled in the application.
   The clerk asked her *whether or not* she had filled in the application.
   The clerk asked her *whether* she had filled in the application *or not*.

Noun clauses often begin with information words *who, what, where, when, why, which,* **and** *how.* These clauses are in statement form (subject before the verb), *not* in question form.

1. "Where did Joe store the containers?"
   He told her *where Joe had stored the containers.*
2. "How is he?"
   Mrs. Bates wants to know *how he is.*
3. "Which dress do you prefer?" the saleswoman asked.
   The saleswoman asked me *which dress I preferred.*
4. "What subject is she going to discuss?"
   She explained *what subject she was going to discuss.*
5. "Who was the speaker last night?"
   Talia mentioned *who the speaker was last night.*

NOTE: When direct questions do not begin with informational question words such as *what, where, when, why,* and *how,* use the informational question word in statement order. Compare:

"What is your name?"
"Can you tell me *what your name is*?"

"Why did they leave early?"
"Do you know *why they left early*?"

"How many books does Charlie have to buy?"
"Would you let me know *how many books Charlie has to buy*?"

Avoid the following kinds of errors:

(wrong): (Do you remember who was Henry the VIII's sixth wife?)
RIGHT: Do you remember *who Henry the VIII's sixth wife was*?
(wrong): (He asked her did she like to dance?)
RIGHT: He asked her *if she liked to dance.*
RIGHT: He asked her *whether (or: whether or not)* she liked to dance.
(wrong): (She pointed out him that she won't be in class the next day.)
RIGHT: She pointed out *(to him)* that she *wouldn't be* in class the next day.
(wrong): (We hoped if Sue could return soon.)
RIGHT: We hoped *that* Sue could return soon.
(wrong): (Yesterday a reporter announced that several homes have been destroyed.)
RIGHT: Yesterday a reporter announced that several homes *had been destroyed.*
(wrong): (He thought he can remember the woman's name but he can't.)
RIGHT: He thought he *could* remember the woman's name but he *couldn't.*
(wrong): (I don't know as I can recall her name.)
RIGHT: I don't know if (or: whether) I can recall her name.

EXERCISE IV. 1.

Fill in the blanks with the correct form of the verb in the parentheses.

1. We were asked not to disturb the baby because he (sleep) _____ .
2. He mentioned that he (be) _____ in court the previous day.
3. When Laura was stopped by the officer, she insisted that she (cross, not) _____ the intersection on a red light.
4. Since it was a beautiful day, Rafael thought he (hike) _____ in the forest for a few hours.
5. When the press secretary claimed that he (have, not) _____ any information, the reporters (leave) _____ the room.
6. Fred believed that his friend (promote) _____ by his employer a month or so ago.
7. The legislator noticed that there (be) _____ nine signatures on the bottom of the letter.
8. The article stated that everyone on the sinking ship (save) _____ .
9. Didn't they tell you that they (watch) _____ television now?
10. The instructor wanted to know if we (have) _____ any questions.

EXERCISE IV. 2.

Change the following direct speech to formal indirect speech. Use the past tense of the reporting verb in the parentheses. The subject is given.

1. "Betty is an excellent student." (tell)
   I _____
2. "She's going on a business trip next week." (say)
   She _____
3. "Are you planning to take a speech course?" (want to know)
   He _____
4. "Paul hasn't eaten breakfast yet." (think)
   We _____
5. "How long has she been married?" (wonder)
   Joe _____

EXERCISE IV. 3.

Practice asking and answering questions such as the following.

1. What did she say?
2. What did he want to know?
3. What did they ask you?
4. What did the reviewer say about the film?
5. What did the reporter say about the news?
6. What did the weather forecaster say about the weather?
7. What did she say that she was doing?
8. What did you tell them about your future plans?

EXERCISE IV. 4.

Underline the indirect or direct speech errors in each of the following sentences. Correct the error as in number 1. (Use the formal sequence of tenses.)

                                           resided
1. The director was told last week that Dusit <u>resides</u> in San Diego.
2. When I saw him last night, he said that he is soon going to look for a job.
3. Mrs. Vasquez promised that she will help us with the party Saturday.
4. Did the reporter announce when would the politician declare his candidacy?
5. They apparently knew that he divorced his wife and remarried.
6. I believe that Johann had to leave next Friday.
7. Can you tell me when will she be conducting a seminar?
8. Last month a few students asked me do I like teaching.
9. Heinz shouted that he can't answer the door because he's in the shower.
10. As soon as Fedora heard Dick's voice on the telephone, she could tell that he has just awakened.

Five

THE CONDITIONAL FORM

Conditional clauses **describe an activity that may or may not occur, depending on circumstances.** They frequently begin with *if* or *unless.* The conditional form is used in four ways: present general, future possible, present unreal, and past unreal. In examining the following examples, you will recognize that you studied the present general in the Present Time section, and the future possible in the Future Time section. Note that conditional clauses may precede or come after the main (independent) clause.

Present general:	He gets good grades *if (or: when) he studies.*
	He doesn't get good grades *unless he studies.*
Future possible:	If it doesn't rain, the party will be outdoors.
	Unless it rains, the party will be outdoors.

NOTE: In the sentences above, notice the difference between an *if* clause and an *unless* clause. The *if* clause has the effect of "cooperating" with the main clause action. The *unless* clause has the potential effect of "cancelling" the main clause action.

Conditional unreal clauses describe imagined situations rather than true or real situations. Such clauses are said to be in **the subjunctive mood,** "subjunctive" meaning "unreal." The unreal situation may, in fact, be the exact opposite of the truth. *Past form verbs are used in unreal situations.*

Compare:

Future possible:	If I *have* time, *I'll call* her. (I may have time)
Present unreal:	If I *had* time, I *would call* her. (but I don't have time so I can't call her)
Past unreal:	If I *had had* time yesterday, I *would have called* her. (but I didn't have time yesterday, so I couldn't call her)

Use the present unreal form to describe an imagined situation **in the present or in the future.** Note the verb forms in the following chart.

"If" Clause	Main Clause
Use past tense of the action verb	Use *would, could, might,* + simple form of verb
If George had a million dollars, If Nino took voice lessons, If she worked overtime, If Miss Wilson didn't have a secretary,	he could travel all over the world. he might become a great singer. she could make extra money. she would have to type the reports herself.
Use only the *were* form of *be* no matter what the subject	Use *would, could, might*
If I were you, If you were here, If she were an accountant, If there were a radio in his room,	I would tell him about the plan. we might go deep-sea diving together. she wouldn't have to hire one he could listen to the news.
Sometimes *were* + infinitive is used to speculate about the future.	Use *would, could, might*
If Ken were to become a doctor, (*or:* if Ken became a doctor) If George were to buy a small car, If they were to grow vegetables,	he would practice medicine in his home town. he might save money on gasoline. they could preserve them for the winter.

(wrong):	(We could shop now if the store was open.)
RIGHT:	We could shop now if the store *were* open.
(wrong):	(If Gladys comes on time every day, she wouldn't miss the review.)
RIGHT:	If Gladys *came* on time every day, she wouldn't miss the review.
(wrong):	(If the consul speaks English, he wouldn't need a translator.)
RIGHT:	If the consul speaks English, he *won't* need a translator.
RIGHT:	If the consul *spoke* English, he *wouldn't* need a translator.

Use the past unreal form to describe an imagined situation **in the past.**

"If" clause	Main Clause
Use past perfect of the action verb	Use *would have, could have, might have,* + past participle of the verb
If Moi had recorded the data, If I hadn't taken my friend's advice, If he had set his alarm, If he had had some money,	he could have written a fine report. I would have regretted it later. he wouldn't have been late for class. he would have been able to buy a new suit.
Use only the *had been* form of *be*	Use *would have, could have, might have*
If she had been at the party last night, If they had been happy, If the test had not been difficult, If we had been there,	she could have met Raul. they might have continued to live together. she probably would have passed. we might have been able to help.
Even if the action of the main clause is in the present or future, use the past perfect of the verb in the *if* clause if the imagined situation is in the past.	Use *would, could, might*
If Humberto had bought new guitar strings, If I had studied Spanish, If they had invested in that stock,	he would play for the class today. I could speak Spanish with my South American cousin. they might be wealthy now.

(wrong):   (If they would have tasted it, I'm sure they would have liked it.)
                    xxxxxxxxxxxxxxxxxxxxxxxx

RIGHT: If they *had tasted* it, I'm sure they would have liked it.

(wrong):   (Nothing would have grown, if the area wasn't irrigated.)
                                                    xxxxxxxxxxxxxxxxxxxxxxx

RIGHT: Nothing would have grown, if the area *hadn't been irrigated.*

(wrong):   (Gary and Miguel would cheer for our team if they had been watching the game
                                      xxxxxxxxxxxxxxxxx
              last Saturday.)

RIGHT: Gary and Miguel would have cheered for our team if they had been watching (*or:*
              had watched) the game last Saturday.

(wrong):   (Stan could of changed the tire if he had a spare one.)
                    xxxxxxxxxxxx   xxxxx

RIGHT: Stan *could have changed* the tire if he *had had* a spare one.

Besides *if* and *unless,* other words expressing a conditional state may be used. Numbers 1
through 4 below are in the future possible.

If he comes while I am out, ask him to wait.
If he *should come* while I am out, ask him to wait. (*should* expresses feelings of doubt)

If it rains or if it doesn't rain, we're going to go to the ball game Sunday.
Even if it rains, we're going to go to the ball game Sunday.
Whether or not it rains, we're going to go to the ball game Sunday.

If they can get tickets, they're going to go to the theater tonight.
They're going to go to the threater tonight *provided that* they can get tickets.

If they don't know the way, we will give them directions.
In case they don't know the way, we will give them directions.
In the event that they don't know the way, we will give them directions.

If is **sometimes omitted** in conditional *unreal* clauses.

If Mike were interested in becoming a pilot, he would take the pilot training course.
Were Mike interested in becoming a pilot, he would take the pilot training course.

If he had completed school, he wouldn't have had to take extra courses.
Had he completed school, he wouldn't have had to take extra courses.

If the wall is removed, the room will be larger.
Were the wall removed, the room would be larger.
If the wall were to be removed, the room would be larger.
Were the wall to be removed, the room would be larger.
If the wall had been removed, the room would have been large enough for the concert last
week.
Had the wall been removed, the room would have been large enough for the concert last week.

(wrong):   (Were the flowers planted earlier, they would have been in bloom for the garden
                    xxxxxxxxxxxxxxxxxxxxxxxxxxxxxxxxxxxxx
              party last week.)

RIGHT: *Had the flowers been planted* earlier, they would have been in bloom for the garden
              party last week.

(wrong):   (Had he not promoted, he would have never remained with the company.)
                    xxxxxxxxxxxxxxxxxxxxxxxxxxxxxx   xxxxxxxxxxxxxxxxxxxxxxxxxxxxxxxxxx

RIGHT: *Had he not been promoted,* he *would never have remained* with the company.

Clauses beginning with *as if* and *as though* are often in the subjunctive mood. (*As if* and *as though* clauses have the same meaning.) They are used to express actions that appear to be true but are probably *not true. Past form verbs* are used in these clauses. When the action in the *as if* or *as though* clause takes place at the same time as the action in the main clause, use *past tense.* Other tenses may be used in the main clause. Use the *were* form of *be.*

1. She has eaten the meal *as though she liked it.* (Later she confessed that she had disliked it.)
2. At the game last night, he was talking *as though he were a professional baseball player.*
3. There's a statue in the park that looks *as if it could walk away.*

As if and *as though* may be used in a future possible sense if the action is likely to happen. In this case do not use subjunctive mood verbs.

1. It looks as if the plane will take off on time. (likely)
2. According to the forecast, it appears as though there will soon be a storm. (likely)

(wrong):   (The author writes as if he feels every emotion of his characters.) (unlikely)
            xxxxx
RIGHT: The author writes as if he *felt* every emotion of his characters.

When the action in the *as if* or *as though* clause takes place *earlier* than the action in the main clause, use *past perfect* in the *as if* or *as though* clause. Use the *had been* form of *be.*

1. She acts excited, as though she *had received* some wonderful news.
2. Minasyan spoke English as though he *had been born* in the United States.
3. Every time I see him, I feel as if we *had met* years ago.
4. Sheila seemed shocked. She acted as though she *had seen* a ghost.
5. He was wet from head to foot when we saw him. He looked as if he *had been swimming* (or: *had swum*) with all of his clothes on.

(wrong):   (The antique Persian carpet looks as if it were woven recently.)
            xxxxxxxxxxxxxxxx
RIGHT: The antique Persian carpet looks as if it *had been woven* recently.
(wrong):   (Bertha played the organ as if she took a great many lessons.)
            xxxxx
RIGHT: Bertha played the organ as if she *had taken* a great many lessons.

Sentences with *wish* are in the subjunctive mood.
   Wish **is used to express present desire that is contrary to fact and to express regret about a past experience.** *Wish* **is followed by a *that* noun clause.**
   When expressing **present desire,** use the **past tense or the past modal** in the *that* clause. Use the *were* form of *be.*

1. He wishes that he *knew* the names of all the employees.
2. I wish (that) I *could play* the cello.
3. They wish they *didn't have to repeat* the course.
4. Sometimes he wishes he *were* back in his native country.
5. Do you wish that your home *were heated* by solar equipment?

(wrong):   (She wishes that they will remember her birthday.)
                                   xxxxx
RIGHT: She wishes that they *would* remember her birthday.
(wrong):   (He wish there was a swimming pool near his house.)
            xxxxxx   xxxx

RIGHT: He *wishes* there *were* a swimming pool near his house.
(wrong):   (They wish they have a larger home.)
            ^^^^^^^
RIGHT: They wish they *had* a larger home.

When using *wish* to express **regret about a past experience,** use the **past perfect or the past perfect modal** in the *that* clause. Use the *had been* form of *be.*

1. Lee Yoo wishes that he *had taken* a trip abroad before starting college.
2. Francette wishes that she *hadn't told* Pierre about losing the money.
3. They said that they *wished* they *had saved* more money. (In formal English, the past tense of *wish* is used with a reporting verb.)
4. Stan told us he wished he *had been warned* about the storm before he went sailing.
5. Andy wishes that he *could have gone* to the moon with the astronauts. (*or: would have been able to go* to the moon with the astronauts.)

(wrong):   (Displeased with the leader's policies, many wish they didn't vote for the man.)
                                                                    ^^^^^^^^^^^^^^^^^
RIGHT: Displeased with the leader's policies, many wish they *hadn't voted* for the man.
(wrong):   (Bill wishes he were there when the wedding took place.)
                             ^^^^^^^
RIGHT: Bill wishes he *had been* there when the wedding took place.
(wrong):   (He wishes that he could avoid the accident last week.)
                                    ^^^^^^^^^^^^^^^^^^
RIGHT: He wishes that he *could have avoided* the accident last week (or *had been able to avoid* the accident last week).

Wish is often used **in shortened clauses** as a response.

1. Did he see the exhibit last week? No, but he wishes he had. (had seen the exhibit)
2. She plays the piano beautifully. I wish I could.
3. Bob doesn't have to work next Saturday. Sue wishes that she didn't.

EXERCISE V. 1.

Fill in the following blanks using the correct form of the verb or the modal.

1. She would have returned the books if she (remember) _____ .
2. If we (repair, not) _____ the roof last summer, the living room (be) _____ wet now.
3. The Nolans will have to get a permit if they (remodel) _____ their house.
4. The sky is so red, it looks as it if (be) _____ on fire.
5. I wish the agenda (change, not) _____ at last night's meeting.
6. Chung (cook) _____ a Chinese dinner for us last night if he (have) _____ the proper ingredients.
7. If she (be) _____ free now, she (get) _____ a job as a social director on a big ship, but she wants to keep her present job.
8. If your friend makes a very important scientific contribution, she (receive) _____ a Nobel prize.
9. Ann wishes that she (receive) _____ a better salary so that she could move to a larger apartment.
10. The bedspread was beautiful! It looked as though it (make) _____ by hand many centuries ago.

EXERCISE V. 2.

The verb error is in *the second clause* of each of the following sentences. Underline the error and correct it.

1. She spoke in a very low voice as though everyone was asleep.
2. If they had had any extra time, they would visit the Tower of London.
3. Please tell him that I wish he stops making so much noise.
4. You won't have to pay a fine if you returned the book on time.
5. The yellow rose in the garden was so perfect, it looked as if it was artificial.
6. If my guests should arrive early, please tell them I would be back soon.
7. Many people would still be afflicted with polio if a vaccine weren't discovered.
8. Don't you wish that the cost of living was as inexpensive as it used to be.

EXERCISE V. 3.

Practice asking and answering the following questions.

1. If you could choose anything you wanted, what would you choose?
2. If you had a camera, what would you photograph?
3. What are some subjects that you wish you knew more about?
4. Have you ever known anyone who spends money as if he were rich?
5. If you had more free time, what would you do?
6. Where would you have gone last summer if you had had an opportunity to travel?
7. What are some things that you wish you hadn't said or hadn't done?
8. If you could have three wishes, what would they be?

MIXED EXERCISE 6: PART A

Fill in the circled letter that represents the *correct* form. Be able to give a reason for your selection.

1. The Easter parade _____ by huge crowds, even though it rained. Ⓐ Ⓑ Ⓒ Ⓓ
   A. was saw
   B. was seen
   C. was seeing
   D. has seen

2. He probably could have passed the exam if he _____ well-prepared.
   A. were
   B. was
   C. had been
   D. has been
   Ⓐ Ⓑ Ⓒ Ⓓ

3. While the secretary _____ his desk, he found the long lost report.
   A. had been clearing
   B. is clearing
   C. has been clearing
   D. was clearing
   Ⓐ Ⓑ Ⓒ Ⓓ

4. This morning she mentioned on the telephone that she _____ tonight.
   A. wouldn't be going
   B. won't be going
   C. isn't going
   D. will not be going
   Ⓐ Ⓑ Ⓒ Ⓓ

5. The adverse publicity _____ the company a great deal of money. Ⓐ Ⓑ Ⓒ Ⓓ
   A. may costs
   B. expects to cost
   C. could be cost
   D. must be costing

6. Generally Mr. Rubin is available for consultation but today he _____ some friends.   Ⓐ Ⓑ Ⓒ Ⓓ
   A. entertains   C. is entertaining
   B. has been entertained   D. is being entertain

7. If the Titanic had had additional lifeboats, more people _____ .   Ⓐ Ⓑ Ⓒ Ⓓ
   A. could be saved   C. could have been save
   B. could have saved   D. could have been saved

8. Thoroughly confused, the investigator hesitated to report _____ .   Ⓐ Ⓑ Ⓒ Ⓓ
   A. what did he see   C. what had he seen
   B. what he had seen   D. what he was seen

9. Josie doesn't work in the factory any longer and _____ .   Ⓐ Ⓑ Ⓒ Ⓓ
   A. either does her husband   C. her husband doesn't too
   B. also doesn't her husband   D. neither does her husband

10. That plant looked as if it _____ in a long time.   Ⓐ Ⓑ Ⓒ Ⓓ
    A. hadn't been watered   C. didn't watered
    B. hasn't any water   D. wasn't watered

MIXED EXERCISE 6: PART B

Fill in the circled letter that represents the *incorrect* form. Be able to explain why the word or phrase you have chosen is not acceptable and how you can correct it.

1. Billy <u>tried</u> to get a large group <u>to clean</u> up the park but he <u>has found</u> <u>only</u> one
          A   B   C   D
   person willing to help.   Ⓐ Ⓑ Ⓒ Ⓓ

2. The officer explained <u>to the driver</u> that he <u>had broke</u> the law by his failure to
                           A   B
   signal <u>while</u> he was turning <u>left</u>.   Ⓐ Ⓑ Ⓒ Ⓓ
         C   D

3. Mrs. Murray <u>will like</u> to speak to you as soon as you <u>have finished</u> doing your
                A   B
   exercises, and she <u>says</u> to tell you that it <u>will take</u> just a few minutes.
                 C   D   Ⓐ Ⓑ Ⓒ Ⓓ

4. Our friends <u>have</u> a son who is only <u>nine years old</u> but sometimes he acts as if he
               A   B   C
   <u>was</u> nineteen.   Ⓐ Ⓑ Ⓒ Ⓓ
    D

5. You <u>have better</u> be careful when you <u>drive</u> because the roads, according to the
         A   B   C
   newcast, are very <u>slippery</u>.   Ⓐ Ⓑ Ⓒ Ⓓ
                 D

6. <u>Don't you think</u> that she <u>would have helped</u> you yesterday if she <u>were</u> <u>able</u> to?
         A   B   C   D
                                                         Ⓐ Ⓑ Ⓒ Ⓓ

7. The young executive <u>was told</u> that if the computer didn't <u>function</u> properly, he
                      A   B
   <u>will</u> have to use alternative <u>means</u>.   Ⓐ Ⓑ Ⓒ Ⓓ
    C   D

8. If the drilling platform <u>had built</u> <u>to withstand</u> the violent storms, it <u>wouldn't have</u>
                              A   B   C
   <u>collapsed</u>.   Ⓐ Ⓑ Ⓒ Ⓓ
    D

9. The nurse said <u>us</u> to enter the room <u>very</u> quietly because the patient, who <u>had</u>
                   A   B
   <u>just had</u> an operation, <u>might be sleeping</u>.   Ⓐ Ⓑ Ⓒ Ⓓ
       C   D

10. Ordinarily, he <u>would have never</u> considered accepting a position before gradu-
     A   B
    ation but he <u>wanted to work</u> with the <u>eminent</u> scientist.   Ⓐ Ⓑ Ⓒ Ⓓ
                       C   D

Six

VERBALS

A *verbal* is derived from a verb. The four kinds of verbals discussed in this section are infinitives, gerunds, verb words, and Present Participles.

Verbs must be followed by the correct *verbal*.

Infinitive:	She **forgot** *to put* her name on her paper.
Gerund:	Troy **enjoys** *dancing*.
Verb word (or simple verb):	She **let** him *borrow* her car.
Present participle:	The police **caught** the boy *stealing*.

INFINITIVES

Infinitives are used in the following ways:

1. To complete the meaning of the verb.
   The child **started** *to cry*.
   They **agreed** *not to leave* before 5:00 P.M.
2. To complete the meaning of adjectives.
   Stewart seems **anxious** *to leave*.
   Magdy was **careful** *not to upset* her parents.
3. To show purpose and reason. (The full expression is *in order to*.)
   He works overtime *to earn* extra money.
   They studied hard *in order to pass* the test.
4. After expressions with *too*.
   We arrived **too late** *to see* the first act.
   She may be **too tired** *to go*.
5. After expressions with *enough*.
   She wasn't **strong enough** *to lift* the box.
   He had **enough patience** *to help* everyone.
6. To describe skill ability with *how*.
   Haim **knows how** *to make* beautiful kites (*not: knows to make*).
   Celia **has learned how** *to sew* (*or:* **has learned** *to sew*).
7. After information words (*what, which, where, how*, etc.), infinitives instead of noun clauses may be used. Compare the first two sentences below.
   I don't know which road I should take.
   I don't know **which** road *to take*.

She can't decide **how many** people *to invite*.
Do you know **where** *to register?*
She couldn't make up her mind **what** *to wear*.

8. As a subject or as an object. Words that are combined with the infinitive, form an infinitive phrase.
   To get eight hours sleep each night is not always possible.
   To tease animals is cruel.
   Not to speak more than one language can be a disadvantage.
   Bob's job is *to lock the windows and the doors*.

9. In sentences with *it* as a subject. *It* refers to the infinitive. Compare the first two sentences below.
   To get eight hours sleep each night is not always possible.
   It is not always possible *to get* eight hours' sleep each night.
   It has taken a long time *to finish* the project.
   It's a good idea *to review* the material.

Avoid the following kinds of errors:

(wrong):   (The nurse asked the visitor to quietly open the door.) The infinitive is seldom
            separated.
RIGHT: The nurse asked the visitor *to open* the door *quietly*.
(wrong):   (She gave her son some money for buy roller skates.)
RIGHT: She gave her son some money *to buy* roller skates.
(wrong):   (They didn't know what for to do about the situation.)
RIGHT: They didn't know *what to do* about the situation.

Other Types of Infinitives

A *continuous infinitive* (*to be* **+** *-ing* form) is used to emphasize the continuing sense of an action occurring **at the time of the main verb.**

He said he was happy *to be working* with our staff.
She's delighted *to be studying* art with a famous artist.
Mr. Foley was sorry *to be delaying* us but he had to wait for a telephone call.

A *perfect infinitive* (*to have* **+** *past participle*) is used to describe an activity that occurred **earlier than the main verb action.**

I am sorry *to have caused* you trouble this morning.
She appears *to have understood* the lesson this morning.
Mary Beth can't find her keys. She seems *to have lost* them.

A *perfect continuous infinitive* (*to have* **+** *been* **+** *-ing* form) is used to emphasize the continuing activity that occurred **earlier than the main verb action.**

She claims *to have been sleeping* when the crime occurred.
Ned is perspiring. He appears *to have been exercising* vigorously.

A passive infinitive (*to be* **+** *past participle*) is used to express an **action that occurs to the subject.** (The subject does not do the action.)

Tom hopes *to be promoted* soon.
Pollution is a serious problem that needs *to be dealt with.*
Vera will probably *want to be driven* to the ophthalmologist.

A perfect passive infinitive (*to have* **+** *been* **+** *past participle*) is used to express an action that **happened to the subject earlier** than the action in the main verb.

The telephone is working now; it seems *to have been repaired.*
She is thrilled *to have been invited* to the White House by the president himself.
Many of the sculptures in Venice appear *to have been eroded* by time and the elements.

Avoid the following kinds of errors:

(wrong):   (Leo is fortunate to find his wallet yesterday.)
                       xxxxxxxxxx
RIGHT: Leo is fortunate *to have found* his wallet yesterday.
(wrong):   (The investigative committee claimed to uncover a fraud last week.)
                                                        xxxxxxxxxxxxxxx
RIGHT: The investigative committee claimed *to have uncovered* a fraud last week.
(wrong):   (Doris was displeased to have found out that someone had copied her paper.)
                                    xxxxxxxxxxxxxxxxxxxxxxxxx
RIGHT: Doris was displeased *to find* out that someone had copied her paper.
(wrong):   (The employees expect to give a raise in pay soon.)
                                       xxxxxxxxxx
RIGHT: The employees expect *to be given* a raise in pay soon.
(wrong):   (All the gifts are stilled wrapped in paper. They appear not to be opened.)
                                                                        xxxxxxxxxxxxxxxxxxxxxxxx
RIGHT: All the gifts are still wrapped. They appear *not to have been opened.*

Verbs Followed by Infinitives

Some verbs can be followed by an **object** (a noun or a pronoun) **plus an infinitive.** The object performs the infinitive action.

Myron **taught his daughter** *to drive.*

Some verbs cannot be followed by a **direct object before the infinitive.** In this case, the subject performs the infinitive action.

Jeff **refused** *to sign* the contract.

Still other verbs may be used in either of the above ways.

The company **wants Jody** *to prepare* a financial report.
The **company wants** *to send* a financial report to its stockholders.

Study the following charts, which list the three types of verbs.

Verb + Infinitive			Verb + Object + Infinitive	
afford	fail	plan	advise	order
agree	forget	pretend	allow	permit
arrange	hesitate	refuse	cause	persuade
care	hope	remember	challenge	remind
consent	know how	say	command	request
decide	learn	threaten	convince	require
demand	manage	volunteer	encourage	teach
deserve	mean	want	forbid	tell
expect	need	wish	force	urge
	offer		hire	warn
			instruct	
			invite	

VERB + INFINITIVE *or* VERB + OBJECT + INFINITIVE
ask, beg, dare, expect, help, like, promise, want, wish, would like

Practice using the verbs in the chart above as in the following examples. Notice that the verb, or verb plus object, may be separated from the infinitive by a word, a phrase, or a clause.

1. Natalia **agrees**, after consulting with her advisor, *to take* the course.
2. The research institute can't **afford**, at this time, *to hire* additional staff members.
3. Those who took the nature class last month have **learned** *not to disturb* delicate plant life.
4. She said that she **didn't care** *to see* the recital.
5. Cary **has volunteered** *to supply* the drinks for the picnic.
6. Sam **may refuse**, since he's rather shy, *to make* a speech.
7. She **told them** *to listen* carefully. *or:* She **said** *to listen* carefully.
8. Mrs. Yokota **has advised Elsie** *to review* the material.
9. The director **persuaded the actress** *to use* another interpretation.
10. The instructor **reminded his students** *to bring* their book reports.
11. The forest ranger **permitted us** *to build* a fire in the clearing.
12. Mr. Marcus, the chief buyer, **is expecting his assistants** *to complete* the inventory by the end of the day.
13. Mr. Marcus, the chief buyer, **is expecting** *to complete* the inventory by the end of the day.
14. Jenny **asked Jim** *to work* on the project with Steve.
15. Yuko **asked** *to work* on the project also.
16. Next week Ismael **will be helping the professor** *to gather* data.
17. He **will be helping** *to find* information on early experiments.
18. The child **begged her mother** *to allow* her to stay up late.
19. The child **begged** *to stay up* late.

Avoid the following kinds of errors:

(wrong):   (Julius offered his friend to drive him to the airport.)

RIGHT: Julius *offered to drive* his friend to the airport.

(wrong):   (Alex refused, much to the surprise of the others, answering the question.)

RIGHT: Alex refused, much to the surprise of the others, *to answer* the question.

(wrong):   (Mrs. Genet wants her antiques to give to a museum after her death.)

RIGHT: Mrs. Genet wants her antiques *to be given* to a museum after her death.

(wrong):   (She told to them to listen carefully.)

RIGHT: She *told them* to listen carefully.

RIGHT: She *said* to listen carefully.

NOTE: The verbs that are followed by an object before the infinitive may be changed to passive voice, in which case no object is used before the infinitive.

The store clerks were required to attend a sales meeting.
(wrong):   (The store clerks were required them to attend a sales meeting.)

NOTE: The verbs *hope, decide, agree, pretend,* and *promise* are often followed by a *that* clause instead of by an infinitive; approximately the same meaning is retained.

Compare:

Miss Ross hopes to find a solution soon.
Miss Ross hopes that she can find a solution soon.

The above option, however, is not true of most verbs.

(wrong):   (The earthquake caused that the building collapsed.)
RIGHT: The earthquake caused *the building to collapse.*
(wrong):   (He deserved that he should get the award.)
RIGHT: He deserved *to get the award.*

Infinitives in Short Responses

The *to* of the infinitive is used in **short responses** to questions and statements, and also in short clause endings.

"Why did you take the longer route?" "I *wanted to.*" (*not:* "I wanted.")
"He was surprised when he got an A on his composition." "Yes, he *hadn't expected to.*" (*not:* "Yes, he hadn't expected.")
Becky walks five miles every day because she *likes to.* (*not:* because she likes.)

NOTE: Add *be* to the *to* in the infinitive if the question or statement is in the passive voice.

    "She seemed to be troubled by something." "Yes, she *seemed to be.*"
    "Does he expect to be promoted?" "Yes, he *expects to be.*"

EXERCISE VI. 1.

Using the words in the parentheses, complete the following sentences with the correct form of the infinitive. Add an object before the infinitive when necessary. When you are finished, read the sentences again, paying special attention to the various forms (verbs, adjectives, nouns, pronouns) that the infinitives follow.

1. Last night Rudy invited (come) _____ to his place for dessert.
2. The couple agreed, after talking it over, (move, not) _____ to another apartment.

3. A few small companies have reduced their prices (compete) _____ for a larger share of the market.
4. Mrs. Brooks allowed (use) _____ her kitchen facilities.
5. Irving has managed, at last, (pass) _____ the driver's test.
6. It is possible, even if one attends school part time, (obtain) _____ an advanced degree.
7. The hall clock doesn't work. It needs (repair) _____ .
8. Did she hurt his feelings? She (mean, not) _____ . (Give short response.)
9. We've decided that it's too late (change) _____ our plans.
10. She's of course very pleased (chose) _____ yesterday by the committee to represent them at the convention.
11. Jane's father has been encouraging (apply) _____ for the position.
12. Nojan is disappointed (win, not) _____ the athletic award.
13. Wouldn't it be wonderful (have) _____ a reunion next year?
14. He has failed, even after several attempts, (set) _____ a new speed record.
15. I wish he had been careful (touch, not) _____ the wet paint.
16. The candidate promised, after repeated questioning, (give) _____ reporters an answer the following week.
17. She's a good partner with whom (practice) _____ conversation.
18. Have you asked (give) _____ another assignment?
19. She seemed uncertain as to where (register) _____ for the class.
20. The girls couldn't communicate because neither one knew how (speak) _____ the other one's language.
21. Sometimes it's difficult (make) _____ a decision.
22. Do you have enough time this afternoon (go) _____ to the observatory with me?
23. Mrs. Jackson has been unable (find) _____ her map of the United States. It appears (take) _____ out of the classroom.

GERUNDS

A *gerund* functions as a noun and may be used as a subject, an object, or an object of a preposition. Think of a gerund as a **"noun activity."** Gerunds have an *-ing* ending.

Gerund subject:	*Fishing* is a pleasant activity.
Gerund object:	My husband enjoys *fishing*.
Gerund object of a preposition:	The family is interested *in fishing*.

NOTE: A gerund subject is often used instead of an infinitive construction.

> To fly a kite is fun.
> It is fun to fly a kite.
> *Flying a kite* is fun. (Additional words can be added to the gerund to form *a gerund phrase.*)

   Since a gerund functions as a noun, *the possessive form* of a noun or a pronoun must be used with a gerund. Compare:

Unfortunately, we missed *his speech* about Early Man.
Unfortunately, we missed *his speaking* about Early Man.
(wrong):   (Unfortunately, we missed him speaking about Early Man.)
xxxxxx

Gerunds With Verbs

The following verbs are followed by a *gerund*.

admit	finish	regret
anticipate	imagine	remember
appreciate	mention	resent
avoid	miss	resist
consider	postpone	risk
delay	practice	stop
deny	quit	suggest
discuss	recall	tolerate
enjoy	recommend	understand

Practice the verbs above as in the following examples. (Notice, in some of the examples, the verb or expression is separated from the gerund by a word, a phrase, or a clause.)

1. The supervisor **appreciated Rona's** *finishing* the job before she went home.
2. Heads of the firm **are considering**, if indeed it is feasible, *installing* newly-developed robots.
3. The officer **suggested** their *not walking* alone in remote areas of the park.
4. The brochure **recommends** everyone's *reserving* seats for the concerts.
5. Can you **imagine** *living* in the times of the American frontier?
6. Why don't you **quit**, once and for all, *smoking* cigarettes?
7. Mr. Chapman **can't tolerate** her *being* late so frequently.
8. She tries to **avoid**, if she possibly can, *discussing* controversial subjects.

Avoid the following kinds of errors:

(wrong): (Their mechanic has recommended them to take their car to a foreign car expert.)

RIGHT: Their mechanic has recommended *their taking* their car to a foreign car expert.

The following verbs can be followed by either **a gerund or an infinitive.**

advise	forget	prefer
attempt	hate	remember
begin	hesitate	start
continue	intend	stop
dislike	like	try
forbid	need	

Practice the verbs above as in the following examples.

1. It **began** *raining.*
2. It **began** *to rain.*

3. Miss McLean prefers *contacting* her clients in person.
4. Miss McLean prefers *to contact* her clients in person.

5. His family **have been advising his** *consulting* a lawyer.
6. His family **have been advising him** *to consult* a lawyer.

NOTE: In the following examples the verbs differ in meaning, depending on the form of the verbal.

---

7. Kurt **remembered** (didn't forget to do something) *to give* Kay the message.
8. Brian **remembered** (recalled from the past) *seeing* the painting a few years ago.

9. Florencio **stopped** (halted) *to look* in the store window.
10. Connie **had stopped** (ceased) *biting* her nails when I saw her last week.

11. She promised that she **wouldn't forget** (would remember to do something) *to bring* the music the next day.
12. **I'll never forget** (or: I'll always recall) *my spilling* wine on the hostess's white dress.

NOTE: Need may be followed by a gerund or a passive infinitive. The gerund in this sense has the same meaning as the passive infinitive.

---

13. This typewriter **needs** *repairing.*
14. This typewriter **needs** *to be repaired.*

Avoid the following kinds of errors:

(wrong):   (The dean intends to forbid the students smoke in class.)
            xxxxxxxxx

RIGHT: The dean intends to forbid the students *to smoke* in class.
RIGHT: The dean intends to forbid *students' smoking* in class.
RIGHT: The dean intends to forbid *smoking* in class.

Gerunds With Other Expressions

The following verb idioms and expressions are followed by a **gerund.**

can't stand, can't bear
can't help
have trouble (also have: a good time, a hard time, a problem, difficulty)
mind, never mind
make money
no use
spend time, spend money
take turns

Practice the idioms and expressions above as in the following examples.

1. Claude **spends his free time** *reading* history books.
2. She said that she **didn't mind** *waiting* until we got back.
3. The movie was so sad that they **couldn't help** *crying.*
4. In the debate, each team **must take turns** *presenting* arguments.
5. **Never mind** *cooking.* We'll go out to eat.
6. Steve **makes extra money** *waiting on tables* in the evening.
7. Some of the students seem **to have a hard time** *memorizing* the vocabulary.
8. There's **no use** *worrying;* she'll probably call you soon.
9. **I couldn't stand** *listening* to the loud music last night.
10. That collector **spends his money** *buying* old comic books.

Avoid the following kinds of errors:

        (wrong):   (Emiko, my neighbor, had a wonderful time last summer to go to the Broadway
xxxxxxx

                        shows.)

        RIGHT: Emiko, my neighbor, **had a wonderful time** last summer *going* to the Broadway
shows.

Prepositions, including prepositions that follow verbs, must be followed by a noun or a pronoun. Since a **gerund** functions as a noun, it can be the object of a preposition.

Practice following verbs plus prepositions with *gerunds,* as in the following examples. (See Verbs with Prepositions in Section VII.)

1. Some people **disapprove of** *marching* as a means of protesting.
2. He **apologized** to them **for** *taking up* their time.
3. One can always **depend on** their *being* helpful.
4. We walked in the rain **without** *carrying* umbrellas.
5. The experience was **like** *floating* on a cloud.
6. **Besides** *working* eight hours every day, he works three hours at night.

Avoid the following kinds of errors:

        (wrong):   (Tito was capable of to do the work unassisted.)
xxxxxxxx

        RIGHT: Tito was capable of *doing* the work unassisted.

Idioms and Two-Word Verbs with prepositions, (such as *feel like, "be" used to, keep on, look forward to*) must be followed by a noun, pronoun, or gerund. (See Idioms in the Supplement.)

1. It was such a lovely day, we **felt like** *taking* a walk along the beach.
2. Henry Thoreau, a well-known American writer, **had been used to** *living* very simply when he wrote "Walden Pond."
3. At his wife's insistence, Mr. Neiman **cut out** *working* twelve hours a day.

Avoid the following kinds of errors:

        (wrong):   (The child was irritable because he wasn't used to stay up late.)
xxxxxxxxxx

        RIGHT: The child was irritable because he wasn't used to *staying up* late.

Gerunds are used in many common expressions with the verb *go.*

go camping	go hunting	go skating
go dancing	go jogging	go skiing
go fishing	go sailing	go swimming
go hiking	go shopping	go walking

Practice the *go* expressions as in the following examples.

1. The girls *went shopping* last night.
2. We*'re going to go sailing* next weekend.
3. The Petrovich family *will have gone camping* by the time we finish summer school.

Avoid the following kinds of errors:

        (wrong):   (The Chang brothers aren't home. Every Sunday they go to sail.)
xxxxxxxxxx

        RIGHT: The Chang brothers aren't home. Every Sunday they go *sailing.*

Gerunds are also a part of many expressions with the preposition *by*, when it means "by what means."

Practice the *by* expressions as in the following examples.

1. Beatriz was able to take a trip *by arranging* her schedule.
2. He didn't have a car, so he got to the station *by walking*.
3. *By being* prepared, one can usually do well on a test.

Avoid the following kinds of errors:

(wrong):   (The truth was learned by question the witness.)
                                     xxxxxxxxxxx

RIGHT: The truth was learned by *questioning* the witness.

Perfect Form of the Gerund

Perfect gerunds are used to make clear that the gerund activity was completed before the action in the main verb.

having **+** *past participle* of the verb

Regular gerunds, however, may be used with approximately the same meaning. Compare:

perfect gerund   Our *having read* the book spoiled the film for us.

regular gerund   Our *reading* the book spoiled the film for us.

1. Mike seems worried about his *having omitted* a number of questions.
   or: Mike seems worried about his *omitting* a number of questions.
2. *Having been* a pediatric nurse a few years ago was an advantage for Victoria as a mother.
   or: Being a pediatric nurse a few years ago was an advantage for Victoria as a mother.
3. Yung appreciates *having won* the school prize for academic excellence.
   or: Yung appreciates *winning* the school prize for academic excellence.

Avoid the following kinds of errors:

(wrong):   (Them having had a good education was of great benefit in getting good jobs.)
                 xxxxxxxxx

RIGHT: *Their* having had a good education was of great benefit in getting good jobs.

Passive Form of the Gerund

Gerunds may also be used **in the passive form.**

being **+** past participle.

1. The children are enjoying *being entertained* by the clowns.
2. *Being carried* on his father's shoulders made it possible for little Benny to see the parade.
3. The members of the tour are looking forward to *being taken* through the palace.

Avoid the following kinds of errors:

(wrong):   (The cat didn't appear to enjoy holding.)
                                          xxxxxxxxxxxx

RIGHT: The cat didn't appear to enjoy *being held.*

Perfect Passive Form of the Gerund

Perfect passive gerunds are used to make clear that the passive gerund activity was completed before the action in the main verb.

having been **+** *past participle*

Regular passive gerunds with *being* may be used with approximately the same meaning. Compare:

perfect passive gerund   The child told us about *having been taught* two languages at the same time.

passive gerund   The child told us about *being taught* two languages at the same time.

1. They are discussing the problem of their *having been evicted.* or: They are discussing the problem of their *being evicted.*
2. She appreciates *having been given* an extension on repaying the loan. or: She appreciates *being given* an extension on repaying the loan.
3. Mako's *having been asked* to give a speech completely surprised her friend. or: Mako's *being asked* to give a speech completely surprised her friend.

Avoid the following kinds of errors:
(wrong):   (The defendant didn't recall having been inform of his rights.)
                                    xxxxxxxxxxxxxxxxxxxxxxxxxxxx
RIGHT: The defendant didn't recall *having been informed* of his rights.

EXERCISE VI. 2.

Complete the following with the *correct* form of the infinitive or the gerund.

1. He finished (work) _____ at 3:00 P.M.
2. The children didn't want to walk because they were used to (pick up) _____ at school each day by their mother.
3. Although the majority appeared (be) _____ disinterested, the speaker kept right on (talk) _____ .
4. Would you mind (turn on, not) _____ the radio?
5. Javad is considering (take) _____ the job because he needs (get) _____ additional experience.
6. A few years ago she wouldn't have been able, even in an emergency, (communicate) _____ in English.
7. The woman admitted, after several hours of (question) _____ , (use) _____ someone else's credit card.
8. Tony is fortunate, as is his friend, (find) _____ by the rescue team when he went (hunt) _____ last week.
9. He decided (risk, not) _____ , after (have) _____ such a successful career, (lose) _____ his license.
10. Sometimes she dreams of (carry) _____ away on a white horse by a handsome young prince.
11. It was difficult to understand (reduce, they) _____ the amount of money allocated for education.
12. She couldn't help, even though she tried not to, (laugh) _____ at the odd clothing which her friend was wearing.
13. You must practice, in order to improve (speak, you) _____ and (write) _____ .
14. Members were told that the organization couldn't afford, due to unforeseen expenses, (purchase) _____ new furnishings.
15. Mrs. Ting has managed, despite other obligations, (go) _____ to college and (work) _____ the past year by carefully (arrange) _____ her schedule.
16. They told us that they very much looked forward to (visit, we) _____ them and that they had many things (discuss) _____ with us.

VERB WORDS

A *verb word* is an **infinitive without *to*.** In the infinitive *to walk,* the verb word is *walk.* A verb word is often called the simple base or **root form of the verb.**

A verb word follows modals and expressions such as the following.

can	shall	must	would rather
could	should	had better	would (you) please
will	may		
would	might		

Practice as in the following examples. Notice that the modal or expression may be separated from the verb word.

1. **Would you please**, if you have time, *come* to my office today.
2. She **must**, before she drives anywhere, *buy* automobile insurance.
3. You **had better** *not visit* him until the doctor tells you to.
4. Chan **would rather**, if it's all right with everyone, *cook* dinner than go out.

Avoid the following kinds of errors:

(wrong): (We'd better, since we're not sure, to ask one of the students what the assignment
          xxxxxxxxx

          is.)

RIGHT: We'd better, since we're not sure, *ask* one of the students what the assignment is.

Auxiliaries followed by a **verb word** are:

do,   does,   did

Yun Bi stated that she **didn't** *own* a car but that she **did** *own* a sailboat.
Do the birds in that region of the world *migrate* to other areas?

Avoid the following kinds of errors:

(wrong): (Billy did, contrary to his parents' belief, to call home last night, but the tele-
          xxxxxxxxxx

          phone was out of order.)

RIGHT: Billy did, contrary to his parents' belief, *call* home last night, but the telephone
         was out of order.

Let and *make* are **followed by a verb word.**

1. The sergeant **made** the recruits *run* four miles before breakfast.
2. Mr. Rampal believes in **letting** his children *learn* from their mistakes.
3. I wish she**'d let** her dog, the one that barks all night, *come* into the house.

Avoid the following kinds of errors:

(wrong): (Mrs. Flanders made the boys, whose boots were muddy, to take off their boots
          xxxxxxxxxxxxxx

          before coming into the house.)

RIGHT: Mrs. Flanders made the boys, whose boots were muddy, *take off* their boots before
         coming into the house.

The verbs listed below are **followed by a verb word** *or* **a present participle.**

hear,   feel,   see,   watch,   notice,   observe

1. The speaker could hear the audience *whisper/whispering*.
2. When they were at the seashore, they saw artists *paint/painting*.
3. It's interesting to watch construction workers *build/building* a foundation.
4. As they sat on the deck, they felt the wind *blow/blowing* on their faces.
5. Janet spent hours observing the children *play/playing*.
6. While he was exploring the area, he happened to notice workmen *install/installing* a micro-wave transmitter.

Avoid the following kinds of errors:

(wrong):   (He reported that he had noticed her locked the door before she left.)
xxxxxxxx

RIGHT: He reported that he had noticed her *locking* (or lock) the door before she left.

Catch, report, find are followed **by a present participle.**

1. The police **caught** the thief *stealing* the diamond bracelet.
2. We **found** Peter in one of the dressing rooms *rehearsing* his lines.
3. The commentator **has just reported a** man *sitting* on the top of a flagpole.

Avoid the following kinds of errors:

(wrong):   (The photographer tried to catch the bird feed its young.)
xxxxxx

RIGHT: The photographer tried to catch the bird *feeding* its young.

The **causative *have* is followed by a verb word.** The causative is used when the subject gets, or asks, or hires someone to do something for him.
     Compare the two sentences below.

The Mendozas *are going to hire an architect to design* their house.
The Mendozas *are going to have an architect design* their house.

1. The police chief *had* **two of his men** *investigate* the complaint.
2. The instructor *plans to have* **an expert** *teach* the computer software course.
3. Since last September the theater manager *has had* handicapped **students** *work* in the theater.
4. The company *will have had* its **consultants** *test* the new products by next week.

NOTE: Sometimes a present participle, instead of a verb word, is used to emphasize a continuing action over *a period of time*.

---

1. The drama coach *had* **the cast** of the play *rehearsing all morning*.
2. By the time the bell rang, the teacher *had had* her **students** *writing* sentences *for three hours*.

Avoid the following kinds of errors:

(wrong):   (Sydney forgot to have his secretary, who had just left, to confirm his appoint-
xxxxxxxxxxxxxxx
          ments for the next day.)

RIGHT: Sydney forgot to have his secretary, who had just left, *confirm* his appointments for the next day.

(wrong):   (He had just had the waitress locking the back door when a customer came in the

xxxxxxxxxx
front door.)

RIGHT: He had just had the waitress *lock* the back door when a customer came in the
front door.

Proposals

Proposal verbs **are followed by verb words in** *that* **clauses. Proposal expressions contain** *that*
noun clauses and are used to suggest or require a certain procedure. These expressions are
often used to emphasize or to state officially. The word *that* is sometimes implied.

ask (that)	suggest (that)	insist (that)
request (that)	advise (that)	urge (that)
propose (that)	demand (that)	prefer (that)
recommend (that)	require (that)	move (that) (parliamentary procedure)

Practice the proposal verbs above as in the following examples.

1. Clem's advisor **recommended (that)** Clem *take* fewer units next term.
2. The company **has suggested** we *write* to them for further information.
3. The manager **asks that** people in the theater *not smoke*.
4. At the opening of the concert, the conductor **urged that** everyone *be* willing to listen to the strange contemporary music.
5. Chandra said that she **preferred that** a driving instructor, rather than a friend, *teach* her to drive.
6. The monitor **should insist that** students *not talk* during the test.

Use *be* plus the *past participle* **for the passive voice.**

7. Lu **has demanded (that)** he *be told* about any schedule changes.
8. At the meeting, Mr. Simon **moved that** all decisions *be postponed*.
9. The controller **may propose that** production *be delayed* a month.

Avoid the following kinds of errors:

(wrong):   (The administration requires that formal dress is worn for the presentation.)

xxx
RIGHT: The administration requires that formal dress *be worn* for the presentation.
(wrong):   (Her friends insist she should come early.)

xxxxxxxxxxxxxxxxx

NOTE: No modals or auxiliaries may be used with the verb word.

RIGHT: Her friends insist she *come* early.

Proposal clauses, like proposal verb expressions, are used to suggest or require a partic-
ular procedure. These clauses are followed by verb words in *that* clauses.

It is important (that)	It is imperative (that)	There is a requirement (that)
It is essential (that)	I believe it's urgent (that)	He saw the notice (that)
It's necessary (that)	It's preferable (that)	There has been a motion (that)
We saw a proposal (that)	He plans to request (that)	The rule is (that)
He thinks it's vital (that)	It was suggested (that)	A recommendation was made (that)

1. **There was a notice** on the bulletin board **that** all students who need housing *go* to Room 742.
2. **It's necessary** one *make* reservations for that particular restaurant a week ahead of time.
3. He said that **it was urgent** he *see* the manager.
4. If she wishes to get the job, **it's imperative** she *get in touch* with Mr. Mohler at once.
5. **There's a college regulation that** applications for the fall *be filed* with the registrar before May.
6. **A motion has been made that** the meeting *be dismissed*.

Avoid the following kinds of errors:

(wrong):   (The speaker said that it was essential we don't interrupt him.)
                                                                       xxxxxxx

RIGHT: The speaker said that it was essential we *not interrupt* him.

NOTE: Although *would rather* has the same meaning as *prefer*, do not use *would rather* in a proposal form. Use the past tense in the *that* clause.

(wrong):   (I would rather that he come tonight.)
                                          xxxxxxxx

RIGHT: I would rather that he *came* tonight.

(wrong):   (She would rather that he not visit her at this time.)
                                                xxxxxxxxxxxx

RIGHT: She would rather that he *didn't visit* her at this time.

Most words that are used in proposal forms may also be used in other, less formal, forms.

It is important to return their call.
He suggested attending the show.
She urged him to be careful of avalanches.
There is a notice from the county office to appear in court.

Be sure to use the customary form of the verb in *that* clauses that do not follow proposal verbs or clauses.

I hope that your friend wins the race.
He has decided that he will study abroad next year.
Delphine thinks that Manulis should buy the stereo with recording equipment.

Avoid the following kinds of errors:

(wrong):   (Gordon hopes that Sheila accept his invitation.)
                                            xxxxxxxx

RIGHT: Gordon hopes that Sheila *accepts* his invitation.

(wrong):   (He believes that the political prisoner be released.)
                                                      xxxxxxxxxxxxxxxxx

RIGHT: He believes that the political prisoner *should be released*.

Carefully compare the verbal forms of the following. A few alternate forms are presented here for the first time.

He helped her get on the horse.
He helped her to get on the horse.

Jean doesn't need to make an appointment.
Jean need not make an appointment.
Jean need only come to the office and a counselor will speak to him.

He doesn't dare to challenge the expert.
He dare not challenge the expert.

Would you mind (*or:* Do you mind) my opening the window?
Would you mind if I opened the window?
Do you mind if I open the window?

Would you please close the door?
Would you mind closing the door?

I suggest going to a film.
I suggest our going to a film.
I suggest that we go to a film.
Let's go to a film.

Rich prefers playing basketball to playing baseball.
Rich prefers to play basketball than to play baseball.
Rich prefers to play basketball rather than baseball.
Rich prefers we play basketball rather than baseball.

EXERCISE VI. 3.

Practice asking and answering the following questions. Answer in complete sentences.

1. Do you practice speaking English every day?
2. Did your roommate consent to cook every night?
3. Have your friends promised to visit you?
4. Did you let him use your telephone?
5. Does your car need repairing? (*or* to be repaired?)
6. Did she ask you not to tell anyone?
7. Did the instructor have you correct your own papers?
8. Did you refuse to do what she asked?
9. Did they encourage you to work hard?
10. Are you looking forward to having a vacation?
11. Do you mind your friend's smoking?
12. What do you suggest your instructor do?
13. Do you plan to spend your time hiking and swimming?
14. Have you suggested that your friend go with you?
15. Is it important that you be in class tomorrow?
16. Has he recommended that you apply early?
17. Did they appreciate your helping them?
18. Has your friend quit smoking?
19. Are you pleased to have passed the last test?
20. Do you miss being with your family?
21. Would you rather that that they didn't telephone you late at night?
22. Have you become used to getting up early?
23. What do you feel like doing?

EXERCISE VI. 4.

In the following sentences, underline the correct form.

1. Harvey was asked what time he would be through (to rehearse) (rehearse) (rehearsing).

2. He no doubt regretted (to not be able) (not being able) (not able) to see Melanie when she was in Seattle.
3. They didn't feel like, perhaps because of the weather, (to go) (go) (going) to the baseball game.
4. The instructor would rather that we (didn't hand in) (don't hand in) (not hand in) a late paper.
5. Before she buys a new car, she's going to have her mechanic, a man she truly trusts, (looking it over) (to look it over) (look it over).
6. The counselor recommends, after examining the aptitude test, Mary (majoring) (major) (should major) in a scientific field.
7. The notification requested that everyone, with no exceptions (be) (being) (is) at the orientation.
8. The strong wind caused the fire, which apparently had been set by an arsonist, (to spread) (spread) (spreading) quickly across the field.
9. The professor let his students, much to their surprise, (opened) (open) (to open) their books (for find) (for finding) (to find) the correct answers.
10. Boris didn't mention (him receiving) (having been received) (his having received) an award, so we were surprised (to hear) (hearing) (to heard) about it.
11. Apparently, the other tenants didn't mind (me playing the piano) (my playing the piano) (me play the piano) until 11:00 P.M. last night.
12. The marine biologists have just found a whale on the beach (to have) (have) (having) difficulty (to breathe) (breathing) (to be breathing). Although they keep (trying) (to try) (try) to tow it out to sea, the whale refuses (remaining) (remain) (to remain) in deep water.
13. The young bride insisted on (that she be carried) (being carried) (to be carried) across the threshold by her new husband.
14. She's all out of breath. She appears (to have been running) (to be running) (to run).
15. It was fascinating (watch) (being watched) (to watch) the young men (surf) (to surf) (be surfing) on the high ocean waves.

MIXED EXERCISE 7: PART A

Fill in the circled letters that represents the *correct* form. Be able to give a reason for your selection.

1. You can close your umbrella. The rain seems _____ .   Ⓐ Ⓑ Ⓒ Ⓓ
   A. to stop   C. to have stopped
   B. to have been stopped   D. having stopped

2. Mr. Lara has several stores, _____ ?   Ⓐ Ⓑ Ⓒ Ⓓ
   A. doesn't he   C. does he
   B. has he   D. don't he

3. Shawn said that he wasn't quite ready and that his hair _____ .   Ⓐ Ⓑ Ⓒ Ⓓ
   A. needed to comb   C. needs to have combed
   B. needs combing   D. needed to be combed

4. After the fire had been put out, the firefighters recommended _____ an alarm device.   Ⓐ Ⓑ Ⓒ Ⓓ
   A. the occupants' getting   C. the occupants' get
   B. them getting   D. the occupants to get

5. How high did he force _____ ?   Ⓐ Ⓑ Ⓒ Ⓓ
   A. the horse jumping   C. to jump the horse
   B. the horse jump   D. the horse to jump

6. Whenever the child's mother was out of sight, the child _____ .   Ⓐ Ⓑ Ⓒ Ⓓ
   A. would cry   C. cry
   B. had been crying   D. began cry

7. If she _____ come soon, they'll have to go without her.   Ⓐ Ⓑ Ⓒ Ⓓ
   A. didn't   C. don't
   B. won't   D. doesn't

8. The manager insisted _____ by check.   Ⓐ Ⓑ Ⓒ Ⓓ
   A. they don't pay   C. they not pay
   B. that they shouldn't pay   D. them not to pay

9. What kind of advice _____ to you?   Ⓐ Ⓑ Ⓒ Ⓓ
   A. has gave   C. was gave
   B. has been given   D. he has given

10. Lack of understanding and communication _____ trouble between teenage
    children and their parents.   Ⓐ Ⓑ Ⓒ Ⓓ
    A. frequently causes   C. frequently had been causing
    B. is frequently causing   D. causing

MIXED EXERCISE 7: PART B

Fill in the circled letter that represents the *incorrect* form.

1. Isn't the family planning to move to Washington if Mr. Rivkin will be elected to
   _____A_____B_____C___
   office?
   __D__   Ⓐ Ⓑ Ⓒ Ⓓ

2. Although it was very late when Mr. Zeng began doing the job, he managed, with
   _____A_____B____
   his friend's assistance, finishing before the building was locked.   Ⓐ Ⓑ Ⓒ Ⓓ
   _____C_____D_____

3. In what country he told you that he had lived before he came to the United
   ____A_____B_____C_____D____
   States?   Ⓐ Ⓑ Ⓒ Ⓓ

4. The Air Transportation Commission issued an order that all planes were to
   _____A_____
   inspect within the following three months.   Ⓐ Ⓑ Ⓒ Ⓓ
   __B_____C_____D_____

5. Nancy did not like him working late every night; in fact, this situation made her
   _____A_____B_____
   feel lonely and neglected.   Ⓐ Ⓑ Ⓒ Ⓓ
   __C_____D____

6. In case you have been looking for your friend, he's in the typewriter room
   _____A_____
   compose a letter to his parents to tell them that he won't be coming
   ___B_____C_____D_____
   home for Thanksgiving this year.   Ⓐ Ⓑ Ⓒ Ⓓ

7. The mayor <u>proposed</u> that the police commission <u>should</u> immediately investi-
             A   B

   gate <u>the charges</u> that <u>had been made</u> by some of the citizens in the community.
          C   D   Ⓐ Ⓑ Ⓒ Ⓓ

8. Some of the discoveries that <u>were described</u> by writers <u>in biblical</u> times <u>have</u>
                                     A   B

   <u>been found</u> by present day scientists <u>to have been</u> true.   Ⓐ Ⓑ Ⓒ Ⓓ
       C   D

9. If a person <u>should observe</u> someone <u>acting</u> violently toward another person, he
                  A   B

   <u>doesn't need</u> <u>become</u> directly involved, but he ought to at least notify the
       C   D

   police.   Ⓐ Ⓑ Ⓒ Ⓓ

10. <u>Before one votes</u> on the propositions, <u>it's truly vital</u> that he or she <u>becomes</u>
         A   B

    <u>familiar</u> with the reasons for <u>voting</u> both for the proposition and against the
        C   D

    proposition.   Ⓐ Ⓑ Ⓒ Ⓓ

Seven

PARTS OF SPEECH

NOUNS

A *noun* is used as a subject, as an appositive (a further identification of the noun) and as the object of a verb, a preposition, or an infinitive.

Mr. Allen (subject), the art *teacher* (appositive), has just sold an oil *painting* (object of a verb) of a *scene* (object of a preposition) which appears to be a winter *landscape*. (object of an infinitive)

Nouns fall into two classifications, *countable* and *uncountable*. *Countable nouns* are those that can be pluralized and counted. Most nouns simply have an *s* added for the plural, but some are changed in other ways, as in the following examples.

deer–deer	man–men	wife–wives
dish–dishes	child–children	mouse–mice
baby–babies	tooth–teeth	parenthesis–parentheses
woman–women	goose–geese	potato–potatoes

The *mice* that *were used* in the experiment *have died.*

   Uncountable nouns are those that are not pluralized. They are thought of *as a single unit.* Such nouns are abstract, mass, or collective in sense, as in the following examples.

Abstract		Mass		Collective	
advice	intelligence	gas	water	luggage	furniture
courage	information	sugar	cheese	jewelry	news
honesty	peace	rain	rice	food	money
fun	knowledge	sand	tea	jury	clothing
wealth	love			humankind	

The luggage is still on the plane.

Clothes is a plural word. *Clothing* is a singular word.

Warm *clothes are* a necessity for winter.
Warm *clothing is* a necessity for winter.

Some nouns end in _s_ but are singular in meaning.

news	statistics	economics
mathematics	measles	home economics
United States	mumps	physics

The news last night *was* depressing.

Some nouns ending in _s_ refer to only one item, but because the item has two parts, a plural verb follows.

pants	scissors	clippers
trousers	shears	binoculars
glasses	tweezers	

The *shears* which she uses to cut hair *are* very sharp.

NOTE: The term *pair of,* often used with these nouns, is singular. The *pair of shears* which she uses to cut hair *is* very sharp.

Some nouns can be used in either a singular or a plural sense without a change in form.

fish (salmon, trout, etc.)	buffalo	jury
deer (antelope, elk, etc.)	team	family
sheep	class	

There *were* many fish in the sea. The fish that he caught *was* delicious.
The *jury is* out of the room. The *jury* (members) *are* still disagreeing.
The *class was* interested in having an open house for parents.
The *class* (members) *have brought their* parents to the open house.

Nouns that are derived from adjectives are plural since the word *people* is implied. The article *the* must be used.

The sick (people) are less fortunate than *the healthy.*
There are more opportunities for *the educated* than there are for *the uneducated.*

When a noun is used as an adjective, do _not_ use a plural form.

(wrong):   (We bought two desks lamps yesterday.)
RIGHT: We bought two *desk* lamps yesterday.

When quantity-plus-noun is used as an adjective, do not use the plural form. (Notice the use of a hyphen in the two-word adjective.)

(wrong):   (We had a twelve pages assignment yesterday.)
RIGHT: We had a *twelve-page* assignment yesterday.

Don't drop the _s_ when a singular noun ending in _s_ is used as an adjective.

(wrong):   (The mathematic teacher was absent yesterday.)
RIGHT: The *mathematics* teacher was absent yesterday.

Possessive nouns usually refer to people, animals, places, and time.

Our *city's* mayor has been reelected.
She read the article in *yesterday's* newspaper.

NOTE: A possessive apostrophe is generally not used with material or abstract things.

(wrong):   (The table's leg is broken.)
RIGHT: The *leg of the table* is broken. *or:* The table leg is broken.

Add an apostrophe after the *s* to show possession for the plural form of nouns.

Sometimes the Dean can solve the *students'* problems.
Mrs. Baylor has completed a study on *birds'* nests.

Add an apostrophe *s* to the second subject of a compound subject and to the second word of a compound noun.

Mary and John's house is on the corner. (*not:* Mary's and John's)
The baseball players' wives often see the games. (*not:* baseball's players')

NOTE: To form the plural of a compound noun, add *s* to the main word.
      Mrs. Dickson gets along well with all her *daughters-in-law. (not: daughter-in-laws.)*

Many nouns can be formed from verbs, adjectives, or other nouns: *to befriend; friendly; friend; friendship.* The nouns below illustrate common suffixes (endings).

applica*tion*	teach*er*	relation*ship*	physic*ist*
abil*ity*	social*ism*	emerg*ency*	musi*cian*
content*ment*	decis*ion*	compet*ence*	deliv*ery*
kind*ness*	bio*logy*	import*ance*	weal*th*

NOTE: Don't pluralize names of school subjects or abstract concepts: *contentment, socialism, literature, competence, importance, wealth.*

(wrong):   (The importances of his philosophy should be recognized.)
RIGHT: The *importance* of his philosophy should be recognized.

ARTICLES

The *indefinite article, a* or *an,* is used to refer to **a single countable noun** that is one of many and not one in particular. *An* is used before words that begin with a vowel or a vowel sound, that is an unvoiced consonant.

Would you like *a sandwich?*
I am eating *an apple.*
You have *an hour* to finish the test. (The *h* is unvoiced.)
He bought *a history* book. (The *h* is voiced.)

NOTE: When *u* is the first syllable of a word, *a* rather than *an* is used: *a university, a united family, a unit.*

The *definite article, the,* is used before any noun (singular, plural, or uncountable) that is identified as **special or specific, a particular item or items.**

She thanked me for *the information.*
I used to enjoy *the chicken sandwiches* that my mother made me.
It was *the only photograph* that he had of his grandmother.
We didn't care for *the play* that we saw last night.

Do not use an article with a plural or uncountable noun that is used in a general rather than in a specific sense.

We have planted carrots in the garden this year.
She enjoys music of all kinds.
The company installed telephones in each office.
Would you prefer to drink milk or coffee?

   Compare the following pairs:

His mother gave him a dime.
The dime which his mother gave him is in his pocket.

Although dimes are smaller than nickles, dimes are worth more.
She spent the dimes in her purse on telephone calls.

She admires honesty.
She admired the honesty of his speech.

Use *a, an,* or *the* for single designations of uncountable nouns, such as *piece of, slice of, loaf of, cup of, box of, gallon of, teaspoon of.* Do not use *a, an* or a number directly before an uncountable noun.

Shawn has bought *a piece of furniture* for his den.
(*not*: Shawn has bought a new furniture for his den.)
                              xx
He has only *one gallon of gasoline* left.
(*not*: He has only one gasoline left).
                       xxxxx
Please give me *a teaspoon of sugar.*
(*not*: Please give me a sugar.)
                       xx

Use *the* with the superlative form of comparison. (See Adjectives.)

Louella has *the least* interest in sports of all the students.

The city hall is *the tallest* building in town.

Use *the* before ordinal numbers (first, second, third, etc.). Ordinal numbers *precede* the noun.

I asked him the question for *the second* time.
That is *the fifth* game he has won.

Do not use *the* (or any other article) before nouns that are followed by cardinal numbers (one, two, three, etc.).

Go to *gate three.*
We are finished with *chapters two and three.*
Will you please turn to *page thirty*?

Use *a, an,* or *the* before hyphenated adjectives preceding singular nouns.

Last week the governor went on *a three-day* boating trip.
She is taking *the eight-mile* hike instead of *the fifteen-mile* hike.
Don handed in *an eleven-page* essay.

Use *the* before the names of specific countries, states, and cities which are officially identified by a preceding noun.

She lives in *the Republic of France.*
Our daughter thinks that *the state of Oregon* is beautiful.
There are many tall buildings in *the city of Chicago.*

Use *the* before the names of specific rivers, seas, canals, forests, deserts, and oceans.

Steamboats are used to transport people to various destinations along *the Mississippi River.*
The Panama Canal is an important shipping route.
A variety of cactus plants grows in *the Mojave Desert.*

Use *the* when the word *university* or *college* comes before the name.

Shelley attended *the University of California,* but her brother attended *Glendale College.*
Masumi has been studying music at *the College of Fine Arts.*
My brother graduated from *Harvard University.*.

Do not use an article before names of streets, cities, states, parks, or possessive names.

They walked through *Central Park* yesterday.
I will meet you on *Montana Street* in front of *Joe's store.*
Are you going to *Paris* next summer?
Babs used to live in *North Dakota.*

Do not use an article before games such as baseball, golf, tennis.

Every Saturday they play *football.*
Tennis is her favorite sport.

When the words *school, church,* or *work* are referred to as regularly attended places, no article is used.

They go to school each day. (They attend *the school* on First Street.)
What time do you go to work in the morning?

When meals are referred to in a *general* sense, no article is used.

She met her friend for lunch yesterday.
They generally have tea at 4:00 P.M. every day.

When meals are referred to in a *specific* sense, use the article *the*.

We enjoyed the dinner which our hostess had prepared for us.

Use *the* for one or more of a countable group.

Two of the policemen wore civilian clothing.
Many of the people (*many people*) (*many of them*) waved.

***Some* and *a lot of* are used for uncountable and plural countable nouns.**

Rosa has a lot of knowledge about car motors.
He owns some good books.
There are a lot of roses in the museum garden.

Use *the* with the words *past, present,* and *future* but *not* with the words *present times, past times,* and *future times*.

He has worked with the same firm from the time he was twenty to the present (or: *to the present time*).
Undoubtedly there will be exciting new inventions in future times.

Avoid the following kinds of errors:

(wrong):   (Miss Ziv got two advices, one from her friend and one from me.)

RIGHT: Mis Ziv got *two pieces of advice,* one from her friend and one from me.

(wrong):   (He was placed in fifth level of English.)

RIGHT: He was placed in *the fifth* level of English.

(wrong):   ("It is a honor to be here," said his guest.)

RIGHT: "It is *an honor* to be here," said his guest.

(wrong):   (Have you seen good movie recently?)

RIGHT: Have you seen *a good movie* recently?

(wrong):   (Every day the Smiths eat the dinner at 6:00.)

RIGHT: Every day the Smiths eat *dinner* at 6:00.

(wrong):   (Next week he plans to look for the job.)

RIGHT: Next week he plans to look for *a* job.

(wrong):   (Please read the page two.)

RIGHT: Please read *page two.*

(wrong):   (The librarian removed one of reference books from shelf.)
                                    xxxxxxxxxxxxxxxxxxxxx   xxxxxxx

RIGHT: The librarian removed one of *the reference books* from *the shelf.*

EXERCISE VII. 1.

Fill in the blanks with *a, an, the,* or no article. (✗)

1. A few of ___the___ notices had been taken down before Jenny got there.
2. They told me that they had ___✗___ respect for their employer.
3. He mentioned that ___the___ information he had been given was useful.
4. Benita enjoys wearing ___✗___ jewelry.
5. For many people, ___✗___ childhood was not a happy time.
6. This is ___the___ first time that the child has seen ___an___ elephant.
7. Her teacher was born in ___the___ town of Williamson.
8. She is wearing ___the___ beautiful red dress her mother bought her.
9. It takes ___✗___ courage to begin a new life in a strange country.
10. She said ___the___ stories he told her were about ___the___ years he had worked in ___the___ country of Australia.
11. He purchased ___a___ new pair of reading glasses.
12. Have you finished ___✗___ chapter eight of ___the___ novel that we're reading in our class this month?
13. Can you lend me ___a___ pencil so that I can finish ___the___ test?
14. She was so tired that she took ___a___ two-hour nap.

EXERCISE VII. 2.

There is at least one error in each sentence. Underline the error (or errors) and correct them.

1. She asked the waitress for three-minutes egg.
2. It is a third time that I have heard that news.
3. Have you ever been on the campus of University of Colorado?
4. I have eaten the raw fish several times.
5. He was a honorable man who truly cared about people.
6. The teacher asked us to turn to the page thirty-four.
7. I would like to call you. Do you have the telephone?
8. That zoo has largest animal in the world.
9. Which do you generally prefer to eat, the fish or the chicken?
10. The house was advertised as having hardwood floors and security system.
11. Mrs. Wohl still has two childs living at home; the others are in college.
12. One of hospitals is seeking mental health professional.
13. Peter and Susan went to the Fred's restaurant last night.
14. My favorite fabric is the cotton.
15. Behind a house in which he lives, there are a lot of orange tree; therefore he can drink the glass of orange juice every day.
16. Mr. Aronovitch usually carries only one luggage on his trips.
17. Sandy needs to have two typewriter's keys repaired.
18. Pacific Ocean borders west coast of the United States.
19. When Janet went to the market, she bought the lettuce, the apples, and the fish.
20. Every Sunday, the two gentlemen can be seen playing the chess.
21. Peace-keeping force included troops from several countries.
22. Why don't you ask for an information about train schedules?
23. Marco Polo was an explorer who came from city of Venice.

24. She seemed to be *the* only one who enjoyed statistics class.
25. Some think that life was easier in the past times than it is in the present times.

VERBS

Verbs are used to describe an action or a state of being. They can be in the active voice or in the passive voice. Most action verbs are regular, that is, *ed* is added to form the past tense and the past participle.

call   called   called

To review principal parts of irregular verbs, see the Supplement. The principal parts of the verbs listed below are particularly confusing to students. *Transitive verbs* are verbs that can take an object. *Intransitive verbs* do *not* take an object.

		Transitive				Intransitive	
Present	Past	Past Part.	Present Part.	Present	Past	Past Part.	Present Part.
lay	laid	laid	laying	lie	lay	lain	lying
raise	raised	raised	raising	rise	rose	risen	rising
set	set	set	setting	sit	sat	sat	sitting

Compare the **transitive** and **intransitive** verbs in the sentences below.

When he came home, he *lay* on the bed. (intransitive)
When she came home, she *laid* her *books* on the table. (transitive)

The sun *has risen* over the mountains.
For many years Farmer Brown *has raised corn*.

Because there were no chairs, Don *sat* on the floor.
When dinner was ready, Maureen *set* the *plates* on the table.

Avoid the following kinds of errors:
(wrong): (Last year the rate of inflation raised by 20 percent.)
RIGHT: Last year the rate of inflation *rose* by 20 percent.
(wrong): (Susie's cat has been laying there for several hours.)
RIGHT: Susie's cat *has been lying* there for several hours.

Only transitive verbs can be used in the passive voice.

(wrong): (The unconscious girl was lain on the bed.)
RIGHT: The unconscious girl *was laid* on the bed.
(wrong): (The white coat is belonged to Muriel.)
RIGHT: The white coat *belongs* to Muriel.

The following pairs of verbs are often confused with each other.

affect–effect	tell–speak
hung–hanged (past tense)	lend–borrow
bring–take	used to–be used to
leave–let	suppose–be supposed to

Study the following groups of sentences to see how these verbs are used.

Smog affects plant and animal life. (*affect:* to influence physically or emotionally)
Scientists have effected a cure for many diseases. (*effect* (verb): to produce)
The drug had a bad effect on her. (*effect:* (noun) a result)

He hung the picture on the wall. (clothing, pictures, etc. are *hung*)
In the days of the early Western settlement, cattle thieves were sometimes hanged. (People are *hanged,* i.e. put to death by suspending by the neck.)

Dan brought us some lovely flowers. (One *brings* when one comes to a place.)
When she left, she took a sweater with her. (One *takes* when one leaves from a place.)

Stu leaves water for his dog when he goes to work. (*leave:* to cause something to remain)
He left the room. (*leave:* to depart)
Mrs. Callihan let her daughter watch the program. (*let:* to permit)

He told us that he was an optometrist. (*tell*: to inform someone)
She will speak about communication. (*speak:* to express ideas orally; it is *not* a reporting verb)

Sue has just lent Robert her pen. (*lend:* to give for temporary use)
Dana borrowed a dollar from Fred. (*borrow:* to receive for temporary use)

We used to play the game "Jacks" when we were children. (*used to:* in the past but not anymore)
They are used to the noise; it doesn't bother them. (*be used to:* to be accustomed to)

Tom used the mail order service for his business last year. (*use:* to make use of)
Bob isn't here. I suppose he has gone home. (*suppose:* to assume)
The auditors are supposed to check the accounts. (*be supposed to:* should)
Suppose you found some treasure. What would you do? (*suppose*: to imagine)

Avoid the following kinds of errors:

(wrong):   (Are you going to borrow her your car?)
RIGHT: Are you going *to lend her* your car?
(wrong):   (She supposed to meet me at nine o'clock.)
RIGHT: She *is supposed* to meet me at nine o'clock.
(wrong):   (Patty hanged her new dress in the closet.)
RIGHT: Patty *hung* her new dress in the closet.
(wrong)   (Some of the fish have been effected by the chemicals.)
RIGHT: Some of the fish have been *affected* by the chemicals.

Two-Word Verbs

Many idioms are composed of **verb–preposition combinations**. They are sometimes called **"two-word verbs." Some two-word verbs may be separated**, in which case the object may be placed between the verb and the preposition.

John *filled out* the application.

John *filled* the application *out*.

John *filled it out*. (*not:* John filled out it.)
_{xxx}

Other two-word verbs may not be separated.

I *came across* an old letter. (*not:* I came an old letter across.)
_{xxxxxxxxxxxxxxxxxxxxxxxxxxxxxxxxxxxx}

NOTE: Idioms and two-word verbs are explained and demonstrated in the Supplement. The two-word verbs that are preceded by the initials N.S. (nonseparable) may not be separated; therefore, the object must come after the preposition.

Verbs Followed by Indirect Objects

An indirect object refers to the one to whom something is given or for whom something is done.

He gave a book to me. (*book* is the direct object)

He gave me a book. (*me* is the indirect object)

(wrong):   (He gave to me a book.) The prepositional phrase must follow the direct object.
_{xxxxxxxx}

The following verbs are frequently followed by an indirect object:

tell	offer
give	show
sell	hand
buy	mail
bring	lend
send	read
make	write

Practice using the above verbs as in the following examples.

I sent Harry a letter.

She told her child a story.

Consuela made her husband a sweater.

Would you do me a favor? (*Do a favor* is idiomatic.)

Avoid the following kinds of errors:

(wrong):   (Consuela made for her husband a sweater.)
_{xxxxxxxxxxxxxxxxxxxxxx}

RIGHT: Consuela made *her husband* a sweater.

RIGHT: Consuela made a sweater *for her husband*.

EXERCISE VII. 3.

Review the irregular verbs in the Supplement.

EXERCISE VII. 4.

Review the two-word verbs in the section on Idioms.

EXERCISE VII. 5.

Underline the correct verb in the parentheses.

1. The English teacher asked the students (to bring, to take) their compositions to school the next day.
2. As soon as he (lay, laid) his head on the pillow, he fell asleep.
3. A question (was risen, was raised) as to the budget director's credibility.
4. She (hung up, hanged up) her coat as soon as she entered the house.
5. Akiko has knitted (for her boyfriend, her boyfriend) some socks for his birthday.
6. Microfilm (uses, is used) to photograph papers and documents.
7. Lloyd is tired; he (is lying, is laying) on the sofa.
8. Would you please (borrow, lend) me your dictionary?
9. As she (come, came) toward him, she (began, begin) to laugh.
10. When her mother was ill, Diane (took the responsibility over, took over the responsibility) of caring for the children.
11. After the new books had been (lain, laid) on the library table, they were sorted by the librarians.

EXERCISE VII. 6.

Fill in the blanks with the past tense and the past perfect of each verb.

become	became	become	fall	fell	fellen	bleed	bled	bled
bite	bited	biten	lay	laid	laid	choose	chose	chosen
lie	lay	lain	keep	kept	kept	find	fund	fund
drink	drunk	drinken	hold	held	held	drive	drove	driven
build	built	built	know	knew	known	rise	rose	risen
forgive	forgave	forgiven	lend	lent	lent	speak	spoke	spoken
go	went	gone	lose	lost	lost	take	took	taken
buy	bought	bought	grow	grew	grown	raise	raised	raised
stick	stuck	stuck	shake	shaked	shaked	sit	sat	sat
fight	fight	fight	blow	blew	blown	win	won	won

ADJECTIVES

An *adjective* describes (modifies) a noun or a gerund. Adjectives do not change in gender or number.

> soft pillows; excellent essay; interesting information; tall women

The usual order of adjectives is demonstrated in the following example.

	number	general description	size	color	type	material	
Sam owns	two	handsome	large	white	Texan	leather	hats.

Present and Past Participles as Adjectives

The *present participle* before a noun describes **what the noun is actively doing**.

swaying trees
moving train
boiling water
sinking ship

The *present participle* also describes the general use of the noun or **what the noun customarily does**.

washing machine
dining table
growing children
landing gear

The *past participle* describes **what happened to the noun (usually earlier).**

baked potato
signed contract
injured hand
frozen meat
lost puppy

The use of the present and past participle of words such as those listed below is sometimes confusing.

amusing–amused   exciting–excited
interesting–interested   confusing–confused
boring–bored   discouraging–discouraged

The present participle of these words describes **a judgment or an opinion** (how a situation appears to someone).

The book is *interesting. or*: It's an *interesting* book. (in my opinion)
(wrong):   (The book is interested. It's an interested book.)
They thought the exhibit was *boring*. The *boring* exhibit did not hold their attention.
The question was *confusing*. It was a *confusing* question.

The past participle of these words describes how the subject itself has been influenced or affected by an outside force or stimulus.

Yong Lee is *interested* in the book. (The book is the external stimulus.)
(wrong):   (Yong Lee is interesting in the book.)
Sascha was *confused* about the directions.
Lana felt *embarrassed* about the situation.

NOTE: The (adjective *open*) rather than the past participle *opened* is used to modify nouns. The window is *open* and the door is *closed*. A bird flew in through the *open* window. (Passive: The window was *opened* by the janitor.)

Present or past participles often replace clauses that describe nouns. The participle comes before or after the noun and is set off by commas.
  Compare:

Becky, *who was crying*, waved good-bye to her friends. (adjective clause)
Becky, *crying*, waved good-bye to her friends. *or: Crying*, Becky waved good-bye to her friends. (present participle as adjective)

When the participle is combined with other words, the group of words is called *an adjective phrase* or a *modifying adjective phrase*. (See "Using Participles" in Section VIII.)

Crying softly, Becky waved good-bye to her friends.
Becky, *crying softly*, waved good-bye to her friends.

Forgiven by its master, the dog wagged its tail.
The dog, *forgiven by its master*, wagged its tail.

Adjectives After State of Being Verbs and Linking Verbs

Adjectives are used after some form of a *be* verb or a linking verb. The following **linking verbs** are treated like *be* verbs in that they link or connect the adjective to the noun.

seem	taste
sound	become
feel	get
smell	grow
remain	turn
appear	

(*Get, grow* and *turn* mean, "become.")

1. **Jane** *is* **tired.**
2. **Jane** *seems* **tired.**
3. **Jane** *feels* **tired.**
4. The **roses** in her garden *were beautiful.*
5. The **music** from the new stereo *sounds wonderful.*
6. The **children** *grew restless* during the film.
7. His **ideas** *appear to be trite* and *boring.*
8. This chilled **drink** which she has given us *tastes bitter.*
9. Some **employees** *are becoming confused* about the retirement policy.

Adjectives of Emotion Followed by Adverbial *That* Clauses

That clauses are often used after **adjectives and past participles that express emotion.**

He is *happy* **that his application has been accepted.**

She was *concerned* **that she might not qualify for the diving event**.

Below is a list of **common adjectives and past participles** that can be used with *that* clauses.

afraid	excited	satisfied
angry	glad	shocked
annoyed	happy	sorry
ashamed	hopeful	sure
concerned	pleased	surprised
depressed	positive	thrilled
disappointed	proud	upset
disgusted	sad	worried

Comparison of Adjectives

The comparative form of an adjective or an adverb contrasts (or compares) *two*. Think of the two as two sides; there may be one or more on one side and one or more on the other side. Use *than* in the comparative form.

Lin is *taller than* his brother Wang.
This **dress** is *more attractive than* the other dresses.
The **members** of the green team seemed *stronger than* the **members** of the red team.

The superlative form of an adjective describes the one that stands out from a group of three or more. The article *the* must precede the superlative adjective. Use *of* or *in* in the superlative form.

Raymond has *the largest* stamp collection *of* the collectors.
Last night's play was *the most exciting in* the series.

Comparison of *Regular* Adjectives

	Positive	Comparative	Superlative
One-syllable words:	tall	taller	the tallest
Two-syllable words ending in *y, er, ow, le*	pretty	prettier	the prettiest
	clever	cleverer	the cleverest
	yellow	yellower	the yellowest
	stable	stabler	the stablest
All other words of two or more syllables	careful	more careful	the most careful
	intelligent	more intelligent	the most intelligent

1. Our classroom is sunnier than the one across the hall.
2. Mr. Cho was the cleverest man she had ever met.
3. The Greek philosophers may have been the most influential of all the philosophers.
4. Su Ling appears to be more responsive than her sister.

Sometimes the full comparative or superlative phrase is only implied.

Today's test is more difficult. (*implied*: than yesterday's test)
I buy fruit at the open market because it tastes the best. (of all)

Sometimes a comparative adjective or adverb refers to a single subject which is compared to itself.

Willie looks happier today. (than he did yesterday)
Since it has been repaired, the machine works more efficiently.

Sometimes double comparatives are used. Notice the similarity in structure.

The deeper the roots are, *the stronger* the tree is.
The longer she practiced, *the more accurately* she typed.
The higher the mountain (is), *the harder* (it is) to climb.

Sometimes a prepositional phrase expressing "of the two" is used in the comparative form.
The article *the* must precede the comparative adjective or adverb.

I think this painting is *the more interesting of the two*.
Unquestionably, *of the two students*, Asa works *the harder*.

Comparison of *Irregular* Adjectives

Positive	Comparative	Superlative
much	more	the most
many	more	the most
little	less	the least
good	better	the best
bad	worse	the worst

1. Mary had *the worst* case of measles of all the children.
2. His recent art works seem to have *less* appeal than the earlier ones.
3. Don't you think her pronounciation is *better* than it was?
4. Jed had *the least* difficulty of all the students figuring out the problem.

Avoid the following kinds of errors:

(wrong):   (The Himalayas in Central Asia are the most highest mountains in the world.)

RIGHT: The Himalayas in Central Asia are *the highest* mountains in the world.

(wrong):   (The view from the top of the hill was even more lovelier than the view at sea level.)

RIGHT: The view from the top of the hill was even *lovelier* than the view at sea level.

(wrong):   (Of the two courses, Tomasa thought that geology was the most fascinating.)

RIGHT: Of the two courses, Tomasa thought that geology was *the more fascinating*.

(wrong):   (The child had the worse case of measles the doctor had ever seen.)

RIGHT: The child had *the worst* case of measles the doctor had ever seen.

(wrong):   (Following the instructions on how to assemble the toy was confused.)

RIGHT: Following the instructions on how to assemble the toy was *confusing*.

(wrong):   (Kunya has a rare green beautiful jade ring.)

RIGHT: Kunya has a beautiful rare green jade ring.

(wrong):   (Between them, Dr. McCaffery has the greatest insight.)

RIGHT: Between them, Dr. McCaffery has *the greater* insight.

(wrong):   (Among the inventors at the convention, Mr. Ito seemed cleverest.)
                                                                          xxxxxxxxxxx
RIGHT: Among the inventors at the convention, Mr. Ito seemed *the cleverest*.
(wrong):   (The World Trade Center is taller as the Empire State building.)
                                                   xxx
RIGHT: The World Trade Center is taller *than* the Empire State building.

The phrases *the same as, as — as, similar to,* and *different from* are used in **comparing equality and inequality in adjectives**.

Brazil has about *the same* amount of coal *as* Norway.
Albert's essay was *as* amusing, if not more amusing, *as* Dana's (not: than Dana's).
                                                                        xxxxxxx
The architecture in London is very *different from* the architecture in New York City.
Jane's ideas were *similar to* Albert's.

The following sentences illustrate how **indefinite adjectives and pronouns** are used in **comparative form**. Note that *any* becomes *any other*, *someone* becomes *someone else*, *all* becomes *all (of) the other*, *somewhere* becomes *somewhere else* and so on. When *prefer* is the verb, the preposition *to* is placed before the second noun or gerund. *Would rather* is also commonly used in comparative forms.

He prefers fishing *to any other activity* (not: than any other activity).
                                                              xxxxxxx
Eric and Ida would rather visit Hawaii than *anywhere else* (not: than anywhere).
                                                                              xxxxxxxxxxxxx

In the following sentences, **the comparative form shows increasing degree.**

As summer approached, the days seemed *longer and longer*.
Gradually, he became *more and more* upset over the noise.

More is also used **in a noncomparative sense.**

Would you like *more* milk? (additional milk)
She asked for *more* time to complete the test.

The following adjectives are **conclusive in meaning** and therefore they cannot be used in comparative forms: *unique, perfect, pregnant, fatal, dead, empty.*
(wrong):   (This rose is more perfect than the other rose.)
                                   xxxxxxxxxxxxxxxxxx
RIGHT: This rose is *perfect*.

Adjectives With Countable and Uncountable Nouns

Use *much, a great deal of,* or *a lot of* with *uncountable nouns.* (*Much* is usually used only with negative verbs.) Use *many* and *a lot of* with *countable nouns.* (*A lot of* is usually used only with positive verbs.)

The meteorologist wasn't able to give *much information* about the hurricane.
Mrs. Greenberg has *a great deal of knowledge* about plants.
They had *a lot of fun* playing croquet.
There aren't *many eggs* left in the refrigerator.
Fedora and Harry have *a lot of friends* (or: *many friends,* or: *a great many friends*).

More **may be used with both countable and uncountable nouns.**

At one time there were *more* trains in the United States than there are today. (or: *many more* trains) (or: *a great many more* trains)

There appeared to be *more* fruit on the ground than on the tree. (or: *much more* fruit)

Use *little, less,* and *the least* with *uncountable nouns.* Use *few, fewer, the fewest* with *countable nouns.* The word *amount* is used with an *uncountable noun,* whereas the word *number* is used with a *countable noun.*

He has *little respect* for most politicians.

She has *less difficulty* in science than she does in English.

Of all the teachers, Mr. Font gave *the least homework* (or: *the least amount of homework*).

There were *few* imported *cars* in the showroom.

Some companies offer good insurance rates to those who have had *the fewest violations* (or: *the fewest number of violations*).

Jim feels that *the fewer possessions* he has, the better.

There is a difference between *little* and *a little,* and between *few* and *a few. Little* means *not much; few* means *not many. A little* and *a few* mean "some."

I can't make a pie because there is *little sugar.* (not much sugar)

There is *a little sugar* for your coffee. (some sugar)

She doesn't seem very friendly; she has *few friends.* (not many friends)

Although Lida has been here only a short time, she has already made *a few friends.* (some friends)

NOTE: When *only* is added, the article *a* must be used.

There is *only a little gas* left in the car.
Only a few tickets are left for the show.

Use the following adjectives with both *countable* and *uncountable* nouns: *other* (meaning "additional"); *the other* (meaning "the second of two"); *some* (use in positive statements); *any* (use in negative statements and in questions).

There is *some dressing* in the salad.

Some people enjoy baseball and *other people* enjoy football.

Janet couldn't find *any books* on child care in the bookstore.

The red tie is attractive but *the other tie* is even more attractive.

Do you have *any change* for a dollar?

Use the following adjectives with *singular countable nouns: each, every, either, neither, another* (meaning "one more").

Each year more is learned about the universe.

The librarian has catalogued *every book* in the fiction section.

I enjoy *either one,* the red wine or the white wine.

Neither course was what Antonio had in mind.

Would you care for *another cup* of tea? (not: other cup of tea)

Additional Rules About Adjectives

Use a **plural form of measure with adjectives** and a **singular form of measure with nouns.**

The table is *three-feet wide.* It is a *three-foot* wide *table.*
The hike was *four and a half miles.* We took a *four-and-a half* mile hike.
My friend Mary is a *five-foot-two-inch* tall *woman.* She's *five-feet-two-inches tall.*

The word *helpless* applies to **people and animals.** The word *useless* usually applies to **things and ideas** but occasionally can also apply to people.

The animal, trapped under a fallen tree, appeared *helpless.* (powerless)
The police tried to revive the man but it was *useless.* (of no value)
In any kind of an emergency situation, her cousin seems *useless.* (ineffectual; incapable)

Adjectives referring to **color of hair** are: *red-haired, black-haired, brown-haired, light-haired,* and so forth.

No one seemed to know the *red-haired man* talking to the blonde girl.

The adjectives below illustrate some **common suffixes (endings).**

help*ful*	child*ish*	numer*ous*
use*less*	sens*ible*	dramat*ic*
politi*cal*	comfort*able*	monet*ary*
attent*ive*	health*y*	essen*tial*
depend*ent*	crowd*ed*	relig*ious*
milit*ant*	bor*ing*	

Avoid the following kinds of errors:

(wrong): (Since she didn't have many bread, she couldn't make sandwiches.)
RIGHT: Since she didn't have *much* bread, she couldn't make sandwiches.
(wrong): (The farmer had a great deal of potatoes that he couldn't sell.)
RIGHT: The farmer had *a great many* potatoes that he couldn't sell.
(wrong): (Mrs. Blake has had small opportunity to travel.)
RIGHT: Mrs. Blake has had *little* opportunity to travel.
(wrong): (Please serve few kinds of drinks to our guests.)
RIGHT: Please serve *a few* kinds of drinks to our guests.
(wrong): (Of the two chairs which one do you prefer, the gray chair or other chair.)
RIGHT: Of the two chairs which one do you prefer, the gray chair or *the other* chair (or: the other one).
(wrong): (The city of Chicago had trouble getting rid of its large amount of rats.)
RIGHT: The city of Chicago had trouble getting rid of its large *number* of rats.
(wrong): (He said that he didn't have some interest in politics.)
RIGHT: He said that he didn't have *any* interest in politics.
(wrong): (He complained that he had much more problems than he used to.)
RIGHT: He complained that he had *many more* (or: *a great many more*) problems than he used to.

(wrong):   (Although the captain tried everything possible, he was useless to save the
xxxxxxxxx
             drowning man.)

RIGHT: Although the captain tried everything possible, he was *helpless* to save the drown-
           ing man.

(wrong):   (Presumably there are less diseases in the frigid zones than there are in the torrid
xxxxx
             zones.)

RIGHT: Presumably there are *fewer* diseases in the frigid zones than there are in the torrid
           zones.

(wrong):   (They would rather live in Wyoming than anywhere in the United States.)
xxxxxxxxxxxxxx

RIGHT: They would rather live in Wyoming than *anywhere else* in the United States.

(wrong):   (He thought his method was more efficient than all the methods.)
xxxx

RIGHT: He thought his method was more efficient than *all the other* methods.

(wrong):   (On the top of the seven-and-a third-feet pole was a birdhouse.)
xxxxxxxxxxxxxxxxxxxxxxxxxxxxxxx

RIGHT: On the top of the *seven-and-a third-foot* pole was a birdhouse.

ADVERBS

An adverb describes (modifies) an action verb, an adjective, or another adverb. Adverbs
are used to refer to **manner, time, quality, and quantity.**

Compare the use of adjectives and adverbs in the following sentences.

He is slow.
He **works** *slowly*. (describes an action verb)

She appears to be a rapid typist.
She appears to be an *extremely* **rapid** typist. (describes an adjective)
She types *extremely* **rapidly**. (describes an adverb)

Rahman's family is Rahman's primary interest.
Rahman is *primarily* **interested** in engineering.
Also: Rahman is *primarily* an engineer. *or:* *Primarily*, Rahman is an engineer.

NOTE: Used in the same manner as *primarily* are the adverbs *chiefly, basically, mainly, prin-
       cipally, fundamentally;* also, *ordinarily* and *normally* (*usually*).

Principally, he **seems** to be an honorable man.
Teresa was *basically* **sensitive** to those around her.
Dr. Kim **is** a mathematician *mainly*.
Ordinarily he is at home, but last week he had to go to Cleveland.

Avoid the following kinds of errors:

(wrong):   (Although Terry sometimes works as a plumber, he is chief an engineer.)
xxxxxxx

RIGHT: Although Terry sometimes works as a plumber, he is *chiefly* an engineer.

Some adjectives and adverbs have the same form.

fast   late
early   high
hard   enough

Compare:

She is a *fast* runner.
She runs *fast*.

He was *early*.
He arrived *early*.

There was *enough* food for everyone.
Everyone had *enough*.

Adverbs (*not* adjectives) modify present and past participles.

Mr. Papadopoulos is *gradually learning* to operate the computer.
Rapidly recovering from his illness, Reuvan was able to do a little work.
Loved by all who knew him, the coach was *deeply missed*.
Proudly sponsored by a federation of hospitals, the programs on nutrition have been educational
to all.

Avoid the following kinds of errors:
(wrong):   (Careless written, the composition had to be done over.)
RIGHT: *Carelessly* written, the composition had to be done over.
(wrong):   (Easy finding his way, he reached his destination early.)
RIGHT: *Easily* finding his way, he reached his destination early.

Comparison of Adverbs

Comparison of Regular Adverbs

Positive	Comparative	Superlative
softly	more softly	the most softly
beautifully	more beautifully	the most beautifully
often	more often	the most often
soon	sooner	the soonest
hard	harder	the hardest

Comparison of Irregular Adverbs

Positive	Comparative	Superlative
well	better	the best
badly	worse	the worst
little	less	the least
much	more	the most

Below are examples of both **regular and irregular adverbs** in the positive, comparative, and superlative degree.

1. The professor suggested that each student go over the material *carefully*.
2. Tom was *more easily* convinced than Pete to vote for the proposition.
3. *Slowly but surely*, Sydney found a solution to the problem.
4. It was *the most poorly* constructed building that he had ever seen.
5. He has *less* than most people but he seems to enjoy himself *the most*.
6. Mrs. Parnell is *the hardest* working woman that I know.
7. Of the two pianists, Francie plays *the more musically*.
8. Having finished his work *quickly*, Charles hurried home.
9. *Swiftly*, the tiger sprang at the zebra.
10. The house, *brightly* painted an orange color, draws attention from those passing by.
11. Entering the room *silently*, Miss Izen sat down unnoticed by anyone.
12. Zev played *worse* today than yesterday.
13. She listened carefully but she didn't speak *much*.
14. The buildings deteriorated *more* quickly than anyone had anticipated (or: *much more* quickly).

Best is sometimes used as an adverb with past participles.

The composer Georges Bizet is *best remembered* for his opera *Carmen*.

Best sometimes means "most advisable."

It is *best* not to dwell on past mistakes.

The following sentences illustrate the comparison of equality and inequality in adverbs.

1. Mr. Huxley speaks French *as fluently as* Mr. Cousteau.
2. She tried to express her feelings *as sincerely as* she could.
3. The legislator debated the issue *as effectively as* he could.
4. The train appeared to be going *as fast as*, perhaps even faster than, a plane.
5. The pump doesn't work *as well as* it did.
6. An advertisement for a hair product used to proclaim that blondes had *twice as much* fun *as* brunettes (not: two times as much fun).
7. Claude got a good grade but he had done *half as much* work *as* the others.
8. The country of India has almost *three times as many* people *as* the United States (not: three times more people than).

Other Adverbs

"Enough"
Place *enough* after an adjective and an adverb but before a noun.

Yeon Soo doesn't feel *ill enough* (sufficiently ill) to remain home.
The manager spoke *loudly enough* for everyone to hear.
There are *enough books* for everyone in the class.
There is *more than enough food* to go around. (*more than enough* means "in excess of an adequate supply")

"Such" and "So"

Such refers to a noun and *so* **refers to an adjective.** Both are followed by a *that* clause, written or implied.

It was *such* a cold *day* that we decided to stay inside.
It was *so cold*, we decided to stay inside. (*or:* It was *so a cold a day*)

Other Forms With "Such" and "So"

He told us *so strange a story* that we could hardly believe it.
As we were looking at antique automobiles, Pat said he owned *such an automobile.* (an automobile such as that or similar to that one)
The president thought the problem *so serious* (thought that the problem was so serious) that he discussed it on television.
He left early because he was *so uncomfortable.* (*implied*: so uncomfortable that he didn't wish to remain)

"So" and "Such" with "Little," "Few," "Much," "Many"

He had *so little education* that he had difficulty getting a job.
He had *such a small amount of education* that he had difficulty getting a job.

So few of the rare bird's *eggs* had hatched that the scientist was disappointed.
Such a few number of the rare bird's *eggs* had hatched that the scientist was disappointed.

There was *so much data* that it took a long time to sort it out.
There was *such a large amount of data* that it took a long time to sort it out.

The lecturer was asked *so many questions*, he couldn't answer them all.
The lecturer was asked *such a large number of questions, he couldn't answer them all.*

"Very" and "Too" with "Little," "Few," "Much," "Many"
Very means "a high degree." "*Too*" means "excessively" and must be followed by an infinitive, or an infinitive must be implied.

Ronit enjoyed the play *very much.*
He complained that he had eaten *too much.* (or: *much too much*) (or: *far too much*)

NOTE: *Too much to be comfortable* is implied.

After his date, Ralph had *very little money* left.
He had *too little* (or: *far too little*) *money* to buy a new battery.
Mr. Berman had *very few customers* yesterday.
Selma has *too few credits* to graduate.
One day the earth may have *too many* (or: *far too many*) *people* to sustain.
Ned didn't have *very much fun* at the party but Troy had a lot of fun.

We learned *many* good ideas at the workshop.
There weren't *very many* people at the concert.
Some days there is *a lot of* smog in the air but today there isn't *very much* smog.
There is *a lot of* difference between the two states.
There *isn't much* difference between the two opinions.

Additional use of **Most** and **Much**

Most is sometimes used instead of *very.*

The Everglades in Florida are *most* (*very*) interesting.
That dress is *most* becoming to you.

Much is sometimes used instead of *a lot.*

We must hurry because there is *much* to do.
Much has been said on that particular subject.

NOTE: Don't use *too, so,* or *real* instead of *very.*

(wrong): (This car needs repairing; it doesn't run too (so) well.)
RIGHT: This car needs repairing; it doesn't run *very* well.
(wrong): (Javier did real well on the test.) *Real* is an adjective, and means "not artificial."
RIGHT: Javier did *very* well on the test.

Farther and Further: *Farther* refers to distance. *Further* refers to a continuance or to an additional amount.

Santa Barbara is *farther* from Los Angeles than Ventura.
After lunch, Dr. Moore spoke *further* on the subject of motivation.
Tony needs *further* experience in public speaking.

Quite and Pretty: Adverbs *quite* and *pretty* mean "to a large degree." (These words are not used in this sense in the negative.)

This essay is *quite* good.
Miss Saunders has been able to rent a *pretty* large apartment.

NOTE: Quite with a negative means "not completely."

Dinner isn't *quite* ready.
Jean wasn't *quite* sure what had happened to his friend.

Somewhat and Rather: Adverbs *somewhat* and *rather* mean "to some degree," "more or less."

Mr. Minassian has completed his business and he's *rather* anxious to return home.
The letter, written in pencil, was *somewhat* difficult to read.

NOTE: Don't use *kind of* or *sort of* instead of *somewhat* or *rather*. *Kind of* and *sort of* mean ''the type of,'' and precede a noun.

(wrong):   (She thought the assignment was sort of confusing.) (kind of)

RIGHT: She thought the assignment was *somewhat (rather)* confusing.

RIGHT: What *kind of* test were you given?

Almost, Nearly, Just About: *Almost, nearly,* and *just about* mean ''not yet or fully, but close to completion.''

Majorie was *almost* finished with her term paper.

The boy was *nearly* drowned by the huge wave.

When we stopped to pick her up, she was *just about* ready.

NOTE: Don't use *most* instead of *almost, nearly,* or *just about*. *Most* means ''the majority.''

(wrong):   (Most all of the students passed the course.)

RIGHT: *Almost all* of the students passed the course.

RIGHT: *Most of the students* passed the course.

Anymore and Yet: *Anymore* means ''no longer.'' *Yet* means ''up to now.''

The Alfords don't attend the dances *anymore*.

The Alfords *no longer* attend the dances.

(wrong):   (The Alfords don't attend the dances yet.)

Sylvia has *yet* to be paid for the many services she has rendered.

Sylvia hasn't *yet* been paid. (*Also:* Sylvia hasn't been paid *yet*.)

Avoid the following kinds of errors:

(wrong):   (Physical tired after two games of golf, Ken lay on the grass.)

RIGHT: *Physically* tired after two games of golf, Ken lay on the grass.

(wrong):   (Some chickens lay much more eggs as other chickens.)

RIGHT: Some chickens lay *many more* eggs *than* do others.

(wrong):   (My hometown is twice more populated than it used to be.)

RIGHT: My hometown is *twice as* populated *as it* used to be.

(wrong):   (Enrique works slower than the other technicians, but he is particular conscientious.)

RIGHT: Enrique works *more slowly* than the other technicians, but he is *particularly* conscientious.

(wrong):   (Antonia likes Marco better than any boy in school.)

RIGHT: Antonia likes Marco *more* than *any other* boy in school.

(wrong):   (Neil didn't attend classes as regular as he should have.)

RIGHT: Neil didn't attend classes as *regularly* as he should have.

(wrong):   (He real foolish became involved with groups that preach hatred.)

RIGHT: He *very foolishly* became involved with groups that preach hatred.

(wrong):	(The more uncomfortably he felt, the lesser he participated.)
RIGHT:	The more *uncomfortable* he felt, the *less* he participated.
(wrong):	(Basic, the robot is too efficient but the concern is that it will replace a great amount of people.)
RIGHT:	*Basically,* the robot is *very* efficient but the concern is that it will replace a great *number* of people.
(wrong):	(It was so hot day, no one felt like working.)
RIGHT:	It was *such a hot day,* no one felt like working.
RIGHT:	It was *so hot a day,* no one felt like working.
(wrong):	(Ida has further to walk than Sofia.)
RIGHT:	Ida has *farther* to walk than Sofia.

Position of Adverbs

Frequency adverbs are placed before an action verb, after the *be* verb, before or after the auxiliary of the action verb, and at the beginning or the end of a sentence.

They *usually* **pay** their rent the first of each month.
He **is** *frequently* absent. He **is** *frequently* **working** while classes are being held.
She **has** *often* **viewed** the stars through a telescope. (*also:* She *often* **has viewed** the stars through a telescope. *also: Often* she **has viewed** the stars through a telescope.)
Sometimes Jeff has been too busy to attend the social events. *also:* Jeff has **sometimes** been too busy to attend the social events.)

The adverb *still* is placed before the action verb but after the *be* verb. In negative sentences, *still* comes before the auxiliary.

Katrina *still* **lives** at home with her parents.
Mr. Rubin **was** *still* with a client when we called him.
A commission *still* **hasn't** been appointed.

Recently and *lately* are placed at the beginning or the end of a sentence and at the end of a dependent clause. *Recently* may also be placed after the auxiliary.

Recently scientists have been studying primitive tribes in Brazil.
Although the desk had been constructed *recently* (or: had *recently* been constructed), it strongly resembled an antique.
There has been a lot of discussion about life on other planets *lately.*

Certainly, probably, and *possibly* are placed before the action verb or the auxiliary. They are placed before or after *be* verbs or at the beginning of the sentence.

They **have** *certainly* **traveled** a great deal.
They *certainly* **have traveled** a great deal.

That lecture *certainly* **was** interesting.
That lecture **was** *certainly* interesting.

She **will** *probably* **be** here soon.
She *probably* **will be** here soon.
Probably she **will be** here soon.

Manner adverbs are adverbs telling "how" or "in what manner" an action was done. They are placed before or after the action verb, after the *be* verb, or at the begining or end of a clause or a sentence.

Ms. Spiro *slowly* **walked** out of the room.
Ms. Spiro **walked** *slowly* out of the room.
Carefully, Rachel **cut** the pattern.
The clouds **were** *rapidly* disappearing.
The clouds **were** disappearing *rapidly.*

Avoid the following kinds of errors:

(wrong):   (Sidney enjoys still playing his clarinet.)
            xxxxx
RIGHT: Sidney *still* enjoys playing his clarinet.
(wrong):   (When there's an important exhibit, Ben stays sometimes in town.)
                                                xxxxxxxxxxxxxx
RIGHT: When there's an important exhibit, Ben *sometimes* stays in town.
(wrong):   (Dinah has been making lately her own clothes.)
                                    xxxxxxx
RIGHT: *Lately,* Dinah has been making her own clothes.
(wrong):   (My husband still was in the office when Bruce called.)
                        xxxxx
RIGHT: My husband was *still* in the office when Bruce called.

EXERCISE VII. 7.

Fill in the blanks with the correct form in parentheses.

1. Although Mr. Clark receives a small salary, he manages to deposit money in the bank _____ (regular, regularly)
2. The _____ child hid behind his mother when the stranger approached. (frightening, frightened)
3. The capital of Japan was _____ Kyoto. (original, originally)
4. When the chef had tasted the soup _____ , he added additional seasoning. (careful, carefully)
5. Of all the subjects he studied, he found political science to be _____ . (the more interesting, most interesting, the most interesting)
6. Catherine explained the case to the judge _____ an experienced lawyer. (eloquent like, as eloquently as, as eloquent as)
7. Having saved _____ money, Ernestine was able to buy her mother a lovely new lamp. (little, a little, only little)
8. More corn is produced in the United States than in _____ country in the world. (any, all other, any other)
9. This month I have _____ number of students than last month. (fewer, less, few)
10. The saw which he had was completely _____ for cutting down a large tree. (useless, unuseless, helpless)
11. Plant cells, which are filled chiefly with cellulose, aren't _____ animal cells. (the same like, the same as, the same than)
12. The china displayed at the museum had been _____ painted in red and gold. (beautiful, beautifully, more beautifully)
13. The auditorium was _____ , some of us had to stand. (such a crowded place, such crowded a place, so crowded place)
14. His condition grew _____ (worser and worser, worst and worst, worse and worse)

15. The farmers are hoping that there will be _____ rainfall this year than there was last year. (a greater amount of, a great many, a greater number of)
16. The children, _____ playing with their sleds, welcomed the winter's first heavy snowfall. (happy, happily)
17. As Carol was waving good-bye to Janet, a cloud appeared and the plane was _____ out of sight. (sudden, suddenly)
18. The more he insisted, _____ she objected. (the more strongly, the more stronger, the stronger)
19. Although Miss Uchida has been ill rather often, she is _____ a healthy person. (fundamentally, fundamental)
20. The great composers Mendelssohn and Mozart died at _____ young age. (an extreme, a real, a very, too)
21. Of the two, Mozart was _____ when he died. (the younger, younger, the more young)

EXERCISE VII. 8.

There is at least one error in each sentence. Underline the errors and make corrections.

1. Among the schools that were mentioned, Roosevelt High School has the greater academic standing.
2. Mr. Sands has to travel more often than anyone in his firm.
3. Most all of the wildlife refuges near the city were bad damaged by the floods.
4. Having quick spent his money, Fred decided to leave Las Vegas.
5. It's a good plan, perhaps even better as the one presented earlier.
6. I don't think Jane types quite as good or accurate as Leah.
7. Eligibility will be conclusive decided after the interview.
8. People certainly did not want to move but because of high poisonous chemicals, it was real dangerous to remain in the area.
9. Mona always enjoyed skiing but she doesn't do it yet.
10. The illegal shipped equipment was discovered by a federal agent.
11. Totally absorbed in what she was doing, Carol didn't hear the loudly ringing of the bells.
12. There have been twice more imported cars this year than in the previous year.
13. Original her plan was to build a house but it proved to be too expensive.
14. There aren't half so many parks in Los Angeles like there are in London.
15. The boxer wasn't near enough heavy to be eligible for the fight.
16. The parents complain that they haven't received too much mail from their son since he left.
17. Gloria has much interests but primary her interests are in the field of administration.
18. Although most all of my friends disliked the film, I thought it was sort of interesting.

PRONOUNS

Pronouns are used in place of nouns.

Types of Pronouns

Subject pronouns	I, you, he, she, it, we, you, they
Object pronouns	me, you, him, her, it, us, you, them

Possessive adjective pronouns	my, your, his, her, its, our, your, their, whose
Possessive noun pronouns	mine, yours, his, hers, ours, yours, theirs
Reflexive pronouns	myself, yourself, himself, herself, itself, ourselves, yourselves, themselves
Demonstrative pronouns	this, these, that, those
Relative pronouns	who, whom, whose, which, that, whoever, whomever

Subject Pronouns

A subject pronoun is used as the subject of a sentence or a clause. When there is a comparison made, the complete clause is not repeated. Auxiliaries and verbs are used as clause endings.

We enjoy surfing as much as *they*.
or: We enjoy surfing as much as *they do*. (*implied*: as much as they enjoy surfing)
Sally has gone to Europe as many times as *he*.
or: Sally has gone to Europe as many times as *he has*.
You men talked more at the meeting than *we* women.
or: *You* men talked more at the meeting then *we* woman *did*.
He is not as tall as *she*.
or: He is not as tall as *she is*.

Avoid the following kinds of errors:
    (wrong):   (I didn't like the film as much as her.)
                                                  xxxxx
    RIGHT: I didn't like the film as much as *she* (*or*: *she did*).

    Use a subject pronoun after a *be* verb.

It was *he* who answered the door.
The person you met last year was *I*. (*or*: I was the one you met last year.)

NOTE: Pronouns *you*, *we*, and *us* may be used before a noun for emphasis.

    (wrong):   (It is us people who require quality education.)
                        xxx
    RIGHT: It is *we* people who require quality education.

Object Pronouns

An object pronoun is used as a direct object, an indirect object, an object of a preposition, or an object of an infinitive.
    Some of the following sentences illustrate object pronouns in *comparison clauses.*

1. I like *her* as much as I do *him* (*implied*: as much as I like him)
2. She spends as much time with *me* as she does with *them*.
3. That problem is between *her* and *him*.
4. Her brother has visited Marla more than *her*. (*implied*: more than he has visited *her*)
5. She wasn't sure, but it appeared to be *him*.
6. They gave presents to *us* three, my sister, my brother, and *me*.

Avoid the following kinds of errors:

(wrong):   (The supervisor gave Tom as much to do as he did she.)
_{xxxxx}

RIGHT: The supervisor gave Tom as much to do as he did *her*.)

Possessive Adjective Pronouns

A *possessive adjective pronoun* **is used as an adjective to describe a noun or** *a gerund.* The pronoun must agree in person, gender, and number with the antecedent (the noun or pronoun to which it refers.)

1. **Ming and Yang** enjoy *their* home very much.
2. **Lydia** is a fine cook. *Her* cooking is excellent.
3. **Ted** reminded us to register. We appreciated *his* reminding us.
4. **You** are very thoughtful. We are grateful for **your** thoughtfulness.
5. Mrs. Khalsa's **son** was married last week. *His* wife is a teacher.
6. She is the one *whose* art was acclaimed.

Avoid the following kinds of errors:

(wrong):   (The students played there instruments. Them performing for us was a nice sur-
_{xxxxxxx}   _{xxxxxxxx}
prise.)

RIGHT: The students played *their* instruments. *Their* performing for us was a nice surprise.

Possessive Noun Pronouns

A *possessive noun pronoun* **is used as a subject, a direct object, an object of a preposition, or an object of an infinitive.**

1. It is not my book; it is *hers*.
2. If you forgot your pencil, you can borrow one of *mine*.
3. Please return those tennis balls to us. They are *ours*.
4. No, that book, isn't *mine*. It must be *yours*.
5. Our children were very friendly with *theirs*.
6. These glasses appear to be *his*.
7. *His* was lost and *mine* was returned.
8. Mary is a friend of *his*.

Avoid the following kinds of errors:

(wrong):   (You may borrow one of my.)
_{xxxxx}

RIGHT: You may borrow one of *mine*.

Reflexive Pronouns

A **reflexive pronoun must refer back to the** *antecedent.* The pronoun must agree with the antecedent.
Reflexive pronouns often emphasize the fact that the action was done without assistance.

1. **Julie** conducted the experiment by *herself*.
2. The **cat** hurt *itself* jumping from the high branch.

3. I *myself* will discuss the problem with her.
4. **Jack** looked at *himself* in the mirror.

NOTE: There are no such words as *hisself* and *theirselves*.

      (wrong):   (The couple painted their house by theirselves.)
      RIGHT: The couple painted their house by *themselves*.

NOTE: Do not use a reflexive pronoun after *similar to, like,* or *such as*.

      (wrong):   (Educated people like ourselves should keep an open mind.)
      RIGHT: Educated people like *us* should keep an open mind.

Demonstrative Pronouns

A *demonstrative pronoun* **is used to point out a particular item or person.** *This* **(singular) and** *these* (plural) refer to items near at hand. *That* (singular) and *those* (plural) refer to items at a distance. Demonstrative pronouns are used as adjectives, subjects, and objects.

That belongs to Mike. (subject)
This pencil needs to be sharpened. (adjective)
I would like to buy some of *these* and some of *those*. (object)
Those are beautiful earrings that you are wearing.
I had *these* chairs upholstered.

NOTE: Use *this kind* or *that kind* for singular and uncountable nouns. Use *these kinds* or *those kinds* for plural nouns.

      Mrs. Hurwitz has *this kind of carpet* and *those kinds of drapes*.

(wrong):   (Alice has this kind of plants in her home.)
RIGHT: Alice has *these kinds* of plants in her home.

NOTE: Don't use the object pronoun *them* before a participial phrase, a relative clause, or a prepositional phrase which identifies people or items.

(wrong):   (The proctor passed out pencils to them taking the test.)
RIGHT: The proctor passed out pencils to *those* (people) taking the test.
RIGHT: The proctor passed out pencils to *those* who were taking the test.
RIGHT: The proctor passed out pencils to *those* in the classroom.

NOTE: Do not use *them* as an adjective or as a subject.

      (wrong):   (Christine owns one of them cameras.)
      RIGHT: Christine owns one of *those* cameras.
      (wrong):   (Them are my friends.)
      RIGHT: *Those* are my friends.

NOTE: Do not use *"here"* and *"there"* directly after demonstrative pronouns.

> (wrong):   (Please give me some of these here and those there.)
>   xxxxxxx   xxxxxxxx
>
> RIGHT: Please give me some of *these* and *those.*

Demonstrative pronouns are often used in comparing things in order to avoid naming the item twice. Compare:

I prefer the paintings of Matisse to the paintings of Renoir.
I prefer the paintings of Matisse to *those* of Renoir.
I prefer the paintings of Matisse to *the ones* of Renoir.
I prefer Matisse's paintings to Renoir's.

NOTE: Do not use *the one* or *the ones* with uncountable nouns.

> (wrong):   (The weather in California is warmer than the one in New York.)
>   xxxxxxxxxxx
>
> RIGHT: The weather in California is warmer than *that* in New York.

Analyze the following sentences. Think about the two items being compared.

The stone in this ring is similar to that (or: the one) in the other ring.
The books in the main library are of a greater variety than those (or: the ones) in the branch library.
She did better on the test this week than that (the one) last week.

Avoid the following kinds of errors:

> (wrong):   (The stone in this ring is similar to the other ring.) It is "stones" that are being
>   xxxxxxxxxxxxxxxxxxxx
>   compared, not "rings."
>
> (wrong):   (Li prefers his own garden to that of his friend's.)
>   xxxxxxxxxxx
>
> RIGHT: Li prefers his own garden to that of his *friend.*
>
> (wrong):   (I think the brakes in your car are better than my (*or: mine ones*).
>   xxxxx   xxxxxxxxxxxx
>
> RIGHT: I think the brakes in your car are better than *those in my car* (*or: those in mine, or: the
>   ones in mine*).

Relative Pronouns

A *relative pronoun* introduces a relative (adjective) clause.
  Who, that, and *whoever* are used as **subjects of relative clauses** that refer to **people.**

The musician *who taught David how to play the violin* is a member of the Cleveland Symphony.
He's the person *that asked for directions.*
You may give this brochure to *whoever wants it.*

NOTE: Don't omit the subject *who* or *that* of a relative clause.

> (wrong):   (Ara is the one received the scholarship.)
>   xxxxxxxxxxxxxxxxxx
>
> RIGHT: Ara is the one *who (that) received* the scholarship.

Whom, that, and *whomever* are used as *objects of verbs in relative clauses* that refer to *people. Whom* and *whomever* are used as *objects of prepositions.*

NOTE: Although the relative pronoun *whom* may appear to occupy a subject position, it is, in fact, an object when a subject of the relative clause is present. (In informal usage the relative subject *who* is more commonly used.)

Bob is the young man *whom* she interviewed. (*She* interviewed *whom.*)
Bob is the young man *who* she interviewed. (informal)
The woman *to whom she spoke* is her teacher.
The woman *that (whom) she spoke to* is her teacher. (Sometimes the preposition is placed at the end of the clause.)
She said you could bring *whomever* you wish.

Avoid the following kinds of errors:

(wrong):   (He's the one whom, I believe, is interested in entomology.)
                       xxxxxxxxx

RIGHT: He's the one, *who,* I believe, *is interested in entomology.*

(wrong):   (He didn't know for who Miss Ryan was substituting.)
                                      xxxxxxxxxxxx

RIGHT: He didn't know *for whom* Miss Ryan was substituting.

NOTE: Whom and *that* may be omitted. Compare:

The girl whom you want to meet is Masami's girlfriend.
The girl that you want to meet is Masami's girlfriend.
The girl you want to meet is Masami's girlfriend.

The person for whom he has worked is his father.
The person whom he has worked for is his father.
The person that he has worked for is his father.
The person he has worked for is his father.

The relative pronouns *which* and *that* are used to refer to *things,* and, as a rule, to *animals.*
Which and *that* may be omitted when used as object in a relative clause.

The book which I borrowed from Carmen has been very useful. (I borrowed *which.*)
The book that I borrowed from Carmen has been very useful.
The book I borrowed from Carmen has been very useful.

Which and *that* may *not* be omitted when used as subject of the relative clause.

Joe's dog, which followed Joe everywhere, had been given to him by his aunt.
Joe's dog, that followed Joe everywhere, had been given to him by his aunt.
(wrong):   (Joe's dog, followed Joe everywhere, had been given to him by his aunt.)
                       xxxxxxxxxxxxxxxxxxxxxxxxxxxxxxxxxxx

The relative pronoun *where* refers to *places.*

This is the city *where* George Washington lived.
This is the city in which George Washington lived.
This is the city which George Washington lived in.

Avoid the following kinds of errors:

(wrong):   (This is the book where I read the story of George Washington.)

(wrong):   (This is the book that I read the story of George Washington.)

RIGHT: This is the book *in which* I read the story of George Washington.

The relative pronoun *whose* is used to show possession. *Whose* generally refers to people, but sometimes to places or things.

It's interesting to meet people *whose culture* differs from our own.
Some official documents, *whose wording* is difficult to understand, are being revised.

Avoid the following kinds of errors:

(wrong):   (Mrs. Estrada, which purse had been stolen, reported the incident to the police.)

RIGHT: Mrs. Estrada, *whose* purse had been stolen, reported the incident to the police.

Use a preposition with the relative pronoun when it is required.

The house *in which* Andrew Carnegie was born is still standing.
(wrong):   (The house which Andrew Carnegie was born is still standing.)

The tourist *in whose* luggage were gold coins, was detained.
The tourist, *whose luggage contained* gold coins, was detained.
(wrong):   (The tourist whose luggage were gold coins, was detained.)

(wrong):   (The tourist in whose luggage contained gold coins was detained.)

The means *by which* he solved the problem remains a mystery.
(wrong):   (The means which he solved the problem remains a mystery.)

Johanna is the woman *with whom* Maria is studying the cello.
(wrong):   (Johanna is the woman whom Maria is studying the cello.)

Don't repeat a preposition.

Ned returned the money to his sister *from whom* he had borrowed it.
(wrong):   (Ned returned the money to his sister from whom he had borrowed it from.)

Don't use the relative pronoun *which* in clauses that are not relative clauses.

The belief that the earth was flat was held for centuries.
(wrong):   (The belief which the earth was flat was held for centuries.)

Use *whoever* instead of *whomever* if the word occupies a subject position, even if it is preceded by a preposition.

Mrs. Van Dan bought the books for *whoever* might be interested.
(wrong):   (Mrs. Van Dan bought the books for whomever might be interested.)

EXERCISE VII. 9.

Fill in the blanks with the correct form of the pronoun.

1. He likes to hike but I like to hike as much as ___*he*___ .
2. We have three bicycles. If you don't have one, you are welcome to use one of ___*ours*___ .
3. Anita's leg is sore. While she was exercising this morning, she hurt ___*it herself*___ .
4. Little James complained that his sister had received more presents than ___*he*___ .
5. The film which Mary and John saw appeared to have impressed her more than ___*him*___ .
6. Both Floyd and Maude have a large collection of records but I think ___*hers*___ is even larger than ___*his*___ .
7. Mrs. Flourney, ___*whose*___ house had been burglarized, decided to have an alarm system installed.
8. My husband and I forgot to bring some things with us. Would you buy toothbrushes for ___*me*___ and ___*him*___ ?
9. The child didn't want any assistance. He insisted on dressing ___*by himself*___
10. She invited all ___*those*___ who had been in her class last term.
11. The market on San Vicente street has more vegetables than ___*the one*___ on Montana street.
12. The secret he told you is strictly between ___*you*___ and ___*me*___ .
13. The buses in town are larger than ___*those*___ in the suburbs.
14. Forms were passed out to ___*those*___ registering for the course.
15. Why don't you show your paintings to ___*whom*___ you think might exhibit them.
16. Parents complain that there aren't enough quality programs on television ___*which*___ are shown for children. — *in which*
17. The drawer ___*~~that~~*___ she keeps her notes is in the middle.
18. This is the town _____ library she found some rare books.   *in whose*

EXERCISE VII. 10.

There is at least one pronoun error in each sentence. Underline the errors and make corrections.

1. My sister is a little bit shorter than me. *I*
2. The psychology lecture today was more interesting to Beth than yesterday. *that*
3. She insisted that it was not her who had awakened the baby.
4. I see where it's going to rain tonight. *his*
5. Between her writing for radio and him playing professional hockey, the couple does very well. *with*
6. The books which he did his research are in the university library.
7. I'm sorry that I didn't remember whom you were.
8. Unfortunately, the magazine where the recipe was printed can't be found. *in which*
9. There's a possibility that it may have been them who called last night.
10. Who did you speak to this morning?
11. There are still them that think men have more intelligence than us women. *we*
12. The stunt job has been offered to whomever is willing to take the risks.
13. She's convinced that people like themselves wouldn't do anything foolish.
14. The thought which she might fail the test never occurred to her. *that*
15. Mrs. Moses makes toys for them children who are in hospitals.
16. They're the family which house was damaged by the wind last week. *whose*
17. The topic about which the trainer was talking about was unfamiliar.

18. The foundation which grants are given to charitable organizations is administered by Mrs. Perle.
19. This here kind of vegetables can't be grown in tropical climates.
20. John is the student whose benefit Ms. Sim repeated the lesson.

PREPOSITIONS

A *preposition*, combined with an object (noun, pronoun, or gerund), forms a *prepositional phrase*, which imparts information about a word in the sentence.
    The list below describes the general use of some common prepositions.

AT

where situated; address; clock time; night; midnight; noon; at present; at first

At present there is no one home.
She goes to school *at night*.
He is *at school* right now.
She arrived *at four o'clock*.
He lives *at 431 Lincoln Street*.
She felt uncomfortable *at first*.

ABOUT

pertaining to a subject or a situation

That book is *about the Civil War*.
He is worried *about his grades*.
He is happy *about returning* to America.
He is sincere *about his desire* to help his people.

FOR

purpose; time length; for whom; in favor of; how much

He went to the store *for some cigarettes*.
A saw is used *for cutting wood*.
She has worked there *for three years*.
He repaired the bicycle *for me*.
He works *for a building company*.
They are *for equal rights for all people*.
He bought a silk shirt *for only ten dollars*.

WITH

anything in hand; accompanied by; descriptive of; converse with

She opened the box *with a knife*.
We went to the theater *with our friends*.
She wore a hat *with a flower* on it.
He discussed the idea *with his boss*.

TO

directly; to a place or to a person

We walked *to the store.*
He spoke *to his mother.*
He gave it *to me.*
We drove *to San Francisco.*

BY

how; by what method; by what person; by what time or date

It was repaired *by a mechanic.*
She improved her English *by practicing.*
He got there *by bus.*
By next week it should be completed.
It was written *by Roberta Cohaney.*

AGAINST

positioned against; opposed to a principle or an idea

He stood *against the wall.*
She was *against busing* children to school.
It is *against her principles* to cheat on a test.
They were *against their daughter's marrying* Fred.

LIKE

similar to

The boy spoke *like a man.*
This perfume smells *like roses.*

OF

pertaining to; in reference to

Many *of the voters* felt that their property taxes were too high.
She is afraid *of the dark.*
She lost one *of her earrings.*
I bought a pound *of sugar.*

FROM

source (origin); from a place; from the activity; from a person; from the beginning

She got a wristwatch *from her parents.*
She was all worn out *from washing* windows.
He just got back *from Chicago.*
He worked *from 8 A.M. to 6 P.M.*

IN

inside a place; projecting future time; month, season, year, evening; in a country, city, etc.

The ticket is *in my purse.*
I will be there *in a few minutes.*
He's coming *in October.*
He studied history *in 1955.*
She likes to read *in the evening.*

She likes to take long walks *in the spring*.
He is *in Chicago* right now.

ON

surface; specific day; specific date; on a vehicle (except car); on a street; on a team

The book is *on the shelf*.
He will arrive *on Sunday*.
She plans to leave *on May 30*.
He is *on an airplane* right now.
He lives *on Pico Boulevard*.
Mike is *on the* college football *team*.

A variety of prepositional phrases are demonstrated below. Some of these phrases are idiomatic. (Reminder! The possessive form is used before a gerund or a gerund phrase, as well as before a noun.)

1. We had confidence *in Robert's ability*.
2. She doesn't approve *of their staying out* late *at night*.
3. The Smiths called *off their fishing plans because of rain*.
4. That baker is famous *for her pies*.
5. There's no point *in my delaying you*.
6. Educators, *on the whole*, are supportive *of those* who, much later *in life*, decide to resume academic study.
7. Everyone was pleased *with Roger's singing*.
8. *Besides using theirs*, we can use two *of ours*.
9. A dinner party was held *in honor of the guest speaker*.
10. As John walked *into the room*, he was asked *by the team captain* to become a member *of the team*.

The student must practice using the correct preposition. Sometimes it is helpful to think of two words as being one word. For example, *recover from* may be thought of as *recoverfrom*: "recoverfrom a cold," "recoverfrom the measles," "recoverfrom an illness," "recoverfrom grief." After such practice, the sound of the word *from* becomes firmly related to the word *recover*. Study the lists below for the correct prepositions. See Idioms in the Supplement for unfamiliar expressions and for further verbs with prepositions.

Verbs with Prepositions

accuse of	experiment with	insist on, upon	object to
approve of	interfere with	keep on	refer to
consist of	sympathize with	rely on, upon	respond to
be in charge of	argue about, with	call off	subscribe to
be in favor of	boast about	put off	arrive at (airport,
remind (one) of	complain about, of	apologize to, for	school, theater, etc.)
take care of	find out about	apply to, for	arrive in (city, state,
take advantage of	forget about	be used to	country)
what's the use of	speak about	compare to	look at, for
argue with, about	think about, of	compare with	preside over
agree with	worry about	contribute to	believe in
compete with	depend on, upon	dedicate to	excel in
communicate with	comment on	devote to	major in
cooperate with	count on	look forward to	participate in

take part in	substitute for	escape from	recover from
succeed in	thank for	prevent from	rescue from
excuse for, from	vote for	prohibit from	save from
forgive for	distinguish from		

Adjectives and Past Participles with Prepositions

afraid of	dependent on, upon	dedicated to	concerned about
appreciative of	founded on, by	devoted to	confused about
ashamed of	insistent on, upon	faithful to	enthusiastic about
aware of	innocent of	indifferent to	excited about
bored of	jealous of	inferior to	happy about
capable of	made of	kind to	nervous about
careful of	proud of	married to	sad about
composed of	regardless of	opposed to	skeptical about
conscious of	sick of	polite to	worried about
considerate of	supportive of	preferable to	adequate for
critical of	suspected of	related to	appropriate for
envious of	thoughtful of	sensitive to	blamed for
fearful of	tired of	similar to	famous for
frightened of	tolerant of	superior to	fit, unfit for
guilty of	acquainted with	derived from	grateful for
hopeful of	covered with	different from	known for
disappointed in	familiar with	divorced from	perfect for
experienced, inexperienced in	finished with	far from	qualified for
interested, disinterested in	pleased with	free from	responsible for
involved, uninvolved in	provided with	prevented from	suitable, unsuitable for
skillful, unskillful in	patient with	prohibited from	affected by
successful, unsuccessful in	satisfied with	protected from	angered by
based on, upon	alert to	good at	attacked by
	attentive to	surprised at, by	caused by
	committed to	upset over	flattered by
	comparable to	divided in, into	offended by
	confined to	anxious about	

Nouns with Prepositions

admiration for	belief in	approval of	comparison to
fondness for	competency in	choice of	devotion to
pity for	confidence in	division of	dedication to
preference for	experience in	fear of	indifference to
reason for	failure in	knowledge of	objection to
responsibility for	faith in	means of	opposition to
respect for	participation in	possibility of	reference to
search for	pleasure in	prevention of	response to
substitution for	pride in	process of	subscription to
sympathy for	satisfaction in	divorce from	argument about
authority on	skill in	escape from	complaint about
dependency on	success in	protection from	concern about
effect on, upon	difference among (3 or more)	attempt at	confusion about
reliance on		access to	doubt about
ability in	difference between (2)	commitment to	ideas about

Prepositional Expressions

ahead of	in place of	make use of	in reference to
in case of	in search of	on account of	in regard to
in care of	instead of	with the exception of	due to
in charge of	in spite of	what's the use of	in connection with
in the course of	in terms of	because of	in agreement with
in favor of	by means of	for the purpose of	except for
in front of	for fear of	in addition to	take a chance on
in honor of	for the sake of	in comparison to	feel like

Noun clauses and phrases beginning with informational words (*why, what, when, how,* etc.) may be used as objects of the prepositions, just as nouns, object pronouns, and gerunds are.

Isaac was interested *in* **how he could improve his reading ability.**
Isaac was interested *in* **how to improve his reading ability.**
Nadis talked *about* **why she had decided to become a naturalist.**

NOTE: Don't use other clauses as objects of prepositions.

(wrong):   (She hung the picture by means of she used her heel.)

RIGHT: She hung the picture by means of *using* her heel.

(wrong):   (Mrs. Cole was angry about Cyrus left the meeting early.)

RIGHT: Mr. Cole was angry about *Cyrus's leaving the meeting early.*

Avoid the following kinds of errors:

(wrong):   (Buford stated that he wasn't familiar for English literature.)

RIGHT: Buford stated that he wasn't *familiar with* English literature.

(wrong):   (Everyone has gone home except Mary and I.)

RIGHT: Everyone has gone home except Mary and *me.*

(wrong):   (There is never any animosity between we sisters.)

RIGHT: There is never any animosity between *us* sisters.

(wrong):   (The early pioneers traveled west by means a covered wagon.)

RIGHT: The early pioneers traveled west *by means of* a covered wagon.

(wrong):   (Renaldo is both capable and experienced to prepare banquets.)

RIGHT: Renaldo is both *capable of* and *experienced in preparing* banquets.

(wrong):   (Compared with freshly picked fruit, this fruit is tasteless.)

RIGHT: Compared *to* freshly picked fruit, this fruit is tasteless.

(wrong):   (Except her wedding ring, Zia wore no jewelry.)

RIGHT: *Except for* her wedding ring, Zia wore no jewelry.

(wrong):   (Uri looked like he had seen a ghost.)

RIGHT: Uri looked *as if* he had seen a ghost.

NOTE: As means "in the role of" or "in the manner of." *Like* means "similar to."

(wrong):   (Mrs. Walsh, like a busy mother of two children, had little time to study.)

RIGHT: Mrs. Walsh, *as a busy mother* of two children, had little time to study.

RIGHT: Jane thought that Jeffrey looked *like his father*.

EXERCISE VII. 11.

Fill in the blanks with the correct prepositions.

1. She lives _____ 311 5th Street.
2. The course will begin _____ January 16.
3. You are permitted to take a small bag _____ the plane.
4. She said that she was tired _____ cooking dinners.
5. The designer preferred not to comment _____ his new models.
6. His grades were far superior this month _____ those of last month.
7. Some of his classes are _____ night.
8. I have no objection, if everyone agrees, _____ your playing your drum.
9. The letter was in regard _____ books that had been ordered.
10. The proposal depends not only _____ her qualifications but also _____ her availability.
11. Since it was their first day on campus, they weren't familiar _____ the location of the engineering school.
12. Living in a large city provides opportunities _____ many cultural experiences.
13. In comparison _____ his compositions a few months ago, his recent compositions are excellent.
14. He felt inordinately responsible, for some reason, _____ the student's dropping out of class.
15. We were prevented by security guards _____ entering the building.
16. She appeared to be offended _____ my inability to recall her name.
17. The advertising plan had to be cancelled because it conflicted _____ the local laws.
18. The stereophonic earphones can be used in connection _____ the new sound system.
19. Firefighters suspected an employee _____ having started the fire.
20. The window was finally opened by means _____ a crowbar.

EXERCISE VII. 12.

Match the words in the first rows with the prepositions in the second rows, as in the first example.

approve —	for	enthusiastic	for
recover	of	similar	of
subscribe	with	suitable	with
authority	to	critical	to
affected	about	different	about
grateful	in	take a chance	in
sympathize	from	compete	from
complain	on	angered	on
involved	by	skillful	by

EXERCISE VII. 13.

Fill in the blanks with the correct passive tense (or the past participle as an adjective) of the verb in parentheses, *plus* the correct preposition.

1. Since he became a zoologist, he (dedicate) _____ the preservation of African wildlife.
2. Donna said that she (please) _____ her performance last night.
3. Frequently my eyes (affect) _____ the smog.
4. In the months ahead, Carol (commit) _____ the completion of her thesis.
5. On several occasions, some members of Congress (oppose) _____ government subsidization of failing businesses.
6. Last night, they (disturb) _____ the noise from the apartment overhead.
7. Four-fifths of the earth's surface (compose) _____ water.
8. The boy (blame) _____ the incident but he had had nothing to do with it.
9. Henry (marry) _____ Helen for twenty-one years.
10. When we entered the room, the conferees (involve) _____ a discussion on methodology.

EXERCISE VII. 14.

Underline the prepositional errors and make corrections.

1. George lives on 321 Madison Avenue.
2. Compared with his living quarters last year, his room is spacious.
3. He takes classes in the night.
4. The witness seemed afraid for describing what he had seen.
5. After serving a year, he received a substantial raise by his employer.
6. She has been studying at three o'clock to six o'clock.
7. The books are in the shelf.
8. Although advanced in age, the dog is tolerant with children.
9. He said he was tired, after so many years, with being a physician.
10. Most children are capable for doing many things.
11. One should have confidence of his own ability.
12. The investigation was in connection to the accident.
13. Although people objected about the new tax, it wasn't revoked.
14. The premier said he looked forward for meeting the president.
15. Leaders can often be insensitive about the needs of the people.
16. After many attempts, he has succeeded to swim across the channel.
17. They told him that they were appreciative for everything he had done.
18. There's a lot of satisfaction with helping others.
19. Swimming in a lake is very different than swimming in an ocean.
20. The parents were excited from the baby's learning to walk.
21. Some Thai dishes seem similar with Chinese dishes.
22. The dish consisted from vegetables, meat, and rice.
23. She took a bus home because she didn't feel for walking.
24. He lets his business interfere into his pleasure.
25. We noticed that the fruit tree was covered by insects.
26. They were not familiar, they said, on the procedure.
27. The applicant was rejected because he wasn't well qualified in the position.
28. Matisse became famous throughout the world from his magnificent paintings.
29. In addition with other complaints, Miss Adams doesn't like the lights in her office.
30. The nurse could easily sympathize, having had back pain herself, for her patient.
31. The Svensons are not disturbed from the overhead planes because they have become accustomed for them.

32. The researcher was finally satisfied, after many months of work, about the results of his experiment.
33. The young man appeared ashamed for his inability to dance.
34. Manufacturers will be prohibited, in the future, to produce unsafe vehicles.
35. The book was so interesting that I wasn't conscious about the time.
36. Each student was asked to contribute, if at all possible, in the discussion.
37. Obviously there wasn't any point for waiting longer.
38. The only protection that they had of the storm was a small tent.
39. The construction workers erected a barricade to protect people against getting hurt.
40. In spite the differences in age, the youngsters get along very well.

MIXED EXERCISE 8: PART A

Fill in the circled letter that represents the *correct* form. Be able to give the reason for your selection.

1. The visitors liked New York City but now they've returned to _____ city.   Ⓐ Ⓑ Ⓒ Ⓓ
   A. they're   C. their
   B. there   D. theirs

2. Rebecca _____ cook for the party.   Ⓐ Ⓑ Ⓒ Ⓓ
   A. helped for us to   C. helped us for
   B. helped in   D. helped us

3. Tessie didn't have _____ money left after her vacation.   Ⓐ Ⓑ Ⓒ Ⓓ
   A. some   C. no
   B. any   D. none

4. _____ being away so often caused a strain in the relationship.   Ⓐ Ⓑ Ⓒ Ⓓ
   A. Him   C. He's
   B. His   D. For him

5. The sculpture was coated with an alloy composed _____ a metal and a chemical.   Ⓐ Ⓑ Ⓒ Ⓓ
   A. of   C. with
   B. from   D. by

6. When Boris finished practicing, he _____ his violin on the piano.   Ⓐ Ⓑ Ⓒ Ⓓ
   A. laid   C. had laid
   B. has laid   D. lay

7. An armistice is an agreement between the two sides to stop _____ .   Ⓐ Ⓑ Ⓒ Ⓓ
   A. to fight   C. with the fight
   B. fight   D. fighting

8. When Joe needs a tall ladder, he borrows _____ .   Ⓐ Ⓑ Ⓒ Ⓓ
   A. his neighbor ladder   C. the ladder of his neighbor's
   B. that of his neighbor's   D. the one from his neighbor

9. Pedro _____ at six o'clock in the morning to go to work.   Ⓐ Ⓑ Ⓒ Ⓓ
   A. raises   C. rises
   B. rises up   D. has risen

10. Mr. Abdel doesn't know very much English yet but he speaks it _____ keep his job. Ⓐ Ⓑ Ⓒ Ⓓ
    A.   good enough to   C.   well enough for
    B.   enough well to   D.   well enough to

11. After spending _____ next several years in the army, the young man probably will acquire skills which he can use in civilian life. Ⓐ Ⓑ Ⓒ Ⓓ
    A.   an   C.   a
    B.   the   D.   (no article)

12. The ambassador's appointment _____ .   Ⓐ Ⓑ Ⓒ Ⓓ
    A.   already was confirmed   C.   has confirmed already
    B.   has already been confirmed   D.   had been confirm already

13. Alice plays tennis with my sister and _____ .   Ⓐ Ⓑ Ⓒ Ⓓ
    A.   me   C.   myself
    B.   I   D.   me myself

14. The balloon was filled with more and more air until it _____ .   Ⓐ Ⓑ Ⓒ Ⓓ
    A.   bursted   C.   busted
    B.   burst   D.   bust

15. My favorite baritone aria is sung in _____ .   Ⓐ Ⓑ Ⓒ Ⓓ
    A.   the Act Two   C.   the Act Second
    B.   second act   D.   the second act

16. Of the two compositions, the first one was _____ .   Ⓐ Ⓑ Ⓒ Ⓓ
    A.   the better   C.   the best
    B.   best   D.   better

17. Thin sheets of copper, covered with a particular chemical, _____ early photographs called daguerrotypes.   Ⓐ Ⓑ Ⓒ Ⓓ
    A.   used to take   C.   were used to take
    B.   were used to taking   D.   were used in take

18. Edward _____ to eat his meals the past week, much less socialize with his friends.   Ⓐ Ⓑ Ⓒ Ⓓ
    A.   has barely had time   C.   barely hasn't had time
    B.   hasn't barely had time   D.   has barely time

19. After overcoming her shyness, Nan grew _____ the other girls.   Ⓐ Ⓑ Ⓒ Ⓓ
    A.   the more popular of   C.   as popular like
    B.   the most popular than   D.   as popular as

20. Have you _____ of the author who wrote the screenplay?   Ⓐ Ⓑ Ⓒ Ⓓ
    A.   found the name out   C.   found out a name
    B.   found out the name   D.   found a name

21. Eggs, although wonderfully nutritious, have _____ of fat content.   Ⓐ Ⓑ Ⓒ Ⓓ
    A.   high number   C.   the high amounts
    B.   a high number   D.   a high amount

22. The master of ceremonies _____ containing the winner's name.   Ⓐ Ⓑ Ⓒ Ⓓ
    A. handed her an envelope   C. handed her a envelope
    B. handed to her an envelope   D. handed an envelope her

23. Clothing, especially women's clothing, _____ by dress designers to promote
    the fashion industry.   Ⓐ Ⓑ Ⓒ Ⓓ
    A. is constantly changing   C. is constantly being changed
    B. are constantly being changed   D. is frequent being changed

24. Rita felt both _____ the interview which she was about to face.   Ⓐ Ⓑ Ⓒ Ⓓ
    A. unprepared and nervous about   C. unprepared for and nervous
    B. unprepared about and nervous   about
        about   D. unprepared for and nervous for

25. _____ by the pollution, many trees in the area did not grow to their full height.
    A. Affected   C. Affecting   Ⓐ Ⓑ Ⓒ Ⓓ
    B. Effected   D. Effecting

MIXED EXERCISE 8: PART B

Fill in the circled letter that represents the *incorrect* form. Be able to explain why the word or the phrase you have chosen is not acceptable and how you can correct it.

1. Between you and I, I don't <u>approve of</u> the manner <u>in which</u> the lawyer is han-
                      A   B   C
    <u>dling</u> the case.   Ⓐ Ⓑ Ⓒ Ⓓ
      D

2. Many airline companies today <u>require</u> that all <u>luggages</u> <u>be inspected</u> before
                                    A   B   C
    passengers are admitted <u>to</u> the waiting rooms.   Ⓐ Ⓑ Ⓒ Ⓓ
                              D

3. The <u>kidney of a fish</u>, <u>like other</u> animals, <u>is used</u> in the process of <u>excreting</u>
              A   B   C
    <u>wastes</u> from the body.   Ⓐ Ⓑ Ⓒ Ⓓ
      D

4. She was in a beauty parlor <u>getting</u> her hair <u>wash</u> when a messenger <u>burst</u> into
                                  A   B   C
    the room <u>to announce</u> that he had a telegram for her. Ⓐ Ⓑ Ⓒ Ⓓ
                  D

5. His knowledge of world affairs seemed <u>to us</u> very limited for <u>a educated man</u>
                                             A   B
    who, we were told, had <u>once</u> taught in a college.   Ⓐ Ⓑ Ⓒ Ⓓ
                            D

6. My friend insists that Haydn, a famous composer and conductor in <u>the</u> eight-
                                                                        A
    eenth century, <u>wrote</u> greater music than <u>all the composers</u> <u>of his day</u>.
                      B   C   D   Ⓐ Ⓑ Ⓒ Ⓓ

7. If people <u>which</u> were <u>mentally</u> disturbed <u>would seek</u> psychological help early in
                  A   B   C
    their ailment, they <u>could probably</u> avoid serious consequences.   Ⓐ Ⓑ Ⓒ Ⓓ
                              D

8. An infection sometimes <u>results</u> when the body is attacked <u>from</u> a bacteria <u>to</u>
                           A   B
    <u>which</u> the body has <u>little</u> resistance.   Ⓐ Ⓑ Ⓒ Ⓓ
     C   D

9. The <u>principal</u> <u>requested that</u> a purchase order <u>be issued</u> for <u>pencils</u> sharpeners
            A   B   C   D
    in every classroom of the school.   Ⓐ Ⓑ Ⓒ Ⓓ

10. The clothing which she <u>had packed</u> in her bag <u>was</u> <u>chiefly</u> suitable for <u>real</u> cold
                            A   B   C   D
    weather.   Ⓐ Ⓑ Ⓒ Ⓓ

11. After they <u>have played</u> bingo, the women went <u>uptown</u> <u>to meet</u> with their friends
                 A   B   C
    <u>for dinner.</u>   Ⓐ Ⓑ Ⓒ Ⓓ
     D

12. The small corner shop <u>who's</u> merchandise is <u>highly</u> in demand is <u>always</u>
                            A   B   C
    <u>crowded.</u>   Ⓐ Ⓑ Ⓒ Ⓓ
     D

13. They couldn't help <u>laughing</u> at the small <u>redhaired</u> boy who <u>had given</u> <u>hisself</u> a
                       A   B   C   D
    haircut with a dull pair of scissors.   Ⓐ Ⓑ Ⓒ Ⓓ

14. After the show the comedian <u>explained us</u> that <u>almost all the stories</u> he <u>had told</u>
                                A   B   C
    us <u>were</u> true.   Ⓐ Ⓑ Ⓒ Ⓓ
     D

15. Jenny is <u>so</u> upset that she <u>has laid</u> on the bed since <u>she</u> and her friend <u>quar-</u>
            A   B   C
    <u>reled.</u>   Ⓐ Ⓑ Ⓒ Ⓓ
     D

16. One <u>had to agree</u> that the <u>more better</u> Vicky felt about <u>herself</u>, the more capable
                A   B   C
    she <u>became.</u>   Ⓐ Ⓑ Ⓒ Ⓓ
     D

17. My little brother always gets <u>exciting</u> about <u>going</u> to the seashore so he wakes
                                  A   B
    up <u>earlier</u> than <u>anyone</u> else in the house.   Ⓐ Ⓑ Ⓒ Ⓓ
     C   D

18. <u>Its</u> <u>not likely</u> that <u>all of the contractors</u> will be able to understand the <u>complicated</u>
    A   B   C   D
    regulations.   Ⓐ Ⓑ Ⓒ Ⓓ

19. Most bankers <u>sincerely</u> believe that <u>finance</u> is one of the <u>poorest</u> <u>understood</u>
                   A   B   C   D
    problems in the country.   Ⓐ Ⓑ Ⓒ Ⓓ

20. The plot of the story is <u>where two sisters</u> meet <u>again</u> after a separation <u>of</u>
                           A   B   C
    twenty-five <u>years.</u>   Ⓐ Ⓑ Ⓒ Ⓓ
     D

21. I <u>suggest</u> that you all <u>are</u> very quiet if you <u>want</u> the party <u>to be</u> a surprise.
       A   B   C   D   Ⓐ Ⓑ Ⓒ Ⓓ

22. The speaker this evening, <u>whom</u> I understand is an authority <u>on</u> <u>crime</u> preven-
                                   A   B C
    tion, <u>will be focusing</u> on self-protection.   Ⓐ Ⓑ Ⓒ Ⓓ
              D

23. Although her dog <u>is not</u> a thoroughbred, it <u>followed</u> orders in the training class
                       A   B
    at the park yesterday, <u>quicker</u> than any of the <u>other dogs</u> that were there.
                                C   D   Ⓐ Ⓑ Ⓒ Ⓓ

24. If the airport <u>were equipped</u> <u>properly</u> before the <u>tragic</u> accident occurred, the
                        A   B   C
    accident might <u>have been averted</u>.   Ⓐ Ⓑ Ⓒ Ⓓ
                         D

25. In addition <u>to</u> <u>all the other</u> sporting events in the marathon, each contestant <u>had</u>
                 A   B
    <u>to go</u> on a <u>three-miles</u> mountain climb.   Ⓐ Ⓑ Ⓒ Ⓓ
    C   D

26. Mr. Schwartz <u>has had</u> <u>a number</u> of jobs in his lifetime, but he's <u>primary</u> <u>an</u> edu-
                    A   B   C D
    cator.   Ⓐ Ⓑ Ⓒ Ⓓ

27. The typewriter, which Ben <u>had used</u> for his thesis, was so old that the letters on
                                   A
    the <u>typewriter's</u> keys were <u>barely</u> <u>visible</u>.   Ⓐ Ⓑ Ⓒ Ⓓ
            B   C   D

28. "Where do you <u>go bowling</u>?" "The <u>very</u> best alleys are <u>at</u> Main Street."
                    A   B C   D   Ⓐ Ⓑ Ⓒ Ⓓ

29. Norton walked into the room <u>confidently</u> since he felt that he had prepared <u>him-</u>
                                           A
    <u>self</u> <u>as good as</u> he <u>possibly could</u>.   Ⓐ Ⓑ Ⓒ Ⓓ
    B   C   D

30. <u>Not being</u> familiar <u>with</u> registration procedure, the student had <u>no idea what</u>
        A   B   C
    <u>should she do</u>.   Ⓐ Ⓑ Ⓒ Ⓓ
    D

31. The twins want <u>get</u> jobs <u>during</u> the summer vacation, a plan <u>which</u> <u>sounds like</u>
                 A   B   C   D
    a good idea to their parents.   Ⓐ Ⓑ Ⓒ Ⓓ

32. The baby-sitter, <u>whose</u> care Mrs. Van Pelt <u>had left</u> her children, <u>fell asleep</u> while
                  A   B   C
    she <u>was reading</u> the children a story.   Ⓐ Ⓑ Ⓒ Ⓓ
          D

33. It was <u>easy to tell</u>, <u>practically</u> from the beginning of the match, that our oppo-
             A   B
    nents had <u>much more</u> expertise than <u>us</u>.   Ⓐ Ⓑ Ⓒ Ⓓ
              C   D

34. Artificial satellites are <u>them</u> which have been put <u>into orbit</u> by <u>scientists</u> for
                     A   B   C
    <u>exploratory and experimental</u> purposes.   Ⓐ Ⓑ Ⓒ Ⓓ
              D

35. Wealthy people like <u>themselves</u>, who <u>have never known</u> deprivation, may not be
                              A   B

    able to empathize with those <u>far less</u> fortunate than <u>they</u>.   Ⓐ Ⓑ Ⓒ Ⓓ
                                       C   D

36. A great number of senior citizens have as <u>action</u> <u>a</u> life as <u>those</u> <u>much younger</u>
                                                   A   B   C   D

    than they.   Ⓐ Ⓑ Ⓒ Ⓓ

Eight

WRITING STRUCTURE AND FORM

SUBJECT–VERB AGREEMENT

The verb must agree with the subject in number and person. Use a singular verb with a singular noun or pronoun, and a plural verb with a plural noun or pronoun.

Ryan *has* two brothers.
They *work* for the telephone company.

Use a singular verb with uncountable nouns. Review the material on uncountable nouns in Chapter Seven.

In all of the classes, *attendance* **has been** *excellent.*

Two subjects joined by *and* are considered plural and must therefore be followed by a plural verb.

Carol and **Janet** *are planning* to visit their parents next Christmas.

The objects of prepositions do *not* change the number of the subject!

A **box** of oranges *was* given to us.
(wrong):   (A box of oranges were given to us.)
                               xxxxxxxxxxxxxxx

NOTE: The following prepositional expressions do *not* change a singular subject to a plural subject: *with, along with, together with, as well as, in addition to, besides.*

Mary, along with her sisters, attends the sessions regularly.
(wrong):   (Mary, along with her sisters, attend the sessions regularly.)
                                           xxxxxxxxx

Singular subjects connected by *or* or *nor* are followed by a singular verb.

John, Mike, or Noriko drives Paula to work each morning.
(wrong):   (John, Mike, or Noriko drive Paula to work each morning.)
                                   xxxxxxxx

When a sentence or clause begins with *there, here,* or with a pronoun such as *who, where, what, which* or *how,* the verb must match the true subject.

There **is**, according to reports, some *doubt* about the outcome.
Here **are** the *books* you ordered.
What **are** your *names?*
How **has** *he* been feeling?
(wrong):   (Here ~~comes~~ the children.)

RIGHT: Here **come** the *children.*

When an infinitive construction is the subject, use a singular verb.

To produce fine paintings **requires** skill and creativity.

When a gerund construction is the subject, use a singular verb.

Growing one's own vegetables **is** pleasurable and gratifying.

When a noun clause is the subject, use a singular verb.

What his sons did when they finished their jobs **was** of no concern to him.

Study the chart below, which lists nouns and indefinite pronouns that are followed by a singular form of the verb, a plural form of the verb, or either one.

Singular		Singular or Plural	Plural
one	salt, advice (etc.)	any	two (etc.)
each	whatever	none	few
every	whoever	some	many
many a . . .	pair of . . .	all	both
everyone	kind of . . .	the rest	several
anyone	sort of . . .	most	others
someone	type of . . .	a lot	people
anybody	the number	either . . . or	persons
somebody	much	neither . . . nor	clothes
nobody	little	half	kinds of . . .
flock	the other	a third (etc.)	types of . . .
herd	another	ten percent (etc.)	sorts of . . .
man/human race	the first, second (etc.)	five dollars (etc.)	children
mankind	a great deal	two hours, miles (etc.)	men (etc.)
clothing	percentage	team, family, jury (etc.)	a number
furniture	either, neither	fish, deer (etc.)	pieces of furniture
	economics, mathematics (etc.)		scissors
	government		glasses

Study the following examples of subject–verb agreement. Note that verbs after quantity pronouns (*some, most, none, half, a lot, all, a third, two percent, the rest*) are determined by the object following the preposition *of. Every, each,* and *many a,* remain single even when there is more than one subject.

1. *Every man, woman, and child* **is** an important being.
2. *All* of the *food* **was prepared** the day before the event.

3. *All* of the meals **were prepared** the day before the event.
4. *A number* of books **were** missing from the shelf.
5. *The number* of books missing *was* indeed large.
6. *A third* of his composition **has been corrected.**
7. *A third* of their compositions **have been corrected.**
8. *Whoever* **finishes** the race first will be this year's champion.
9. *Either* (one) of them **is** competent to do the job.
10. *Neither* of the two pieces **was** familiar to him.

NOTE: In sentences with *either . . . or* and *neither . . . nor* the verb is determined by the subject closer to it.

---

11. Neither Mary nor her *brothers* **are going to** come tonight.
12. Neither Mary's brothers nor *Mary* **is going to** come tonight.
13. Either the sofa or the *chairs* **have been** sold.

NOTE: Use *kind of* with singular verbs and *kinds of* with plural verbs (also true of *sort of* and *type of*). *Kind of* refers to single items and *kinds of* refers to plural items. However, both are sometimes used with uncountable nouns.

---

14. A strange *type* of bug **is** in the garden.
15. Strange *types* of bugs **are** in the garden.
16. What *kind* of rice **is served** in that restaurant?
17. What *kinds* of rice **are served** in that restaurant?
18. In London the *people* **enjoy** the great number of plays performed.
19. *A lot* (or *much*) **has been said** about pollution but *little* **has been done.**
20. *A lot* of industries **are** interested in developing good public relations.
21. *Many* **have wished** that they had a better education.
22. *Many a man and woman* **has wished** that he or she had had a better education.
23. *Ninety percent* of the students in our school **are** pleased with the instruction.
24. A large *percentage* of the students **is** pleased with the instruction.
25. *Three chapters* **were discussed** in class today.

NOTE: Some plural nouns may be thought of as a single collective noun; hence, the verb is singular.

---

26. *Three chapters* a night **was** required reading in Sue's class.
27. *Five hundred miles* **is** a long distance to drive in one day.
28. *One* of the maps **is** missing. *Two* **are** on the wall. *The first* (one) **belongs** to a student and *the second* **belongs** to the teacher.

NOTE: Verb agreement after certain uses of *one* can be confusing. Compare the following sentences, noting the italicized "clues."

One of those men *likes* to drive fast.
He is *the only one* of those men who *likes* to drive fast.
He is one of those *men who like* to drive fast.

Verbs are often separated from the subject by words, phrases, and clauses. No matter how wordy or complicated a sentence may be, or how far the verb is from the subject, make sure the main verb agrees with the main subject. Make sure also that the verb in the dependent clause agrees with the subject of the dependent clause or with the word to which the relative pronoun refers.

The *cost* of renting apartments in some of the cities in the United States **is** considerably higher than *many* have expected it to be.

In each of the departments, the *buyer,* who <u>consults</u> with the clerks to check on shortages, **decides** how much to order. (*Consults,* the verb of the relative clause, is singular because the subject, *who,* refers to the singular *buyer.*)

Avoid the following kinds of errors:

(wrong):   (The elevators in one of the stores doesn't work.)

RIGHT: The elevators in one of the stores *don't* work.

(wrong):   (Neither of the trains are running today.)

RIGHT: Neither of the trains *is* running today.

(wrong):   (A large percentage of goods sold in the United States are foreign.)

RIGHT: A large percentage of goods sold in the United States *is* foreign.

(wrong):   (It's one of those problems that is difficult to solve.)

RIGHT: It's one of those problems that *are* difficult to solve.

(wrong):   (There is a number of people who lives in rural areas today that is considering moving into the cities.)

RIGHT: There *are* a number of people who *live* in rural areas today that *are* considering moving into the cities.

(wrong):   (She think that one of the rats in the science laboratory have escaped.)

RIGHT: She *thinks* that one of the rats in the science laboratory *has* escaped.

(wrong):   (How many had registered were not yet known.)

RIGHT: How many had registered *was* not yet known.

(wrong):   (The Randalls' daughter, as well as her friends, were at the concert last night.)

RIGHT: The Randalls' daughter, as well as her friends, *was* at the concert last night.

(wrong):   (Neither Mrs. Carter or her daughters-in-law is working at the present time.)

RIGHT: Neither Mrs. Carter *nor* her daughters-in-law *are working* at the present time.

(wrong):   (Bob and Ted neither smokes or drinks.)

RIGHT: Bob and Ted neither *smoke nor drink.*

(wrong):   (A flock of Canadian geese, migrating to breeding grounds, were seen flying overhead this morning.)

RIGHT: A flock of Canadian geese, migrating to breeding grounds, *was seen* flying overhead this morning.

(wrong):   (When he arrived in Detroit, he complained that some luggage were missing.)

RIGHT: When he arrived in Detroit, he complained that some luggage *was* missing.

RIGHT: When he arrived in Detroit, he complained that *some pieces of luggage were* missing.

(wrong):   (Sewing, knitting, and weaving are her favorite hobbies; in fact, busy as she is, either activity is usually included in her daily life.) *Either* and *neither* refer to only *two* (or two groups).

RIGHT: Sewing, knitting, and weaving are her favorite hobbies; in fact, busy as she is, *one of the activities* is usually included in her daily life.

EXERCISE VIII. 1.

In the following sentences: (1) circle the subject or subjects of each clause; (2) underline any verbs that do not agree with the subject; (3) make corrections.

1. Jack, along with the other students, think that the campus is getting over-crowded.
2. Every year a percentage of the profits from the college plays are given to the scholarship fund for drama students.
3. Neither the boys nor Mary is going to march in the parade on Saturday.
4. One of the state senators, to whom people often expresses their discontent, *has* have decided to try to combat the new zoning law.
5. The effects of environment versus those of heredity, a subject long argued by those studying human behavior, are still not definitely known.
6. Rice, with vegetables and pineapple, *was* were served with the poultry dish.
7. It was reported on the news this evening that there *was* were a good chance of thundershowers in the mountains.
8. Terry is the only one of the secretaries who still attends classes.
9. The man's harsh comments on the future of the human race were a shock to some of us.
10. In the library every painting on the walls of the reference rooms have been donated by local artists.
11. A great deal of the difficulty they are having is attributable to a lack of communication.
12. Most of the jewelry has been returned but some pieces of jewelry, apparently, has already been sold by the thieves.
13. To visit zoos that simulate the natural habitats of animals *is* are of great interest to zoologists.
14. Most people today seem to accept the fact that the income from their jobs barely exceed their expenses.
15. Although the price of oranges *has* have decreased, the prices of other fruit *have* has increased.
16. Learning about people in ancient times *has* have long interested scholars.
17. Whoever *is* are finished with the test may leave.
18. The ornithologists have reported that a large number of birds is already extinct.
19. Neither of our daughters was interested in opera until recently.
20. Many a father have regretted not spending more time with his children when they were young.

PRONOUN–ANTECEDENT AGREEMENT

The antecedent of a pronoun is the noun or pronoun to which the pronoun refers. The pronoun must agree with its antecedent in number, person, and gender.

> *Kathy and Ann* played *their* violins for us last evening.
> The *dog* with the brown and white spots appears to have hurt *its* paws.

Review the list of nouns and indefinite pronouns on page 130 to determine whether a particular noun or pronoun is a singular or a plural antecedent.

Study the following examples of pronoun–antecedent agreement.

NOTE: Pronouns that refer to antecedents of indeterminate gender include both the male and female gender. Also note that in sentences with either/or and neither/nor, the pronoun agrees in number with the antecedent closer to it.

---

1. *Each man and woman* present at the meeting presented *his or her* opinion.
2. *Neither* of them (John nor Joe) has submitted his report yet.
3. *None* **of the music** was played in *its* original form.
4. *None* **of the pieces** of music were played in *their* original form.
5. *Many a boy and girl* has bruised *his or her* knee riding on a skateboard.
6. *One* of the women in the group discussed *her* feelings openly.
7. *You scientists* sometimes seem unconcerned about the sociological aspects of *your* experiments.
8. Either the Goldman sisters or *Anna* will play *her* own compositions.
9. Either Anna or the Goldman *sisters* will play *their* own compositions.
10. *Both* retired from *their* jobs last year.
11. The *principal* of the school, in addition to the faculty members, gave *her* views on how to increase reading scores.
12. *None* said that *they* had visited the local observatory.
13. *No one* said that *he or she* had visited the local observatory.

Avoid the following kinds of errors:

(wrong): (In a letter to each depositor the Savings and Loan Company gave their views on high interest rates.)

RIGHT: In a letter to each depositor the Savings and Loan Company gave *its* views on high interest rates.

(wrong): Miss Ostrow, together with her associates, expects to sign their names on the contract some time next week.)

RIGHT: Miss Ostrow, together with her associates, expects to sign *her name* on the contract some time next week.

(wrong): (Although it was very warm in the room and the examination was very long, everybody tried to do their best.)

RIGHT: Although it was very warm in the room and the examination was very long, everybody tried to do *his and her* best.

(wrong): (We were told that neither the officers of the club nor the president would read their recommendations at tonight's meeting.)

RIGHT: We were told that neither the officers of the club nor the president would read *his* recommendations at tonight's meeting.

(wrong): (One of the girls has forgotten to take their sweater home.)

RIGHT: One of the girls has forgotten to take *her* sweater home.

A pronoun must have a clear and specific antecedent.

(wrong): (I removed the papers from their folders and threw them out.) The pronoun *them* does not have a clear and specific antecedent since it is not clear whether the antecedent is *papers* or *folders*.

RIGHT: I removed the papers from their folders and threw the papers out.

(wrong): (When Mary ran into Bella, she was surprised.) It is not clear who was surprised.

RIGHT: When Mary ran into Bella, *Mary* was surprised.

(wrong):   (Peter's motorcycle is good transportation for him.) A possessive form of the noun
is *not* an antecedent.

RIGHT: Peter's motorcycle is good transportation for *Peter.*

Refer to those in a particular place as *people*, not they.

(wrong:)   (In Miami, they like to go to the beach and lie in the sun.)

RIGHT: In Miami, people like to go to the beach and lie in the sun.

Nouns and pronouns (not clauses or ideas) are antecedents.

(wrong):   (Pamela was given responsibilities in her childhood. It led to early maturity.)

RIGHT: Pamela was given responsibilities in her childhood. This kind of experience led to early maturity.

(wrong):   (My son enjoys listening to music which he often buys from the record shops.)

RIGHT: My son enjoys listening to music and he often buys records from the record shops.

Use *one* and the possessive *one's* or *his or her* (not *you* or *your*) when the sentence refers to people in general.

(wrong):   (Health experts say that you should exercise daily in order to maintain your health.)

RIGHT: Health experts say that *one* should exercise daily in order to maintain *one's* health (*or*: to maintain *his or her* health).

Don't change the person of the pronoun from its antecedent. Don't change from *one* to *you*, or from *you* to *one*.

(wrong):   (After a person works hard, they need a rest.)

RIGHT: After a person works hard, *he or she* needs a rest.

(wrong):   (If one uses his time well, you can find time for many activities.)

RIGHT: If one uses his time well, *one* (*or*: he or she) can find time for many activities.

(wrong):   (If you are the type of person who needs plenty of sleep, one should retire early.)

RIGHT: If you are the type of person who needs plenty of sleep, *you* should retire early.

Use the impersonal pronoun for a single animal when the sex is unknown.

(wrong):   (Whose cat is she? I don't know, but she apparently is wearing her collar.)

RIGHT: Whose cat is *it*? I don't know, but *it* apparently is wearing *its* collar.

Avoid making errors with the following sound-alike words. (The first in each pair is the possessive form.)

its–it's	their–they're–there
whose–who's	your–you're

(wrong):   Because of a disease, the tree has lost many of it's leaves.
                                                            xxxx
RIGHT: Because of a disease, the tree has lost many of *its* leaves.

EXERCISE VIII. 2.

In the following sentences: (1) circle the antecedent; (2) underline pronouns that are used erroneously; (3) make corrections.

1. Anyone who doesn't understand the lesson should ask their teacher to explain it.
2. Psychologists say that it's good for one to express your feelings.
3. Every boy and girl in the school remembered to bring his note.
4. He has traveled all over the world, which has given him understanding of other styles of life.
5. Neither of the girls would admit that they had forgotten to telephone.
6. If you're careful not to make errors, one should get a high score.
7. It's evident that many a man and woman receives little recognition for their years of service.
8. In Washington, D.C., they are proud of their historical monuments.
9. Members of the landlord's family offered its help to the new tenants.
10. She took the socks out of the shoes and put them away.
11. Somebody left his or her boots under a desk.
12. Nobody has to answer personal questions if they would rather not.
13. Each of the students has demonstrated their comprehension of the lesson.
14. In the basement there was a rat with his foot caught in a trap.
15. We were pleased that you introduced you're family to us.
16. Neither the controller, Mrs. Elton, nor her assistants have submitted their outlines for a budget.
17. When Mr. Patel's mind is occupied with worries, he doesn't function well.
18. Rene's dog, along with the other dogs on the street, rejected its food.
19. The president of the company, Mr. Tehrani, in addition to the members of the board, was not reimbursed for their expenses abroad.
20. Somehow she managed to move the piano by himself.

TYPES OF CLAUSES AND SENTENCES

The general order of a sentence is as follows:

subject	verb	object	place	manner	time
She	wrote	the lesson	on the board	with green chalk	this morning.

NOTE: "Manner" basically tells how, by what means, with whom, how long, how much, and so on.

Sentences often begin with "time."

Next year Joe is going to Africa for six months to photograph lions.

For sentence variety, other forms may be used to begin sentences, such as: 1) prepositions, 2) adjectives, 3) adverbs, 4) conjunctions, 5) participles, and 6) appositives.

1. *In science class* we are learning how to analyze our experiments.
2. *Painless*, the operation takes only ten minutes.
3. *Carefully*, he plucked the thorns from the dog's face.
4. *Because* the elevator didn't function, he had to climb ten flights of stairs.
5. *Disappointed in the results*, Nick decided to try again.
6. *One of the greatest inventors* of all time, Edison was called "The Wizard of Menlo Park."

Independent and Dependent Clauses

An independent clause contains **a subject and a verb and expresses a complete idea.** Every sentence must have at least one independent clause. Therefore, an independent clause, by itself, constitutes a sentence. The subject and the verb of an independent clause are called *main subject* and *main verb*.

The telephone is ringing.

A dependent clause contains **a subject and a verb but *does not* express a complete idea.** Therefore, a dependent clause *does not* by itself constitute a sentence. **Dependent clauses begin with adverbial conjunctions** (see Conjunctions in the next section) **and relative pronouns,** as shown below.

Although she was busy
which had been highly publicized
because they were interested in becoming surgeons
(The package,) after it had been delivered
(Selena), of whom he has spoken several times
if you don't mind waiting for me
when he returns to Seoul, Korea
where she had spent a great deal of time in her youth

Types of Sentences

Sentences may be **simple, compound, complex, or compound-complex. A *simple sentence* contains one independent clause.**
   The electric light was invented by Thomas Edison in 1879. A *simple sentence* may have two main subjects connected by *and* (compound subject), or two main verbs connected by *and* (compound verb), or both.

The *brushes and paint* were kept in a cabinet.
Yesterday John *cleaned* the apartment *and cooked* the dinner.
Space experts and geologists *examined and analyzed* the rocks from the moon.

A *compound sentence* contains two independent clauses connected by *and, or, nor,* or *but*. Words that connect independent clauses are called *correlative conjunctions*.

The city council will meet Tuesday **and** *the public is invited to attend.*

NOTE: Without the correlative conjunction, two sentences would be required.
The city council will meet Tuesday. The public is invited to attend.

The sky is overcast **but** *the air is clear.*
In tomorrow's seminar, Dr. Gooch will demonstrate and discuss new burn treatment **or** *Dr. Gold and Dr. Yoo will debate the subject of tranquilizers.*

A *complex sentence* contains *one independent clause* and one or more dependent clauses.

When the sculpture was unveiled, *everyone cheered.*
Mr. Fuller, who has been in charge of surveys for the county, *will personally inspect the site* before he completes his report.
If George is selected as a delegate, *he'll vote representatively,* even though he doesn't like the candidate.

A *compound-complex sentence* contains *two or more independent clauses* and one or more dependent clauses.

We had eaten all of the rolls and relishes and *we were no longer hungry* by the time the main dish was served.
After the document had been sealed with an insignia that identified the owner, *it was put into the company safe* and *the locking device was set.*
He graduated with a Bachelor of Science degree but *he decided,* when he had reviewed career opportunities, *to return for an advanced degree.*

Avoid incomplete sentences.

(incomplete):	(Since the zoning laws for new construction have been changed.)
COMPLETE:	The zoning laws for new construction have been changed.
COMPLETE:	Since the zoning laws for new construction have been changed, many high-rise buildings will soon be built.
(incomplete):	(The problem of where to store unsold goods that people might request in the future.)
COMPLETE:	There was a problem of where to store unsold goods.
COMPLETE:	The problem of where to store unsold goods that people might request in the future was finally solved.
(incomplete):	(Andy who was declared the most valuable player of the season.)
COMPLETE:	Andy was declared the most valuable player of the season.
COMPLETE:	Andy, who was declared the most valuable player of the season, was offered a job with a professional team.
COMPLETE:	Andy, declared the most valuable player of the season, was offered a job with a professional team.
(incomplete):	(Neil Armstrong a member of the first group of astronauts who walked on the moon.)
COMPLETE:	Neil Armstrong was a member of the first group of astronauts who walked on the moon.
COMPLETE:	Neil Armstrong, a member of the first group of astronauts who walked on the moon, was a hero to many.

(incomplete):	(A series of debates scheduled before the election.)
COMPLETE:	A series of debates were scheduled before the election.
COMPLETE:	A series of debates, scheduled before the election, helped voters to decide how they should vote.
(incomplete):	(The child listening to the story when he fell asleep.) Participles without auxiliaries are *not* verbs.
COMPLETE:	The child was listening to the story when he fell asleep.
COMPLETE:	Listening to the story, the child fell asleep.
COMPLETE:	The child, listening to the story, fell asleep.

Avoid the improper usage of "two main verbs."

(poor form):	(The directions had been given to John were easy to follow.)
GOOD FORM:	The directions that had been given to John were easy to follow.
GOOD FORM:	The directions given to John were easy to follow.
(poor form):	(The naturalist observed the animals took many notes.)
GOOD FORM:	The naturalist observed the animals and took many notes.
GOOD FORM:	The naturalist who was observing the animals took many notes.
GOOD FORM:	The naturalist observing the animals took many notes.
GOOD FORM:	Observing the animals, the naturalist took many notes.
(poor form):	(Mrs. Stone's occupation is teaching computer science spoke about the commercial aspects of computers.)
GOOD FORM:	Mrs. Stone, whose occupation is teaching computer science, spoke about the commercial aspects of computers.
GOOD FORM:	Mrs. Stone's occupation is teaching computer science. In her lecture she spoke about the commercial aspects of computers.
GOOD FORM:	Teacher of computer science, Mrs. Stone spoke about the commercial aspects of computers.
GOOD FORM:	In her lecture, Mrs. Stone, teacher of computer science, spoke about the commercial aspects of computers.

Avoid writing run-on sentences.

When two independent clauses are connected by a comma, the result is a *run-on sentence.*

(run-on sentence):	(Some carried signs, others passed out leaflets.)
GOOD FORM:	Some carried signs. Others passed out leaflets.
GOOD FORM:	Some carried signs and others passed out leaflets.

NOTE: A semicolon (;) may be used to connect two independent clauses if the first independent clause is fairly short and if the second independent clause relates closely to the first.

| GOOD FORM: | Some carried signs; other passed out leaflets. |

(run-on sentence):	(A piccolo is smaller than a flute it is also pitched higher.)
GOOD FORM:	A piccolo is smaller than a flute, and it is also pitched higher.
GOOD FORM:	A piccolo is smaller than a flute; it is also pitched higher.
(run-on sentence):	(I didn't think the movie was very good, there were many inconsistencies.)
GOOD FORM:	I didn't think the movie was very good because there were many inconsistencies.)

GOOD FORM:	I didn't think the movie was very good. There were many inconsistencies.
GOOD FORM:	I didn't think the movie was very good; there were many inconsistencies.

Avoid omitting a subject.

(subject omitted):	(When Jeff is assigned his new post, will leave immediately for Africa.)
GOOD FORM:	When Jeff is assigned his new post, he'll leave immediately for Africa.
(subject omitted):	(As soon as the cable car reached the summit, descended again to the floor of the canyon.)
GOOD FORM:	As soon as the cable car reached the summit, it descended again to the floor of the canyon.
(subject omitted):	(He was in such a hurry when he paid the cashier, forgot to count his change.)
GOOD FORM:	He was in such a hurry when he paid the cashier, he forgot to count his change.

EXERCISE VIII. 3.

Each sentence below contains elements of poor form. Rewrite the following sentences using good sentence form.

1. According to the weather report that was issued this morning.
2. Peter realized his error quickly corrected it.
3. Because there wasn't any food in the refrigerator.
4. A video presentation prepared by the chairman of the conference.
5. After he decides what to do and where to sleep.
6. Helen was unaccustomed to dealing with customers who had complaints, she asked for assistance.
7. If they plan to collaborate, have to meet frequently.
8. If the insects aren't stopped after the farmers spray them with insecticides.
9. The girls are prepared, they know every step perfectly.
10. Myra in the blue dress and Tess in the yellow dress, playing with their dolls like two grown-up ladies.
11. Mr. Blaine, unable to achieve success quickly.
12. A distinguished American writer of the nineteenth century, Ralph Waldo Emerson who had been in demand as a lecturer, was deaded.
13. When they complete the study program that they have been taking, can apply for college credit.
14. Coral skeleton is beautiful, people make jewelry out of it.
15. She expressed her appreciation to everyone had helped her.
16. The book written by the author when he was only fifteen.
17. Although the polar bear lives in an extremely cold climate, doesn't hibernate.
18. The composer's recent opera was performed last night made a strong impression on the audience.
19. The director explaining as he showed the film.
20. The plan to consolidate had been discussed for many weeks, was unexpectedly rejected.

+ three complex sentances

or The plan to consolidate, which was unexpectedly rejected, had been discussed for many weeks.

USING CONJUNCTIONS

Conjunctions are used to combine thoughts and to extend sentences.

When Steve *and* Fred had a vacation, they went to Italy *so that* they could learn about Italian art; *in addition*, they were eager to improve their conversational skills in the Italian language.

Kinds of Conjunctions

***Correlative conjunctions* (connectors) join words, phrases, and clauses with *and, or, nor, but*.**

Last night I washed my hair *and* I wrote a letter to my sister.
Mary *or* John will meet you at the airport.
The cat is neither in the kitchen *nor* in the dining room.
Linda likes jazz *but* Rita prefers country music.

Adverbial conjunctions* introduce dependent adverbial clauses which tell more about the independent clause. Some of these are *because, since, so that, so, although, even though, before, when, while, since, as soon as, after, if, unless, until*. **Adverbial conjunctions may precede or follow the independent clause.**

As soon as Victor arrived, he rented a car.
He'll telephone them *when* he arranges his schedule.

Transitional conjunctions introduce the second of two independent clauses which tells more about the first independent clause. Transitional conjunctions include *therefore, consequently, as a result, however, nevertheless, in addition, furthermore, moreover, besides that, as a matter of fact, in fact, otherwise, for instance, on the other hand, on the contrary, later, afterwards*. **Transitional conjunctions must be preceded by a semicolon when used to extend a sentence.**

He didn't know the meaning of the word; *therefore* he looked it up.

NOTE: Transitional conjunctions may begin a new sentence or may be used at different points in the sentence.

He didn't know the meaning of the word. *Therefore,* he looked it up.
He didn't know the meaning of the word. He *therefore* looked it up.
He didn't know the meaning of the word. He looked it up, *therefore*.

Some Common Conjunctions

Below are examples of conjunctions under general classified headings. Notice the punctuation. Wherever you see a semicolon, you may, instead, begin a new sentence. Notice how the verb tenses in the clauses "go with" each other.

Time

1. Columbus had to wait seven years *before* he was given ships and supplies.
2. *When* the economy is uncertain, people tend to spend less.

3. *Since* he graduated, Tom has been working for an engineering firm.
4. The mirror fell and broke *while* Hector was hanging it on the wall.
5. *As soon as* the snowplow clears the snow, the road will be open.
6. *After* the law is revised, import restrictions will be removed.
7. Feeling tired, Ben took a nap; *later* he resumed working.
8. They talked for about an hour; *afterwards* they took a walk.

Reason, Cause

1. Consumers are interested in solar energy *because* they want to save on fuel costs.

NOTE: Prepositional phrases are sometimes used instead of conjunctional clauses.

---

2. Consumers are interested in solar energy *because of high fuel costs.*
3. *Since* he had never studied English, he enrolled in the first level.
4. She lost a lot of weight *due to the fact* that she had been ill (*also due to her illness*).
5. *Inasmuch as* no witnesses appeared, Bernard lost the case.

Purpose

1. A detour was posted *so that* cars would not travel over the freshly paved roads.

Result

1. Peter didn't like his job; *therefore* he quit.
2. There are many industries in that area; *consequently,* unemployment is low.
3. The road was blocked *so* they had to take another route.
4. He hadn't studied for the test; *as a result,* he failed it.
5. The bridge had been carelessly constructed; *thus* a disaster occurred.

Conditional and Qualifying Situations (Think of *although* as "before the fact" and *however* as "after the fact.")

1. *Although* she has had little experience, she has been effective.
2. She has had little experience; *however,* she has been effective.
3. The firm refuses to endorse the shipment *unless* an agreement is reached.
4. You had better take an umbrella *in case* it begins to rain. (*also:* in case of rain)
5. They dissolved their partnership a year ago *but* they have remained friends.
6. Hakto plays the banjo very well *even though* he has never had lessons.
7. She read the entire contents; she didn't, however, understand the meaning.
8. There had been agreement on most points; *nevertheless,* certain conflicts persisted.
9. *Considering the fact* that he has had little education, he feels fortunate to have such a good job.
   (*also:* considering his lack of education) (*also:* considering that he has had little education)
10. Ahman is a happy man *in spite of the fact* that he is handicapped.
    (*also:* in spite of being handicapped)
11. *Despite the fact* that meat was scarce, they had a healthful diet.
    (*also:* Despite the scarcity of meat)
12. Transportation facilities may improve *if* the proposition is passed.

Addition

1. Tai's wife has been writing a book; *in addition,* she works in the research library every evening.

2. We're not prepared for our trip; *furthermore,* we haven't received our passports yet.
3. I have never gone deep-sea diving; *moreover,* I'm afraid to try it.
4. He sings and dances very well; besides that, he plays the piano.
5. The judge put her on probation *and* made her attend lectures on safe driving.
6. People appear to be careful of what they eat; *also* they exercise more than they used to.

Clarification–Explanation

1. Jenny took flying lessons last year; *as a matter of fact,* she has become an accomplished pilot.
2. Mrs. Chekijian's daughter is often absent; *in fact* she has missed a month of school this semester.
3. She should go to the dentist; *otherwise,* her toothache might get worse.
4. He had better get some sleep *or else* he'll fall asleep in class.
5. He's careless about his personal possessions; *for instance,* he has lost three cameras in the last two years.
6. She's very creative; *for example,* she designed the stage set for the community opera last month.
7. He has a philosophical outlook; *that is,* he accepts life as it is.
8. We couldn't decide what to do. A vacation at the beach sounded very appealing to us; *on the other hand,* we also considered going to the mountains.
9. Some people think he's lazy; *on the contrary,* he's very industrious.
10. She looked as if she were having fun; *actually,* she was bored.

Avoid the following kinds of errors:

(wrong:)   (Pei studied medicine so she could help her people.) So refers to "result."
_{xxx}

RIGHT: Pei studies medicine *so that* she could help her people.

(wrong:)   (The two nations met to discuss a pact; therefore they couldn't agree.)
_{xxxxxxxxxxxx}

RIGHT: The two nations met to discuss a pact; *however,* they couldn't agree.

(wrong):   (Although the road was narrow, but the cars could pass each other.)
_{xxxxx}

RIGHT: Although the road was narrow, the cars could pass each other.

EXERCISE VIII. 4.

Identify the type of clause (independent or dependent) and the type of conjunction (correlative, adverbial, or transitional) in each of the sentences listed under Some Common Conjunctions.

EXERCISE VIII. 5.

Combine the following ideas, as in example number 1, using an appropriate conjunction under the heading suggested in the parentheses. Use a different conjunction in each case. (Check your punctuation.)

1. She went to bed early. She didn't sleep well.   (qualify)
   She went to bed early but she didn't sleep well.
2. Rosa likes to read poetry. She sometimes writes her own poetry. (addition)
3. She eats only low-calorie food. She wants to remain slim. (reason)
4. Lincoln had been a successful lawyer. He became president. (time)
5. Dr. Jenner developed a vaccine for smallpox. Many people were saved. (result)
6. I didn't carry an umbrella. I got wet. (result)
7. Some think that he is unfriendly. He likes people very much. (clarification)

8. Leo arose at 6:00 A.M. He hasn't eaten anything. (time)
9. It's rude to keep people waiting unnecessarily. It's a waste of valuable time. (addition)
10. We'd better hurry. We'll miss the train. (clarification)
11. He was lecturing about the mysteries of the mind. He dropped his notes. (time)
12. Doctors state that exercise is beneficial. One should not overdo it. (qualify)
13. Ingredients must be listed on food products. People will be able to buy wisely. (purpose)
14. Programs showing violence may be harmful to children. Many parents want such programs removed from television. (reason)
15. She won't enroll next fall. She can get a college loan. (conditional)
16. Mark is a marvelous potter. Many of his pieces have been shown in the Frank Lloyd Wright exhibition house. (clarification)
17. The bay has become contaminated with chemicals. It is not safe to eat the fish from the bay. (result)
18. He slept eleven hours last night. He is still tired. (qualify)

EXERCISE VIII. 6.

Complete the following sentences with logical ideas. Be sure that the verb tense in the second clause is compatible with *the verb tense* in the first clause.

1. Our basketball team didn't play well; therefore, _____ .
2. Jafar doesn't dance very well; on the other hand, _____ .
3. Meat was less expensive than fish so _____ .
4. Frank managed to get a good grade in spite of the fact _____ .
5. Serena has stopped smoking; in addition, _____ .
6. I thought the dog was going to bite me; on the contrary, _____ .
7. The dentist told the child to hold very still so that _____ .
8. The bridge must be strengthened; otherwise, _____ .
9. Harold wasn't enjoying the play; however, _____ .
10. The employees agreed to take a salary decrease even though _____ .
11. The lights went out because of a _____ .
12. The heavy snowstorm damaged some of the roofs; furthermore, _____ .
13. We won't need a car when we get there since _____ .
14. They plan to do some traveling before leaving the United States; in fact, _____ .
15. Her friend is very talented. She not only speaks several languages, but also _____ .

ESTABLISHING A VIEWPOINT: TENSE CONSISTENCY

Tenses in a sentence or in a paragraph must be compatible with each other. Select a tense in the time of the action. The verb tense in the first clause establishes time. Don't change to another time period unless the time of the action changes. Time changes are often indicated by words such as: *yesterday, a short time ago, in 1776, last month, formerly, used to, earlier, recently, in the past, at the present time, now, today, this week, in the future, next week, by next month, in October,* and so forth. Compare the following forms:

(poor form):   (Some churches now require couples who wanted to get married to wait for six months. During that time, the couples received counseling.

GOOD FORM:

The church hopes that by this method the divorce rate would be reduced in future years.)

Some churches now *require* couples who *want* to get married to wait for six months. During that time, the couples *receive* counseling. The church *hopes* that by this method the divorce rate *will be reduced* in future years.

(poor form):

(Mr. Pachuki used to prefer to travel by train. He likes the fact that he can rest and work while he was en route to a business appointment. However, presently he is retired and travels only for pleasure. Generally, he flew to whatever country he wishes to visit.)

GOOD FORM:

Mr. Pachuki *used to* prefer to travel by train. He *liked* the fact that he *could* rest and work while he *was* en route to a business appointment. However, presently he *is retired* and *travels* only for pleasure. Generally he *flies* to whatever country he *wishes* to visit.

EXERCISE VIII. 7.

In the sentences or short paragraphs below, underline the verb tenses that do not conform to the verb tense in the first sentence, and make corrections.

1. Carl gets up early every morning. He cooks his breakfast and prepared a lunch before he left for work.
2. There were only ten seconds left in the quarter. Smith throws a long pass to Jones who runs until he scores a touchdown.
3. I had a long conversation with Jackie yesterday. She tells me that she went to Canada last month. In fact, she plans to return there again next summer if her boss gave her a long vacation.
4. Living in London, even if the rate of exchange is better these days, is very expensive. Before you bought anything, you should go to several department stores to learn what range of prices and products were available.
5. Edgar, taking pictures with his new camera, was working quickly. He is afraid that the sun would set before he has a chance to finish the roll of film.
6. The art teacher, Mr. Aok, has planned a field trip for us. Next week we are going to watch a professional sculptor at work. We would be able to observe the manner in which he used a chisel and hammer to carve the wood.
7. A home tour has been planned for next Sunday. Many contemporary houses would be featured. In addition, there is a guide who explains the architectural details of each house. By the end of the tour, those of us who expect to go learn a lot about architecture.

USING PARTICIPLES AND PHRASES

We often use a shortened form of expression in the place of a dependent clause. The shortened form of expression may be a participle or a participial phrase, a prepositional phrase, an infinitive phrase, an appositive or an appositive phrase, an adjective or an adjective phrase, or an adverbial phrase. In the sentences below, compare the sentences containing dependent clauses with those containing the shortened forms. When a phrase is used to describe a noun or a pronoun, **it must be placed before or after the word that it describes.**

Clause:

Mr. McBride, **who was sleeping soundly,** didn't hear the telephone ring.

Participial phrase:	*Sleeping soundly,* Mr. McBride didn't hear the telephone ring.
Also:	Mr. McBride, *sleeping soundly,* didn't hear the telephone ring.
Clause:	Fausto walked into the office **which was at the end of the hall.**
Prepositional phrase:	Fausto walked into the office *at the end of the hall.*
Clause:	Bob went to the library **so that he could study in a quiet place.**
Infinitive phrase:	*To study in a quiet place* (*or:* In order to study in a quiet place), Bob went to the library.
Clause:	Eleanor Roosevelt, **who was a remarkable woman in many respects,** contributed a great deal to humane causes.
Appositive phrase:	*A remarkable woman in many respects,* Eleanor Roosevelt contributed a great deal to humane causes.
Also:	Eleanor Roosevelt, *a remarkable woman in many respects,* contributed a great deal to humane causes.
Clause:	The drapes had to be replaced **because they were old and no longer attractive.**
Adjective phrase:	*Old and no longer attractive,* the drapes had to be replaced.
Also:	The drapes, *old and no longer attractive,* had to be replaced.
Clause:	When you are in doubt, (you) check the answers.
Adverbial phrase:	*When in doubt,* (you) check the answers.

Avoid the following kinds of errors:

(wrong): (An instruction handbook is available to the consumers from the manufacturer.)

RIGHT: An instruction *handbook from the manufacturer* is available to the consumers.

(wrong): (Customers were disappointed who had patronized the store for several years when it went out of business.)

RIGHT: *Customers who had patronized the store for several years* were disappointed when it went out of business.

(wrong): (When only in grade school, Nick's artistic talent was apparent.)

RIGHT: *When only in grade school, Nick* displayed artistic talent.

(wrong): (Complete with diagrams, she had no difficulty assembling the bookcase.)

RIGHT: *Complete with diagrams, the bookcase* was easy for her to assemble.

(wrong): (Collecting seashells as he strolled along the beach, identifying them became a challenge to Harry.)

RIGHT: *Collecting seashells as he strolled along the beach, Harry* found that identifying them was a challenge.

(wrong): (A versatile person, many hobbies attracted Ellie.)

RIGHT: *A versatile person, Ellie* was attracted to many hobbies.

RIGHT: Many hobbies attracted *Ellie, a versatile person.*

Modifying Adjective Phrases with Participles

The present participle, the perfect participle, and the past participle may all be used in phrases modifying nouns and pronouns. Notice, in the following sentences, that **adjective phrases show cause and effect.**

Use the present participle (*-ing* form) when the action in the adjective phrase is *active* and *occurs at the time of the main verb action.* In the following sentences, compare the phrases with the clauses.

While Grandpa Rubin was softly singing a Russian folk song, he carried the child to bed.

Softly singing a Russian folk song, Grandpa Rubin carried the child to bed.

Polly saw a big black bird when she was looking out of the window.
Polly, *looking out of the window,* saw a big black bird.

Doris didn't leave with the others because she hoped to complete the experiment.
Hoping to complete the experiment, Doris didn't leave with the others.

Most of those who were buying goods at the auction were dealers.
Most of those *buying goods at the auction* were dealers.

The instructor dismissed the students who had to rehearse for the play.
The instructor dismissed the students *having to rehearse for the play.*

Since Marvin was a doctor, he rushed over to help the accident victim.
Being a doctor, Marvin rushed over to help the accident victim.

NOTE: The present participle may be used after the time words: *when, since, before, while, after.*
After Randy registered for college, he applied for a room in the dormitory.
After registering for college, Randy applied for a room in the dormitory.

Since Jae spoke with his counselor, he has learned about other career choices.
Since speaking with his counselor, Jae has learned about other career choices.

The company president has delayed making a decision because he is anxious to consider alternatives.
Being anxious to consider alternatives, the company president has delayed making a decision.
Also: Anxious to consider alternatives, the company president has delayed making a decision.
(*Being* may or may not precede the adjective; the meaning is the same.)

Although the machine still functioned, we didn't think it was practical to use.
Although still functioning, the machine, we thought, was not practical to use.

NOTE: Notice, in the sentence directly above, the adjective phrase "although still functioning" refers to the word "machine." Therefore the word "machine" has been placed next to the adjective phrase. An incorrectly placed adjective phrase is called a "dangling modifier."

Use the perfect participle (*having* plus the past participle) when the action is *active* and when it *was completed before the main verb action.* In the following sentences compare the phrases with the original clauses.

Dr. Ray was accepted for the position because he had passed the qualifying test.
Having passed the qualifying test, Dr. Ray was accepted for the position.

Mrs. Oliverio, who had received a bonus check, was able to purchase a new typewriter.
Mrs. Oliverio, *having received a bonus check,* was able to purchase a new typewriter.

Mr. Cawley had been a fireman at one time, so he knew exactly what to do when the fire broke out in the laboratory.

When the fire broke out in the laboratory, Mr. Cawley, having been *a fireman at one time,* knew exactly what to do.

After Raissa had resigned from the police force, a real estate agent persuaded her to enroll in a real estate training class.
After having resigned from the police force, Raissa was persuaded to enroll in a real estate training class.

Also: *After resigning* from the police force, Raissa was persuaded to enroll in a real estate training class.
Also: *Having resigned from the police force,* Raissa was persuaded to enroll in a real estate training class.

Use the past participle (*having been* plus the past participle) when the action is *passive* and occurs *usually earlier than the main verb action.*

George, who was chosen by the student council to give the graduation speech, is considering the subject of space exploration.
George, *having been chosen by the student council to give the graduation speech,* may talk about space exploration.

NOTE: Having been may be omitted. The meaning is the same. Compare:

George, *chosen by the student council to give the graduation speech,* may talk about space exploration.

Since the computer had not been fed the correct information, a serious error was made by the company.
Not having been fed the correct information, the computer caused a serious error to be made by the company.
Not fed the correct information, the computer caused a serious error to be made by the company.

The plants, which had been sadly neglected, appeared unhealthy and diseased.
Having been sadly neglected, the plants appeared unhealthy and diseased.
Sadly neglected, the plants appeared unhealthy and diseased.

The taxi driver hadn't been given directions; therefore he didn't know where to go.
The taxi driver, *not having been given directions,* didn't know where to go.
The taxi driver, *not given directions,* didn't know where to go.

Although the Watts Tower was built from discarded materials, people think it's beautiful.
Although built from discarded materials, the Watts Tower is considered beautiful.

Avoid the following kinds of errors:
    (wrong):   (Announced as the winner of the scholarship, everybody congratulated Dimitri.)
           xxxxxxxxxxxxxxxxxxxxxxxxxxxxxxxxxxxxxxxxxxxxxxxxxxxxxxxxxxxxxxxxxxx
           The adjective phrase is a "dangling modifier." It does not describe the word next to it.
    RIGHT: *Announced as the winner of the scholarship, Dimitri* was congratulated by everybody.
    RIGHT: Everybody congratulated *Dimitri, announced as the winner of the scholarship.*

(wrong): (After working all day, the painting was finally finished.) *The painting,* (above)
did not "work all day"; the adjective phrase refers to a person.
RIGHT: *After working all day, the artist* finished the painting.

NOTE: Don't use past participles after the time words: *after, before, since, while.*

(wrong): (Before left, she locked the door.)
RIGHT: Before *leaving,* she locked the door.

Exception: *When* is sometimes used with a past participle.

When taken with milk, the medicine is more effective.
clause: When it is taken with milk, the medicine is more effective.
(wrong): (Since came to the United States, she has been living with her cousin.)
RIGHT: Since *coming* to the United States, she has been living with her cousin.

Additional Uses of Participles and Phrases

Present and past participles are used to describe and extend the verb action.

The president **drove** through the streets *waving to the crowd.*
Mrs. Sapolsky **returned** to school last month, *motivated by the promise of a job.*
Miss Valdez **sorted out** all the paintings, *selecting a few to hang on the classroom walls.*
Every day Jill **walks** to her shop *accompanied by her dog Star.*

Present participles are used to extend adjective descriptions.

Cindy felt **wonderful** *relaxing on the beach.*
It was very **pleasant** *being carried into the air by the big balloon.*
When I got home, my husband was **busy** *writing letters to his nephews.*
She looked **warm** *wearing a fur coat on a summer's day.*

NOTE: Not all adjectives can be followed by present participles. Present participles are used, as in the above, to describe "a state of being." For the most part, infinitives are used "to proceed with an action."

She was **anxious** *to see* her friend.
I will be **happy** *to help* you.
It's **important** *to pursue* a career that you will enjoy.

Infinitive phrases of purpose that begin a sentence must be placed next to the noun or pronoun to which they refer.

To qualify for the secretarial position, **Joanne** has been renewing her skills.
(wrong): (To qualify for the secretarial position, her skills need to be renewed.)
To achieve a goal, **one** must work hard.
(wrong): (To achieve a goal, hard work is necessary.)

Avoid the following kinds of errors:

(wrong):   (Searched for treasure, robbers in ancient Egypt disturbed the majority of the
             xxxxxxxxxxxx
             kings' tombs.)

RIGHT: *Searching for treasure,* robbers in ancient Egypt disturbed the majority of the kings'
             tombs.

(wrong):   (Monthly financial reports, carefully reviewing and analyzing, were instrumental
                                           xxxxxxxxxxxxxx   xxxxxxxxxxxxxx
             in the manager's business procedures.)

RIGHT: Monthly financial reports, *carefully reviewed and analyzed,* were instrumental in the
             manager's business procedures.

(wrong):   (The ancient Greeks, had a great sense of beauty, left the world magnificent
                                   xxxxx
             works of art and architecture.)

RIGHT: The ancient Greeks, *having had a great sense of beauty,* left the world magnificent
             works of art and architecture.

(wrong):   (Originally hired as a salesman, Mr. Craig's position was changed within a
                                              xxxxxxxxxxxxxxxxxxxxxxxxxxxxxxxx
             month.)

RIGHT: Originally hired as a salesman, *Mr. Craig* was changed to another position within
             a month.

(wrong):   (After introduced the auditor to some of the office staff, the manager accompa-
                    xxxxxxxxxxxxxxx
             nied him to the file room.)

RIGHT: *After introducing* the auditor to some of the office staff, the manager accompanied
             him to the file room.

(wrong):   (To brighten up the room, the walls were painted yellow.)
                                       xxxxxxxxxxxxxx

RIGHT: To brighten up the room, she painted the walls yellow.

(wrong):   (My car, having painted and polished, looks as if it were new.)
                     xxxxxxxxxxxxxxxxxxxxxxxxxxxxxxxxxxxxxxxxxxxx

RIGHT: My car, *having been painted and polished,* looks as if it were new.

RIGHT: My car, *painted and polished,* looks as if it were new.

(wrong):   (Sleeping several hours, Bea and Mark were ready to resume the tour.)
              xxxxxxxxxxxxxx

RIGHT: *Having slept* several hours, Bea and Mark were ready to resume the tour.

EXERCISE VIII. 8.

Each of the following sentences contains an error. The modifying phrase has been incorrectly
placed, or the noun or pronoun to which the phrase refers does not appear next to the phrase,
or an incorrect participle has been used. Correct and rewrite each sentence. When necessary,
alter the wording for good form, but do not change the participial phrases to clauses.

1. When only a child, his father taught Andy the names of plants and trees.
   When only a child, Andy was taught the names of plants and trees by his father.
2. To estimate the success of such a project, a computer was used.
3. Stopped for speeding, the policeman gave Roger a ticket.
4. While having drunk a cup of coffee, Tom spilled it on his homework.
5. Being in a hurry, the route Bill took was through the desert.
6. The table, having made from cherry wood, was, I thought, beautiful.
7. The importer considered many items tried to find one that would sell well.
8. Liano, reporting his dog lost, is searching the city streets for him.
9. Considerably improved, Ed believes his invention will be a success.
10. Before taken the test, the students were given instructions.
11. To earn extra money, it was necessary for Peggy to work overtime.
12. Viewing from afar, the rock formations looked like buildings.

13. The medical advice was appreciated by the patients which the clinic offered.
14. A retired pilot, the new airport installations were of course of great interest to Mr. Sjoberg.

EXERCISE VIII. 9.

Change the dependent clauses in the sentences below to adjective phrases. Notice (as in the first example, which is done for you) that the noun to which the phrase refers is identified in the independent clause.

1. Members of law enforcement agencies met yesterday because they wanted to explore methods of reducing drug-related crimes.
   Wanting to explore methods of reducing drug-related crimes, members of law enforcement agencies met yesterday.
2. Coal, which was actually formed from plants thousands of years ago, has been an important source of energy for the United States.
3. When people rushed to find gold in 1848, they neglected their farms, families, and businesses.
4. Since Mel had read many books on raising children, he thought he was an expert.
5. After the novel had been promoted by the publisher, it sold widely.
6. Sima has great knowledge of glacier movement because she's a geologist.
7. When the two men agreed on the price of the car, they shook hands.
8. The Constitution, which was written after the American states had won their independence, is considered to be a remarkable historical document.
9. Since Carl is a carpenter, he knows how to repair his own roof.
10. An analyst for the aerospace industry, Miss Reuter will show charts that demonstrate recent advances.

PARALLEL STRUCTURE

Use similar forms and structures (matching construction) for related combinations of words, phrases, and clauses.

To join related combinations, use correlative conjunctions: *and, but, than, or,* and *nor.*

Carol knows *how to interpret abstract ideas* **and** *how to write fine essays.*

To connect a related series, use commas.

This morning Gina *baked a pie, cleaned the house, prepared the dinner,* and *did her homework.*

Analyze the following sentences. Notice the similarity of form on each side of the conjunction (connector). Parallel structure is used to avoid unnecessary wordiness and to give good balance, form, and clarity to the sentence.

1. Betty opened the window *and* closed the door.
   (poor form): (Betty opened the window and has closed the door.)
2. The children enjoy playing in the sand *and* swimming in the ocean.
   (poor form): (The children enjoy playing in the sand and they like to swim in the ocean.)
3. The island we visited was beautiful but crowded.
   (poor form): (The island we visited was beautiful but there were too many people.)

4. Mary types slowly *but* accurately.
   (poor form):   Mary types slowly but she is accurate.

5. Sydney would rather read *than* watch television.
   (poor form):   (Sydney would rather read than to watch television.)

6. On Sunday David wants to play tennis, wash his car, *and* take a walk.
   (poor form):   (On Sunday, David wants to play tennis; he would like to wash his car also and not only that, he wants to take a walk.)

7. The environmentalists had a discussion on improving conservation, increasing energy, *and* eliminating pollution.
   (poor form):   (The environmentalists had a discussion on improving conservation, and how to increase energy, and the elimination of pollution.)

8. To listen to fine music *and* to have stimulating conversation with good friends are two pleasures in life.
   (poor form):   (To listen to fine music and having stimulating conversation with good friends are two pleasures in life.)

9. They explained that they had seen the Statue of Liberty *but* that they hadn't been able to see the World Trade Center.
   (poor form):   (They explained that they had seen the Statue of Liberty but weren't able to see the World Trade Center.)

NOTES: Words common to each side of the connector must be repeated when the verb tense changes, when the positive changes to negative (or vice versa), and when different verbs are used to compare a single subject.

---

10. Perle wrote *that they had received our invitation* **and** *that they would attend.*
    (poor form):   (Perle wrote that they had received our invitation and would attend.)

11. Many species of begonia *don't grow well in full sun* **but** *they grow well in shade* (**Also**: *but they do grow well in shade*).
    (poor form):   (Many species of begonia don't grow well in full sun but in shade.)

12. *Jose writes better* **than** *he speaks.*
    (poor form):   (Jose writes better than speaks.)

13. He left early, *not because he was bored,* **but** *because he had to be home by ten o'clock.*
    (poor form):   (He left early, not because he was bored, but he had to be home by ten o'clock.)

NOTE: Repeat ''key'' words, such as in the following sentences.

---

14. She knows *how to* fly an airplane and *how to* navigate a boat.
    (poor form):   (She knows how to fly an airplane and knows to navigate a boat.)

15. Marie was delighted with *how well* Meg arranged flowers and *how well* she composed music.
    (poor form):   (Maria was delighted with how well Meg arranged flowers and how she composed music.)

16. He bought *a* desk and *a* lamp for his room.
    (poor form):   (He bought a desk and lamp for his room.)

17. Amy is going to take next semester off *so that* she can gather some data for her thesis and *so that* she can meet people in her field.
    (poor form):   (Amy is going to take next semester off so that she can gather some data for her thesis and so she can meet people in her field.)

18. Fred came home early not only *because* he had to get a haircut but also *because* he had to go to the bank.

(poor form):   (Fred came home early not only because he had to get a haircut but also he had to go to the bank.)

NOTE: Don't repeat unnecessarily.

---

19. Janie told us that every day she painted pictures and played with blocks.
    (poor form):   (Janie told us that every day she painted pictures and that she played with blocks.)
20. Shura is pleased that she has learned to speak and read in a second language.
    (poor form):   (Shura is pleased that she has learned to speak and learned to read in a second language.)

Special Word Order

The following words must be placed *near the word or words* they describe: *not, only, both, either, neither, not only . . . but also.*

Avoid the following kinds of errors:
Look for the pairs of nouns, verbs, or other elements.

(wrong):   (She not only baked an apple pie but also a lemon pie.)

RIGHT: She baked **not only** *an apple pie* **but also** *a lemon pie.*

(wrong):   (She baked not only a lemon pie but she cooked a big dinner.)

RIGHT: She **not only** *baked* a lemon pie **but** she **also** *cooked* a big dinner.

(wrong):   (She is both a person of great talent and immense charm.)

RIGHT: She is a person **both** *of great talent* **and** *immense charm.*

(wrong):   (Peter only works six hours a day.)

RIGHT: Peter works **only** *six hours a day* (*also:* **just** *six hours a day; also:* **but** *six hours a day*).

(wrong):   (You must either visit me or I will visit you.)

RIGHT: **Either** *you* must visit me **or** *I* will visit you.

(wrong):   (Roger neither saw a bird nor a flower when he was in prison.)

RIGHT: Roger saw **neither** *a bird* **nor** a *flower* when he was in prison.

(wrong):   (Roger saw neither a bird nor smelled a flower when he was in prison.)

RIGHT: Roger **neither** *saw a bird* **nor** *smelled a flower* when he was in prison.

(wrong):   (Everyone is not here yet.)

RIGHT: **Not** *everyone* is here yet.

(wrong):   (Mrs. Marcus grew both gardenias as well as azaleas.)

RIGHT: Mrs. Marcus grew **both** *gardenias* **and** *azaleas.*

RIGHT: Mrs. Marcus grew *gardenias* **as well as** (*or:* **and**) *azaleas.*

(wrong):   (The book is not only interesting but enlightening.)

RIGHT: The book is *not only* **interesting** *but also* **enlightening**.

EXERCISE VIII. 10.

Correct the following sentences using appropriate parallel structure.

1. The office supplies have arrived; paper clips, pencils, file folders, and the stationery is here too.

2. She doesn't like raw oysters but likes raw clams.
3. Let's visit the art gallery first, and then afterwards, having some lunch.
4. One should look over a document carefully before signing and to get advice when needed.
5. When I saw them, he was riding his motorcycle and Gloria rode behind him.
6. He found it not only annoying to be asked for identification each time but insulting.
7. Professor Johnson reported that he had completed the experiment and wrote the conclusions for a scientific journal.
8. Her exercises include bending, stretching, and she also she walks alot.
9. Byron can speak Chinese but not write it.
10. Their insurance program covers dental and medicine expenses.
11. To balance the budget and providing jobs are two goals of the elected official.
12. Willa hasn't had an opportunity yet to work outside of her home because of marrying at an early age and she had to take care of her three young children.
13. It was no easy task to arrange visas, find living quarters, and in addition preparing a program suitable for everyone.
14. It would be wise of her not to interfere and worry about his plans.
15. To be an effective teacher, one needs to know how to convey the material and to determine whether or not it has been understood.
16. A fanatic neither is moderate in his views nor tolerant of other people's views.
17. Not everyone has the same opinion on that issue but can at least listen carefully to another person's opinion.
18. That couple is both attractive as well as successful.
19. A well-rounded musician should be able to play music, arrange music, and also composing music is a good thing to be able to do.
20. Traveling by covered wagon in the early days of America was uncomfortable and it was dangerous as well.
21. The charges were dropped because there wasn't enough evidence and also the prosecutors decided not to pursue the case.
22. The new machinery polishes better than cuts.

EXERCISE VIII. 11.

Combine each line into one sentence using the words in the parentheses. Omit any unnecessary words.

1. Arches, used architecturally, are strong. They are beautiful. (both)
2. An arbitrator listens to both sides in an argument. He helps people come to an agreement. (not only, but also)
3. A neutral substance isn't acidic. Also, it isn't alkaline. (neither, nor)
4. Arnold will attend graduate school. He will teach a class. (both)
5. The company promised to repair the product. If not, they promised to send a replacement. (either, or)
6. He didn't receive compensation. He didn't receive any acknowledgment. (not only, but also)
7. The play was excellent. The play was beautifully performed. (not only, but also)

BASIC RULES OF WRITTEN EXPRESSION

Don't use words and expressions that repeat what you have already expressed, such as *more* with additional, *very* with *highly*, *quiet* with *peaceful*, *repeat* with *again*.

(poor form):	(A few students in the college preparatory course want to repeat the course again.)
GOOD FORM:	A few students in the college preparatory course want to repeat the course.
(poor form):	(I'm glad that Stephen arrived in time to see his friends before they left.)
GOOD FORM:	I'm glad that Stephen arrived in time to see his friends.
(poor form):	(World hunger is a serious problem because many people in the world don't have enough to eat.)
GOOD FORM:	World hunger is a serious problem.
(poor form):	(That professor is very highly thought of.)
GOOD FORM:	That professor is *highly* thought of.

Write in a clear, direct style. Avoid writing awkward, wordy, complicated sentences. Be concise! Get to the point!

(poor form):	(To be sure of having a place to stay, one should, when visiting a foreign city, make a hotel reservation before traveling there.)
GOOD FORM:	Before traveling to a foreign city, one should make a hotel reservation.
(poor form):	(A number of western nations have decided not to have capital punishment anymore because they feel the death penalty doesn't really do much good and besides that, they think it's cruel.)
GOOD FORM:	A number of western nations, considering capital punishment both cruel and ineffectual, no longer practice capital punishment.

Don't repeat a noun with a pronoun.

(wrong):	(The concert that we attended it was excellent.)
RIGHT:	The concert that we attended was excellent.
(wrong):	(Our friends they gave us an anniversary party last month.)
RIGHT:	Our friends gave us an anniversary party last month.
(wrong):	(The coral trees on the boulevard, after they had been trimmed, they grew healthier.)
RIGHT:	The coral trees on the boulevard, after they had been trimmed, grew healthier.

Don't use pronouns "this" or "that" to refer to preceding ideas or statements. Such reference must be *clearly stated*.

(poor form):	(Anticipating an easy victory, the candidate didn't bother to campaign. Later she regretted that.)
GOOD FORM:	Anticipating an easy victory, the candidate didn't bother to campaign. Later she regretted that action.
GOOD FORM:	Anticipating an easy victory, the candidate didn't bother to campaign. Later she regretted not having campaigned. or: Later she regretted that she hadn't campaigned.

Don't use a double negative.

(wrong):   (The child, being of an independent nature, didn't want nobody to help him.)

RIGHT: The child, being of an independent nature, didn't want *anybody* to help him.

(wrong):   (If the builders had known that the land was unstable, they wouldn't have, I'm sure, never built houses on that site.)

RIGHT: If the builders had known that the land was unstable, they wouldn't have, I'm sure, built houses on that site.

Use the correct part of speech.

(wrong):   (The exposed wire caused Sally to get an electricity shock.)

RIGHT: The exposed wire caused Sally to get an *electric* shock.

Arrange words, phrases, and clauses of a sentence in a concise, logical order so that the meaning is clear. Generally speaking, maintain the sentence order: subject, verb, object, place, manner, time.

(poor form):   (He worked for seven months last year in a gas station.)
GOOD FORM: He worked in a gas station for seven months last year.
(poor form):   (Four times they have visited in the past year Disneyland.)
GOOD FORM: They have visited Disneyland four times in the past year.
(poor form):   (The flowers are on the table which are beautiful.)
GOOD FORM: The flowers which are on the table are beautiful.

For the most part, use active-voiced clauses rather than passive-voiced clauses.

(poor form):   (When we were at the beach yesterday, a beautiful sunset was seen.)
GOOD FORM: When we were at the beach yesterday, we saw a beautiful sunset.
(poor form):   (The play that was seen by our friends concerned a biography of Disraeli.)
GOOD FORM: Our friends saw a play about the life of Disraeli.

Separate ideas into well-constructed sentences, using proper punctuation.

(poor form):   (Last week a convention of the Society of American Architects was held in San Francisco one of the speakers presently associated with a local firm spoke about the innovations of architecture in the past decade.)
GOOD FORM: Last week a convention of the Society of American Architects was held in San Francisco. One of the speakers, presently associated with a local firm, spoke about the innovations of architecture in the past decade.

In formal writing, avoid using slang and colloquial expressions such as *broke* (without funds), *cop* (police officer), *cool* (good), *creepy* (frightening), *dope* (drugs).

(poor form):   (The rock concert was real cool.)
GOOD FORM: The rock concert was very good.

Use adverbs rather than wordy prepositional phrases.

(poor form):   (The women, carrying baskets of fruit on their heads, walked in a very graceful manner.)

GOOD FORM: The women, carrying baskets of fruit on their heads, walked very *gracefully*.

REMINDERS:

When describing related ideas, always use parallel structure. Review "Parallel Structure" in this section.

Avoid dangling participles and misplaced phrases. Review "Using Participles" in this section.

Be sure that the verb agrees with the subject and that the pronoun agrees with the antecedent. Review "Subject and Verb Agreement" and "Pronoun and Antecedent Agreement."

Be sure to use correct punctuation. Analyze the punctuation of the sentences in "Using Conjunctions" and "Using Participles."

Avoid errors in word usage. See "Misused Words" and "Common Errors in Word Usage" in the Supplement. Look up words in the dictionary to ascertain accuracy and meaning.

Make sure the spelling is correct. Look up words in a dictionary for spelling accuracy.

Avoid incomplete sentences, run-on sentences, etc. Review "Types of Sentences" in this section.

Do not change tenses without reason. Review "Establishing a Point of View" in this section.

Avoid poor grammar usage. Review each section until you can freely and accurately apply the grammatical structures you have studied to your writing.

Avoid a dull style of writing; avoid a disconnected style of writing; avoid sudden changes of ideas. Sentences in paragraphs should not always begin with a subject (see *Types of Clauses and Sentences,* general form). To provide variety and to move smoothly from one sentence to another, you can begin with *adjectives, adverbs, conjunctions, appositives* and *participial phrases.* Compare the poor form below to the good forms. (Of course a number of good forms are possible.) Notice that in the good forms, each subsequent sentence relates to the preceding sentence. In addition to beginning sentences with a variety of forms, the method of repeating a *key word* helps to ensure a continuity of ideas.

(poor form):   (A galaxy is comprised of clusters of stars. It may have a billion stars. The Milky Way is the most well-known. The sun and the earth are part of it. People are surprised by that.)

GOOD FORM: A galaxy is comprised of clusters of stars. *Each cluster* may contain as many as a billion stars. *Of all the galaxies,* the Milky Way is probably the best known. *As a matter of fact,* the sun and the earth are part of the *Milky Way. When* people learn of this fact, they are often surprised.

GOOD FORM: Comprised of clusters of stars, a galaxy may contain a billion stars in a cluster. *Undoubtedly,* the most well-known *galaxy* is the Milky Way. *Surprising* to many people is the fact that the sun and the earth are part of the *Milky Way.*

LITERARY VARIATION IN SENTENCE ORDER

In literary styles of writing, variation can be achieved in many ways. One way is to reverse the sentence order. Compare:

The child sat in the corner.
In the corner sat the child.

Another way to vary a sentence is to start it with a prepositional phrase of "place."

Across the street from the college is a new museum.
Also: Across the street from the college, there is a new museum.
Out of nowhere, came a policeman.
Also: Out of nowhere, there came a policeman.
In the small box was a beautiful carved stone.
Also: In the small box there was a beautiful carved stone.

For special emphasis, a sentence or clause may begin with a negative adverb. Similar to a question form, auxiliaries are used or the subject and verb are reversed. Compare the first two sentences below.

Does he write to her?
Never does he write to her!

No sooner had he left than she arrived.
Not only is he a biologist, but he is also a chemist.
Emile has returned; however, *not before* his employer contacts him will he resume his position.
The crowd often cheers but *never before* has the crowd cheered as loudly.
Hardly ever is the air in industrial cities truly pure.
Nowhere has it been said that life always goes smoothly.
By not means has he given up his plan to practice medicine.
Rarely, as a boy, did the inventor have any leisure time.
Only after a great deal of practice can one improve one's performance.
Scarcely had he finished when the monitor declared that the time was up.
Seldom does it rain here in the summer.

The *if* that starts a sentence with a pretend-conditional clause can be omitted. Compare the first four sentences and note the changes in structure.

If he could speak English, he would get a better job.
Could he speak English, he would get a better job.

If I had known about such a course, I might have taken it.
Had I known about such a course, I might have taken it.

Had she been home, she could have received the call.
Were I he, I would take a vacation to get some rest.
Were the house completed, they could move in.
Had she kept her receipts, she could have deducted the expense from her income tax.

Endings and clauses are sometimes varied for sentence variety. Compare the following pairs of sentences.

The captain was promoted and so was the lieutenant.
The captain was promoted, as was the lieutenant.

The classrooms have been painted and so have the halls.
The classrooms have been painted, as have the halls.

When he returned to his office, the rug hadn't been cleaned yet, and the drapes hadn't been hung yet.
When he returned to his office, the rug hadn't been cleaned yet, nor had the drapes been hung.

Avoid the following kinds of errors:

(wrong):	(On her bedroom wall, a picture of a movie star is.)
RIGHT:	On her bedroom wall *is a picture* of a movie star.
RIGHT:	On her bedroom wall, *there is a picture* of a movie star.
(wrong):	(Scarcely he had time to prepare for the trip.)
RIGHT:	Scarcely *did he have* time to prepare for the trip.
(wrong):	(Had I been there, I would help her.)
RIGHT:	Had I been there, I *would have helped* her.
(wrong):	(Our friends were eager to see the show, as we were.)
RIGHT:	Our friends were eager to see the show, *as were we.*
(wrong):	(Still in shock, the poor man couldn't move nor couldn't speak.)
RIGHT:	Still in shock, the poor man couldn't move nor *could he speak.*

EXERCISE VIII. 12.

Each sentence below has elements of poor form. On a separate piece of paper, rewrite the sentences, using good form.

1. The senator from the state of Iowa he has announced plans to run for office again in the next election.
2. Doctor Park told us that more than symphony music, he enjoyed the ballet.
3. The machine may not, despite efforts to correct it, never be without defects.
4. Not only the streets were full of holes, but the street lights didn't work.
5. Some prints were not available, others were shown without frames.
6. Having carefully followed the procedure, it was disappointing to Victor when the experiment failed.
7. We noticed a woman sitting at the typewriter about twenty years old.
8. John has to go to an interview for a job tomorrow so he is feeling very nervous because he's worried about all of the questions that he will have to answer when he is at the interview.
9. Yesterday a telegram was received by Mr. Naro while he was teaching.
10. Everyone enjoys the beauty of the national parks. There was a great variety of flora and fauna which park guests could learn about by going on guided walks with the rangers.

11. Activities will be planned for young adults and adults who are mature.
12. When the rate for loans was lowered, an improved economy is expected.
13. Melvin spent the evening reading, listening to a record he had just bought, and he reviewed the notes of his speech.
14. Gaston invited the woman to dance with him who was wearing a white dress.
15. Finally someone provided a logical solution to the problem that made sense.
16. Unable to find his way home, the North Star helped to guide him.
17. It was real great to see all of my friends again.
18. When he learned of his dog's death, he grew depressed and unhappy.
19. After assisting in the administration of training programs, Mrs. DiCarlo appointed as chief of staff.
20. Limericks used to be popular but rarely they are written anymore.
21. Before Luba signed her name, studied the petition carefully.
22. However there are laws to protect consumers, there is a lack of enforcement.

EXERCISE VIII. 13.

Rewrite the sentences in the following paragraphs using a variety of forms to achieve a smooth related flow of ideas.

1. It hadn't rained in a long time. Experts examined the water levels. They said they were low. They said people should use less water. A serious situation might develop.
2. Columbus wanted to find a new route to India. He took three ships with him. He left Spain in 1492. The sailors became frightened. They didn't see any other ships. They wanted to turn back.
3. Joe can't get a job. He was released from jail recently. He is suing the city. His jail record can be seen by perspective employers. Joe thinks that's wrong. His jail record should be sealed.
4. The Namib Desert in Africa has a number of unusual plants and animals. The desert looks lifeless. It rarely rains. Scientists like to study the plants and animals. The fog occassionally rolls in from the ocean. They say it must provide some moisture.

EPILOGUE

After studying the material in this book, including the material in the Supplement, the student should be prepared for the comprehensive tests on the following pages. The tests have been designed to measure the student's knowledge of grammar and sentence forms. The questions represent the broad variation of those typically asked on actual TOEFL tests.

The pretest should be taken again followed by Test 1, Test 2, Test 3, and Test 4.

Answers to each test should be carefully checked. The student is advised to review those structures of which he or she is unsure.

TEST 1

Structure and Written Expression
(Time—25–35 minutes)

Directions: In sentences 1–15 select the word or phrase that best completes the sentence and, with your pencil, fill in the circle marked A, B, C, or D, as in the example below.

Peter's jacket cost _____ Jack's.　　　　　　　　　　Ⓐ Ⓑ Ⓒ Ⓓ
(A) twice more than
(B) two times more as
(C) twice as much as
(D) twice more as
The correct answer above is (C).

1. The word "dexterous" is similar in meaning _____ "deft."　　Ⓐ Ⓑ Ⓒ Ⓓ
   (A) with
   (B) like
   (C) to
   (D) as

2. Asked to make a list of jobs for which he felt qualified, the applicant _____ .
   (A) only included those in which he had had experience　　Ⓐ Ⓑ Ⓒ Ⓓ
   (B) included only them in which he had had experience
   (C) included only ones he had had experience in

3. Originally, each suburb surrounding the city wanted control of its own educational system _____ .   Ⓐ Ⓑ Ⓒ Ⓓ
   (A) besides that, it wanted control of its own zoning laws
   (B) and its own zoning laws
   (C) and to have jurisdiction over its own zoning laws
   (D) as well as controlling its own zoning laws

4. Ether and alcohol _____ in chemistry laboratories.   Ⓐ Ⓑ Ⓒ ·Ⓓ
   (A) frequently are used solvents
   (B) are used frequently solvents
   (C) are frequently used solvents
   (D) are frequent used as solvents

5. The council members have recommended that _____ .   Ⓐ Ⓑ Ⓒ Ⓓ
   (A) the district change its boundaries
   (B) the district to change its boundaries
   (C) to change the district its boundaries
   (D) the district changed its boundaries

6. After having drafted and signed the Declaration of Independence, Thomas Jefferson, a Virginia landowner who later became president of the United States, _____ .   Ⓐ Ⓑ Ⓒ Ⓓ
   (A) now one of the most powerful countries in the world
   (B) in 1801
   (C) as he well deserved
   (D) departed from Philadelphia

7. _____ in a recent science competition, three individuals were awarded scholarships totaling $21,000.   Ⓐ Ⓑ Ⓒ Ⓓ
   (A) Judged the best
   (B) They were judged the best
   (C) Judging the best
   (D) Having judged the best

8. By the time congressional meetings resume, most members of Congress _____ .   Ⓐ Ⓑ Ⓒ Ⓓ
   (A) will have a good rest
   (B) who will have had a good rest
   (C) will have had a good rest
   (D) they will have had a good rest

9. Pineapples are not commercially produced in North America, _____ .
   (A) and coconuts aren't neither   Ⓐ Ⓑ Ⓒ Ⓓ
   (B) and neither are coconuts
   (C) and not coconuts either
   (D) and either aren't coconuts

10. Using the sun's rays to conserve energy _____ .   Ⓐ Ⓑ Ⓒ Ⓓ
    (A) it makes sense to most people
    (B) makes sense to most people
    (C) to most people it makes sense
    (D) make sense for most people

11. Statistics show that after the speed limit had been reduced, _____ .
    (A) less accidents took place   Ⓐ Ⓑ Ⓒ Ⓓ
    (B) not so many accidents were happening
    (C) the fewer there were accidents
    (D) fewer accidents took place

12. One of the officials in the foreign country announced that the goals of _____
    had been reached.   Ⓐ Ⓑ Ⓒ Ⓓ
    (A) five-years plan
    (B) the five-year plan
    (C) the five-years plan
    (D) five-year plan

13. The young chick, separated from its mother after hatching, followed the family
    dog around as if the dog _____ .   Ⓐ Ⓑ Ⓒ Ⓓ
    (A) is its mother
    (B) was its mother
    (C) were its mother
    (D) has been its mother

14. The longer the sun shines, _____ .   Ⓐ Ⓑ Ⓒ Ⓓ
    (A) the earth is warmer
    (B) it makes the earth more warm
    (C) the more warmly is the earth
    (D) the warmer the earth is

15. _____ to provide work for young jobless males, the Civilian Conservation
    Corps relieved the high rate of unemployment.   Ⓐ Ⓑ Ⓒ Ⓓ
    (A) Establishing in the 1930's
    (B) Established in the 1930's
    (C) In the 1930's established
    (D) Being establish in the 1930's

Directions: In questions 16–40 select the underlined word or phrase that is *not*
acceptable in standard written English and fill in the circle marked A, B, C, or D, as
in the example below.

Keeping clean is surely one of the most important rule of good hygiene.
      A   B   C   D
The correct answer above is (D).   Ⓐ Ⓑ Ⓒ Ⓓ

16. Despite the fact that there was very little rain, the vegetables appeared healthy
         A   B   C
    and marketable.   Ⓐ Ⓑ Ⓒ Ⓓ
         D

17. Thunderstorms may occur when heated air full of water vapor rises, cools, and
                                  A   B
    forming thick dark clouds.   Ⓐ Ⓑ Ⓒ Ⓓ
      C   D

18. The element carbon is <u>widely</u> <u>found</u> <u>in nature</u> in many forms including both
                         A   B   C

    diamonds <u>as well as</u> coal.   Ⓐ Ⓑ Ⓒ Ⓓ
              D

19. In a corporation <u>whose</u> stock is <u>private</u> owned, the board of directors <u>is elected</u>
                       A   B   C

    <u>by</u> the stockholders.   Ⓐ Ⓑ Ⓒ Ⓓ
    D

20. Computers and other office equipment, which <u>are</u> <u>being used</u> <u>more and more</u>
                                            A   B   C

    by businesses, <u>either can be</u> purchased or leased.   Ⓐ Ⓑ Ⓒ Ⓓ
                     D

21. In order <u>so that one can</u> develop good merchandising skills, <u>one</u> needs <u>to have</u>
                  A   B   C

    experience <u>in</u> buying and selling.   Ⓐ Ⓑ Ⓒ Ⓓ
              D

22. The reason that <u>so many</u> homemakers buy kitchen appliances is <u>that</u> they <u>are</u>
                     A   B

    <u>wanting</u> to do their tasks in a shorter <u>length of time</u>.   Ⓐ Ⓑ Ⓒ Ⓓ
      C   D

23. According to <u>newspaper</u> advertisements, there <u>appears</u> <u>to be</u> a great need
                     A   B   C

    today for <u>economic</u> and science teachers.   Ⓐ Ⓑ Ⓒ Ⓓ
             D

24. The host suggested that, <u>although</u> it <u>is getting</u> late, everyone <u>remain</u> for <u>another</u>
                              A   B   C   D

    cup of coffee.   Ⓐ Ⓑ Ⓒ Ⓓ

25. By the time jet aircraft could fly at a speed <u>faster</u> than <u>sound</u>, train transporta-
                                               A   B

    tion in the United States <u>was declining</u> over several <u>decades</u>.   Ⓐ Ⓑ Ⓒ Ⓓ
                              C   D

26. <u>While traveling</u> <u>through</u> Japan a few years ago, Professor Cummins noticed
         A   B

    that <u>a great many</u> Japanese students <u>are practicing</u> their English with visiting
             C   D

    Americans.   Ⓐ Ⓑ Ⓒ Ⓓ

27. Mrs. Block is one of the women <u>who</u>, I believe, <u>is running</u> <u>for</u> office <u>in</u> this
                                A   B   C

    <u>district</u>.   Ⓐ Ⓑ Ⓒ Ⓓ
      D

28. If the catcher <u>wouldn't have</u> dropped the ball, the game would <u>probably</u> have
                  A   B
    <u>ended</u> <u>with a victory</u> for the New York Yankees.   Ⓐ Ⓑ Ⓒ Ⓓ
      C   D

29. <u>Realistic,</u> there seems to be <u>no way</u> of settling the issue of water rights for
     A   B
    fishermen <u>to the satisfaction</u> of all.   Ⓐ Ⓑ Ⓒ Ⓓ
               C   D

30. <u>For a time,</u> the planet Mars <u>was thought</u> to have <u>some sort of</u> advanced form of
        A   B   C
    life on its surface but now it appears <u>like</u> the theory has been put aside.
                                       D   Ⓐ Ⓑ Ⓒ Ⓓ

31. The fact that there have been <u>only</u> <u>few</u> people <u>attending</u> the meetings <u>has</u> not
                                 A   B   C   D
    discouraged the organizers.   Ⓐ Ⓑ Ⓒ Ⓓ

32. <u>Us</u> members of the community <u>living</u> on the west side of the river have organ-
     A   B
    ized a community watch program for the purpose <u>of</u> combatting the <u>rising</u>
                                                                 C   D
    crime rate.   Ⓐ Ⓑ Ⓒ Ⓓ

33. The question of <u>whether or not</u> one can <u>truly</u> appreciate the works <u>of others</u>
                         A   B   C
    without he himself having done such work <u>often discussed.</u>   Ⓐ Ⓑ Ⓒ Ⓓ
                                                D

34. In *The Scarlet Letter* by Nathaniel Hawthorne, Hester Prynne refused, <u>despite</u>
                                                                        A
    the exhortations of <u>the town</u> officials, <u>naming</u> the father <u>of her child.</u>
                          B   C   D   Ⓐ Ⓑ Ⓒ Ⓓ

35. In a television series <u>named after</u> the book *The Ascent of Man*, Bronowski
                                A
    described many <u>aspects of</u> culture and science <u>from</u> prehistoric times to
                        B   C
    <u>present</u>.   Ⓐ Ⓑ Ⓒ Ⓓ
      D

36. There <u>were</u> no sign of wild animals when Robinson Crusoe, who <u>alone</u> was
           A   B
    <u>alive</u> after the ship had sunk, <u>had reached the island.</u>   Ⓐ Ⓑ Ⓒ Ⓓ
      C   D

37. <u>The only</u> insects that make <u>a food</u> that people enjoy <u>eating</u> are bees, which
       A   B   C
    produce honey in <u>its</u> hives.   Ⓐ Ⓑ Ⓒ Ⓓ
                    D

38. Some organizations are <u>exempt</u> <u>from paying</u> income tax; for example, a welfare
    ⎳A⎳   ⎳B⎳
    organization <u>need not</u> <u>to give</u> money to the Internal Revenue Department.
    ⎳C⎳   ⎳D⎳   Ⓐ Ⓑ Ⓒ Ⓓ

39. Serum, which contains antibodies <u>of the blood</u>, <u>is used</u> in injections <u>so</u> people
    ⎳A⎳   ⎳B⎳   ⎳C⎳
    can avoid <u>getting</u> certain diseases.   Ⓐ Ⓑ Ⓒ Ⓓ
    ⎳D⎳

40. Compared <u>to</u> prices a few years ago, prices of food and clothing today have
    ⎳A⎳
    increased <u>to</u> such a degree that some people can't afford <u>to buy</u> <u>it</u>.
    ⎳B⎳   ⎳C⎳ ⎳D⎳
                                                    Ⓐ Ⓑ Ⓒ Ⓓ

TEST 2

Structure and Written Expression
(Time—25 minutes)

Directions: In sentences 1–15 select the word or phrase that best completes the sentence and, with your pencil, fill in the circle marked A, B, C, or D, as in the example below.

Peter's jacket cost _____ Jack's.   Ⓐ Ⓑ Ⓒ Ⓓ
(A) twice more than
(B) two times more as
(C) twice as much as
(D) twice more as
The correct answer above is (C).

1. The Algonquin Indians of North America were a people who had many tribes
   _____ .   Ⓐ Ⓑ Ⓒ Ⓓ
   (A) but spoken a common language
   (B) but they were speaking a common language
   (C) but who spoke a common language
   (D) but had spoken a common language

2. Labor unions are subject to a large body of laws that are intended to protect the
   unions _____ the rights of their members.   Ⓐ Ⓑ Ⓒ Ⓓ
   (A) in addition with defining
   (B) beside defining
   (C) as well as to define
   (D) and for defining

3. It is sometimes impossible _____ in these times.   Ⓐ Ⓑ Ⓒ Ⓓ
   (A) for remaining optimistic
   (B) to remain optimistic
   (C) remaining optimistic
   (D) for a person remain optimistic

4. Before the detonation of an atomic bomb, never _____ .   Ⓐ Ⓑ Ⓒ Ⓓ
   (A) an explosion of such power had taken place
   (B) had an explosion of such power taken place
   (C) had been such an explosion of power
   (D) there had been an explosion of such power

5. Many people don't realize that Lake Superior, _____ , is in both the United
   States and Canada.   Ⓐ Ⓑ Ⓒ Ⓓ
   (A) which it is the largest fresh water lake in the world
   (B) in the world of which it is the largest fresh water lake
   (C) which the largest fresh water lake in the world
   (D) which is the largest fresh water lake in the world

6. The first clock _____ was invented in the mid-fourteenth century. Ⓐ Ⓑ Ⓒ Ⓓ
   (A) to be historically recorded
   (B) to record historically
   (C) that recorded historically
   (D) to historically be recorded

7. Before returning to the United States, _____ .   Ⓐ Ⓑ Ⓒ Ⓓ
   (A) an agreement from the two parties the special envoy obtained
   (B) an agreement by the special envoy was obtained from the two parties
   (C) the special envoy from the two parties obtained an agreement
   (D) the special envoy obtained an agreement from the two parties

8. In spite of having been one of the world's greatest golfers, Bobby Jones,
   _____ , never became a professional.   Ⓐ Ⓑ Ⓒ Ⓓ
   (A) chose to remain an amateur
   (B) choosing to remain an amateur
   (C) he remained an amateur
   (D) chosen to remain an amateur

9. Many of us wonder _____ will lead to the creation of colonies in space.
   (A) that the current space activities   Ⓐ Ⓑ Ⓒ Ⓓ
   (B) if the current space activities
   (C) if the current space activities going on these days
   (D) about the current space activities

10. The study of aging has become important because the average age of the pop-
    ulation _____ .   Ⓐ Ⓑ Ⓒ Ⓓ
    (A) is increasing
    (B) increases
    (C) has increasing
    (D) was increasing

11. There hasn't been any rain _____ .   Ⓐ Ⓑ Ⓒ Ⓓ
    (A) since two months
    (B) in the past two months
    (C) for two months ago
    (D) since it has rained two months ago

12. In spite of the airline strikes and other inconveniences, people, according to statistics, _____ . Ⓐ Ⓑ Ⓒ Ⓓ
    (A) enjoy anyway to travel
    (B) are enjoying to travel
    (C) find traveling an enjoyable activity to do
    (D) enjoy traveling

13. Although some snakes serve a useful purpose to mankind, the tendency is to be _____ fearful of all snakes. Ⓐ Ⓑ Ⓒ Ⓓ
    (A) somewhat
    (B) real
    (C) kind of
    (D) awful

14. The police questioned the suspects _____ . Ⓐ Ⓑ Ⓒ Ⓓ
    (A) one by one
    (B) one at the time
    (C) one and the next
    (D) by single ones

15. Socrates, the great Greek philosopher, was ordered to _____ . Ⓐ Ⓑ Ⓒ Ⓓ
    (A) give to himself a poison called hemlock
    (B) give a poison to himself, it was called hemlock
    (C) give himself a poison called hemlock
    (D) poison, with a drink called hemlock, himself

Directions: In questions 16–40 select the underlined word or phrase that is *not* acceptable in standard written English and fill in the circle marked A, B, C, or D, as in the example below.

Keeping clean is surely one of the most important rule of good hygiene.
     A   B   C   D
The correct answer above is (D). Ⓐ Ⓑ Ⓒ ⓓ

16. Neither George Washington or Abraham Lincoln had ever seen an airplane fly
                        A   B   C
    during his lifetime. Ⓐ Ⓑ Ⓒ Ⓓ
          D

17. The idea which the world may be destroyed by nuclear weapons has raised
            A   B   C
    questions about the justification of their development and use. Ⓐ Ⓑ Ⓒ Ⓓ
                                                    D

18. Economists have warned that a lengthy recovery period may be the result of
                                  A   B
    allowing unemployment to raise too much. Ⓐ Ⓑ Ⓒ Ⓓ
          C   D

19. If <u>certain</u> drugs were taken together, they <u>can cause</u> a person <u>to become</u>
   A   B   C
 <u>extremely</u> ill.   Ⓐ Ⓑ Ⓒ Ⓓ
  D

20. Joe Louis, <u>born</u> in Alabama, was the <u>world's</u> heavyweight boxing champion <u>in</u>
     A B   C
 <u>1937</u> to 1949.   Ⓐ Ⓑ Ⓒ Ⓓ
  D

21. The Dow Jones Average <u>indicates</u> the <u>daily</u> average value <u>of</u> stock shares that
         A   B   C
 are <u>purchase and sold</u> through stock exchanges. Ⓐ Ⓑ Ⓒ Ⓓ
      D

22. One group was <u>satisfied</u> <u>with</u> the explanation <u>whereas</u> the other group wanted
       A B   C
 to explore the subject <u>farther</u>.   Ⓐ Ⓑ Ⓒ Ⓓ
        D

23. The actress will soon <u>in November</u> begin <u>rehearsing</u> <u>for</u> the <u>opening</u> of a Broad-
         A   B C   D
 way show.   Ⓐ Ⓑ Ⓒ Ⓓ

24. The J. Paul Getty museum was <u>so</u> <u>heavy</u> endowed that it has virtually <u>millions</u> of
          A B   C
 dollars <u>to spend</u> annually on acquisitions.   Ⓐ Ⓑ Ⓒ Ⓓ
     D

25. Since 1782, the bald eagle, which <u>signifies</u> <u>power</u> and courage, <u>is</u> the national
            A   B   C
 emblem of <u>the</u> United States.   Ⓐ Ⓑ Ⓒ Ⓓ
     D

26. Sheep are <u>among</u> the most important animals that <u>has been domesticated</u>
     A   B
 because they provide food and clothing; <u>moreover</u>, they are used <u>in making</u>
             C   D
 other products such as soap and glue.   Ⓐ Ⓑ Ⓒ Ⓓ

27. To ride in a Venetian gondola and to see the beautiful art of Florence <u>are</u> <u>but</u>
                     A B
 two attractions that draw a great <u>amount</u> of tourists to Italy <u>yearly</u>. Ⓐ Ⓑ Ⓒ Ⓓ
          C   D

28. <u>Not being</u> able to speak the language of the country <u>which</u> we were visiting, we
  A   B
 naturally had difficulty <u>to make</u> ourselves <u>understood</u>. Ⓐ Ⓑ Ⓒ Ⓓ
         C   D

29. <u>Contradicted</u> the testimony that he had given <u>earlier</u>, the witness appeared to
       A   B

    be <u>confused</u> and he subsequently asked <u>to be dismissed</u>.   Ⓐ Ⓑ Ⓒ Ⓓ
           C   D

30. The shoe buyer said that since she <u>couldn't get away</u> at this time, one of the
                                      A   B

    experienced <u>clerks</u> <u>were going</u> to be sent to Europe to do some comparative
               C   D

    shopping.   Ⓐ Ⓑ Ⓒ Ⓓ

31. When changes in society <u>took place</u>, good qualities of the past, those that are
                      A

    worth <u>keeping</u>, sometimes vanish, <u>unfortunately</u>, <u>along with</u> bad qualities.
         B   C   D   Ⓐ Ⓑ Ⓒ Ⓓ

32. Perhaps a <u>little known</u> fact about Mark Twain, <u>which</u> real name was Samuel
              A   B

    Clemens, was that at one time, <u>hoping to</u> make a fortune, <u>he</u> prospected for
                                 C   D

    gold.   Ⓐ Ⓑ Ⓒ Ⓓ

33. Although <u>primary</u> a vegetarian, <u>the chimpanzee</u>, a four- or five-foot tall member
             A   B

    of the ape family, likes <u>eating</u> meat <u>occasionally</u>.   Ⓐ Ⓑ Ⓒ Ⓓ
                            C   D

34. The farmer realized that <u>he'd</u> better, if he didn't want to have a total loss, <u>to</u>
                        A

    <u>harvest</u> his crop <u>earlier</u> <u>than</u> usual.   Ⓐ Ⓑ Ⓒ Ⓓ
      B   C   D

35. The guard on duty reported <u>the police</u> that he had heard a <u>strange</u> crying noise
                              A   B

    which seemed <u>to be coming</u> from just <u>outside</u> the basement.   Ⓐ Ⓑ Ⓒ Ⓓ
                 C   D

36. Although the designer had all <u>kinds</u> of fabric samples, <u>but</u> she couldn't <u>make up</u>
                               A   B

    her mind <u>which one</u> to select.   Ⓐ Ⓑ Ⓒ Ⓓ
          C   D

37. The baby sitter <u>told the children</u> that after they <u>had chose</u> the story they
                      A   B

    wanted, she <u>would read</u> it to them.   Ⓐ Ⓑ Ⓒ Ⓓ
       C   D

38. One has only <u>to see</u> the architecture of several generations ago <u>to realize</u> that
             A   B

    people have grown <u>more taller</u> <u>over the years</u>.   Ⓐ Ⓑ Ⓒ Ⓓ
                   C   D

39. After the third <u>such</u> incident, the police admonished the young mother not to
               A
<u>leave</u> her child walk <u>freely</u> on the streets because something <u>might happen</u> to
  B   C   D
him.   Ⓐ Ⓑ Ⓒ Ⓓ

40. It is <u>far</u> better for one to drink milk, <u>where</u> one gets <u>healthful</u> nutrients, than to
     A   B   C
drink coffee, which contains no nutrients <u>at all</u>.   Ⓐ Ⓑ Ⓒ Ⓓ
                                    D

TEST 3

Structure and Written Expression
Time—25 minutes

Directions: In sentences 1–15 select the word or phrase that best completes the sentence and, with your pencil, fill in the circle marked A, B, C, or D, as in the example below.

Peter's jacket cost _____ Jack's.   Ⓐ Ⓑ Ⓒ Ⓓ
(A) twice more than
(B) two times more as
(C) twice as much as
(D) twice more as
The correct answer above is (C).

1. In the War of 1812, the British living in Canada _____ .   Ⓐ Ⓑ Ⓒ Ⓓ
   (A) helped the Indians for fight the Americans
   (B) helped the Indians fight the Americans
   (C) helped the Indians for fighting Americans
   (D) helped the Indians to fighting the Americans

2. The drama critic judged _____ .   Ⓐ Ⓑ Ⓒ Ⓓ
   (A) the third episode in the series to be the best
   (B) the episode three in the series to be the best
   (C) third episode in the series is the best
   (D) the third episode in the series is the best

3. The balance sheet, prepared by the accountants, _____ that the company
made a profit last month.   Ⓐ Ⓑ Ⓒ Ⓓ
   (A) has shown
   (B) has been shown
   (C) showing
   (D) have shown

4. _____ both the largest and northernmost state in the United States, Alaska has the smallest population.   Ⓐ Ⓑ Ⓒ Ⓓ
   (A) Despite it is
   (B) In spite being
   (C) In spite of to be
   (D) Despite being

5. Astigmatism _____ caused by a flat spot on the eyeball.   Ⓐ Ⓑ Ⓒ Ⓓ
   (A) a type of visual impairment
   (B) which is a type of visual impairment
   (C) it's a type of visual impairment
   (D) is a type of visual impairment

6. Mrs. Elvsted, a character in Ibsen's play *Hedda Gabler,* _____ that her husband, being a sheriff had to travel a lot.   Ⓐ Ⓑ Ⓒ Ⓓ
   (A) explained Hedda
   (B) explained to Hedda
   (C) explains to Hedda
   (D) explained for Hedda

7. The atmosphere is denser near the surface of the earth than _____ .
   (A) it is farther away   Ⓐ Ⓑ Ⓒ Ⓓ
   (B) further away from it
   (C) denser farther away
   (D) is farther away

8. Individuals who drive without automobile insurance _____ .   Ⓐ Ⓑ Ⓒ Ⓓ
   (A) may, in the event of an accident, have to pay costly damages
   (B) may, if they have a bad accident, have to pay damages that cost a lot
   (C) may have to pay a lot of money from an accident
   (D) must, in the event of an accident, to pay expensive damages

9. The manager of the hotel requested that their guest _____ after 11:00 P.M.
   (A) shouldn't play music loud   Ⓐ Ⓑ Ⓒ Ⓓ
   (B) not play music loudly
   (C) don't play loud music
   (D) didn't play music loudly

10. The speed of communications today, as opposed to _____ , has greatly altered the manner in which business today is conducted.   Ⓐ Ⓑ Ⓒ Ⓓ
    (A) the one of yesterday
    (B) communications yesterday
    (C) that of yesterday
    (D) communication's speed a long time ago

11. After gaining their independence, _____ their names.   Ⓐ Ⓑ Ⓒ Ⓓ
    (A) a large number of countries has changed
    (B) a large amount of countries have changed
    (C) a great deal of countries have changed
    (D) a large number of countries have changed

12. When the court was in session, the judge would not permit entrance by
    _____ .   (A) (B) (C) (D)
    (A) no one
    (B) anyone
    (C) someones
    (D) none

13. Paul Revere was a hero in colonial America because if it hadn't been for
    _____ , the war at Lexington might have been lost.   (A) (B) (C) (D)
    (A) him having warned the colonists
    (B) his having warned the colonists
    (C) him that he warned the colonists
    (D) he had warned the colonists

14. Agreements between parties that are intended to be legally binding _____ .
    (A) and are called contracts   (A) (B) (C) (D)
    (B) called contracts
    (C) are called contracts
    (D) and that are called contracts

15. If silver _____ scarcer than gold, it will no doubt have a greater value.
    (A) became   (A) (B) (C) (D)
    (B) will become
    (C) becomes
    (D) had become

Directions: In questions 16–40, select the underlined word or phrase that is *not*
acceptable in standard written English and fill in the circle marked A, B, C, or D, as
in the example below.

Keeping clean is surely one of the most important rule of good hygiene.
      A   B   C   D
The correct answer above is (D).   (A) (B) (C) (⑩)

16. Because of increasing less grazing land, a number of wild animals have been
                     A   B   C
    placed on the endangered species list.   (A) (B) (C) (D)
                              D

17. Growing steadily, the company recently added eight additional computer oper-
        A   B   C
    ators to its work force.   (A) (B) (C) (D)
             D

18. Nutritionists exhort people to eat foods with fewer fat content and higher nutri-
                   A   B   C
    tive content.   (A) (B) (C) (D)
    D

19. An important function of the World Health Organization is to improve healthy
                                                              A   B
    and living conditions for the sick and the poor of the world.   (A) (B) (C) (D)
                              C   D

20. Singing two operas at the Metropolitan Opera House, the popular opera star is
       A   B

    awaiting word on her next performance.   Ⓐ Ⓑ Ⓒ Ⓓ
       C   D

21. To get a job in most office, you have to be able to type fifty words a minute,
                    A   B   C

    carry out instructions, and spell well.   Ⓐ Ⓑ Ⓒ Ⓓ
      D

22. Most people think the wolf is a ferocious beast because of their reputation
             A   B

    based on stories and movies; actually it is afraid of people.   Ⓐ Ⓑ Ⓒ Ⓓ
      C   D

23. When John Burroughs died, in 1921, he had written and published twenty
                     A

    nature books and gave the people of America much greater awareness of the
                  B   C   D

    wonders and joys in nature.   Ⓐ Ⓑ Ⓒ Ⓓ

24. The committee is hoping that a concert can be arranged imminently in which
                 A   B

    the works of Bach will play.   Ⓐ Ⓑ Ⓒ Ⓓ
      C   D

25. Floods in the country of Holland have been among the worse of any recorded.
     A   B   C   D

                                           Ⓐ Ⓑ Ⓒ Ⓓ

26. When Cleopatra saw that it was helpless to keep fighting, she killed herself
                 A   B   C

    by letting an asp bite her.   Ⓐ Ⓑ Ⓒ Ⓓ
            D

27. Students studying the paintings of Monet are interesting to learn that
                      A   B   C

    Monet's impressionistic style of painting grew out of visual difficulties.
                                      D   Ⓐ Ⓑ Ⓒ Ⓓ

28. Psychologists tell us that it's perfectly natural to feel like to run away from our
           A   B   C

    responsibilities once in a while.   Ⓐ Ⓑ Ⓒ Ⓓ
              D

29. The executive vice-president wants sometimes not just one, but two secretaries
                            A   B

    to attend the meeting and to transcribe the proceedings.   Ⓐ Ⓑ Ⓒ Ⓓ
                        C   D

30. The two teams are playing the championship game next Saturday to see whom,
                A   B   C

    the red team or the blue team, will win the pennant.   Ⓐ Ⓑ Ⓒ Ⓓ
                                D

31. If one is in doubt about the legality of a particular drug, you can contact
            A   B   C   D

    the Food and Drug Administration.   Ⓐ Ⓑ Ⓒ Ⓓ

32. Most job applicants would rather, according to a survey, that potential employ-
                                                      A

    ers not require them to take a lie-detector test.   Ⓐ Ⓑ Ⓒ Ⓓ
          B   C   D

33. Aspirin, the common name <u>for</u> acetylsalicylic acid, is <u>widely</u> used <u>like</u> a drug <u>for</u>
    A   B   C
    <u>alleviating</u> pain.   Ⓐ Ⓑ Ⓒ Ⓓ
       D

34. When <u>only a young boy,</u> Georges Bizet <u>knew to</u> play the piano very well and <u>as</u>
          A   B   C
    he grew older, he wrote operas, the most famous <u>of which</u> is *Carmen*.
                                 D   Ⓐ Ⓑ Ⓒ Ⓓ

35. Each of the members <u>present</u> <u>have voted</u> to <u>put off</u> <u>moving</u> the headquarters
                    A   B   C   D
    until a suitable location has been found.   Ⓐ Ⓑ Ⓒ Ⓓ

36. Anyone who counts calories is <u>probably</u> <u>aware</u> of <u>the fact that</u> a large apple has
                        A   B   C
    as many calories <u>than</u> a banana.   Ⓐ Ⓑ Ⓒ Ⓓ
              D

37. <u>When asked</u> why <u>he was</u> painting a sunset, the man replied that he was painting
       A   B
    a sunset <u>because</u> he <u>wanted.</u>   Ⓐ Ⓑ Ⓒ Ⓓ
           C   D

38. People who <u>traveled</u> <u>long</u> distances to their jobs, are <u>largely</u> dependent <u>on</u>
              A   B   C   D
    rapid transportation.   Ⓐ Ⓑ Ⓒ Ⓓ

39. Feeling <u>impatiently</u> for someone to return and <u>give</u> <u>him</u> an answer, the student
            A   B   C
    paced <u>up and down</u> the hall.   Ⓐ Ⓑ Ⓒ Ⓓ
          D

40. By the time educators <u>introduced</u> reforms in education, there <u>has been</u> a
                        A   B
    <u>serious</u> decline in <u>achievement</u> in fundamental subjects.   Ⓐ Ⓑ Ⓒ Ⓓ
       C   D

TEST 4

Structure and Written Expression
Time—25 minutes

Directions: In sentences 1–15 select the word or phrase that best completes the sentence and, with your pencil, fill in the circle marked A, B, C, or D, as in the example below.

Peter's jacket cost _____ Jack's.   Ⓐ Ⓑ Ⓒ Ⓓ
(A) twice more than
(B) two times more as
(C) twice as much as
(D) twice more as
The correct answer above is (C).

1. The salmon spends its adult life in rivers and seas but _____ .   Ⓐ Ⓑ Ⓒ Ⓓ
   (A) its eggs are laid in streams
   (B) it lays its eggs in streams
   (C) in streams are laid its eggs
   (D) laid in streams are its eggs

2. Henry Ford's plan was to manufacture cheaper cars _____ .   Ⓐ Ⓑ Ⓒ Ⓓ
   (A) in large quantity, therefore more people would buy them
   (B) in large quantity in order so more people would buy them
   (C) in large quantity so that more people would buy them
   (D) in large quantity so more people will buy them

3. Before arranging a schedule for the conference next week, _____ .
   (A) an agenda will be proposed by the chairman   Ⓐ Ⓑ Ⓒ Ⓓ
   (B) the chairman going to propose an agenda
   (C) the chairman will an agenda prepare
   (D) the chairman will have an agenda prepared

4. A concert _____ will be held next week.   Ⓐ Ⓑ Ⓒ Ⓓ
   (A) in which the musicians' original compositions will be performed
   (B) which performs the musicians' original compositions
   (C) performing the musicians' original compositions
   (D) that the musicians' original compositions will be performed

5. A reward of five hundred dollars will be given _____ can identify the bank rob-
   ber.   Ⓐ Ⓑ Ⓒ Ⓓ
   (A) to whoever
   (B) to whomever
   (C) whomever
   (D) whoever person

6. A fine writer, an excellent storyteller, and _____ , the author, however, lived a
   tempestuous and dissolute life.   Ⓐ Ⓑ Ⓒ Ⓓ
   (A) being a charming person
   (B) very charming
   (C) a charming person
   (D) charming everyone

7. It's the census taker's job _____ the number of people living in a country.
   (A) counting   Ⓐ Ⓑ Ⓒ Ⓓ
   (B) to count
   (C) for count
   (D) he must count

8. On television last night the newscaster announced that the leader _____ .
   (A) is arriving on Saturday   Ⓐ Ⓑ Ⓒ Ⓓ
   (B) will arrive on Saturday
   (C) would be arrive on Saturday
   (D) would be arriving on Saturday

9. One of the tallest buildings in the United States is _____ .   Ⓐ Ⓑ Ⓒ Ⓓ
   (A) the 1,472 feet Empire State Building
   (B) the Empire State Building which is 1,472 foot high
   (C) the 1,472 foot Empire State Building
   (D) the Empire State Building being 1,472 feet tall

10. The United Auto Workers agreed, after much discussion, _____ . Ⓐ Ⓑ Ⓒ Ⓓ
    (A) considering the postponement of a scheduled increase in salary
    (B) to consider postponing a scheduled salary increase
    (C) considered putting off a scheduled salary increase
    (D) considering postponing a scheduled increase in compensation

11. Before anyone could photograph the strange-looking bird, _____ .
    (A) it was flying away   Ⓐ Ⓑ Ⓒ Ⓓ
    (B) it has flown away
    (C) it flew away
    (D) it had been flying away

12. _____ , follow the directions on the bottle carefully.   Ⓐ Ⓑ Ⓒ Ⓓ
    (A) When taken drugs
    (B) When one takes drugs
    (C) When, in taking drugs,
    (D) When taking drugs

13. When their nest was disturbed, the bees _____ .   Ⓐ Ⓑ Ⓒ Ⓓ
    (A) got real mad
    (B) became too angry
    (C) became very angry
    (D) got darned angry

14. The practice of dining late _____ did not start in the United States.
    (A) in the evening   Ⓐ Ⓑ Ⓒ Ⓓ
    (B) at the evening
    (C) at evening
    (D) during evening

15. After 1800, Philadelphia _____ .   Ⓐ Ⓑ Ⓒ Ⓓ
    (A) was no longer the capital anymore
    (B) wasn't the capital yet
    (C) was not the capital no more
    (D) was no longer the capital

Directions: In questions 16–40 select the underlined word or phrase that is *not* acceptable in standard written English and fill in the circle marked A, B, C, or D, as in the example below.

Keeping clean is surely one of the most important rule of good hygiene.
     A   B   C   D
The correct answer above is (D).   Ⓐ Ⓑ Ⓒ Ⓓ

16. Only about a half a year do the swallows spend time in the surrounding area of
       A   B   C   D

    the San Juan Capistrano Mission.   Ⓐ Ⓑ Ⓒ Ⓓ

17. No sooner had the curtain fallen when the audience jumped up from their
            A   B C   D

    seats.   Ⓐ Ⓑ Ⓒ Ⓓ

18. Bill was able to leave the building quickly when the fire broke out but Mary's
                                           A   B

    and Betty's room was on the fifth floor and it was nowhere near an exit.
                               C   D   Ⓐ Ⓑ Ⓒ Ⓓ

19. If the students want advice, they see the counselor, he's usually available.
     A   B   C   D   Ⓐ Ⓑ Ⓒ Ⓓ

20. All of the materials used in making the doll house was from discarded scraps.
                  A   B   C   D Ⓐ Ⓑ Ⓒ Ⓓ

21. In the training session, the instructor mentioned that them who were unsure of
                                             A   B

    what to do could always ask the department head.   Ⓐ Ⓑ Ⓒ Ⓓ
             C   D

22. To avert any criticism, the president had the Secretary of State to address per-
           A   B

    sonally the Congress to acquaint them with the circumstances surrounding the
                                         C   D

    incident.   Ⓐ Ⓑ Ⓒ Ⓓ

23. By means of a sensitive voice-detecting machine, the detective determined
       A   B

    that it was indeed her, the woman he had suspected all along.   Ⓐ Ⓑ Ⓒ Ⓓ
                   C   D

24. Finally realized a life-long ambition, the sculptor, in a ceremony commemorat-
         A   B

    ing the event, donated a statue, which was ten feet high, to the city of his birth.
                                     C   D

        Ⓐ Ⓑ Ⓒ Ⓓ

25. As far as I'm concerned, the Korean cellist has been played more beautifully in
      A   B   C

    last night's concert than I have ever heard him play.   Ⓐ Ⓑ Ⓒ Ⓓ
                                            D

26. Latin, from which the Romance Languages are derived from, is rarely taught in
                                       A   B   C   D

    American schools today.   Ⓐ Ⓑ Ⓒ Ⓓ

27. Ordinarily, Oregon has more enough than rain needed for maintaining vegeta-
        A   B   C   D

    tion in that state.   Ⓐ Ⓑ Ⓒ Ⓓ

28. Surprisingly, the catalogue sent to us had excellent information, beautiful illus-
        A   B C

    trations, and it had an interesting cover.   Ⓐ Ⓑ Ⓒ Ⓓ
                   D

29. The architect had intended, at the very least, to have the plans
                              A   B

    prepare before the loan commitment expired.   Ⓐ Ⓑ Ⓒ Ⓓ
       C   D

30. The prospects of the miner to find gold in that particular location was extremely
                         A   B   C

    poor.   Ⓐ Ⓑ Ⓒ Ⓓ
     D

31. <u>Those</u> pair of silver bookends that the museum had ordered <u>from</u> a European
      A   B

    dealer <u>doing business</u> in Africa, <u>became lost</u> en route to this country.
             C   D   Ⓐ Ⓑ Ⓒ Ⓓ

32. Last <u>month's</u> rainfall was <u>three times</u> <u>more than</u> the average for <u>that period</u>.
            A   B   C   D
                                                          Ⓐ Ⓑ Ⓒ Ⓓ

33. <u>Consider</u> the problems that <u>confronted</u> the expedition, the mountain climbers
        A   B

    decided <u>not to</u> attempt <u>to reach</u> the summit.   Ⓐ Ⓑ Ⓒ Ⓓ
              C   D

34. <u>As careful as</u> possible, and <u>with help</u> from the zookeepers, the veterinarian
         A   B

    examined the panda to see <u>whether</u> <u>she</u> was pregnant.   Ⓐ Ⓑ Ⓒ Ⓓ
                            C   D

35. In spite of <u>looking</u> exceedingly complicated, the machine <u>numbered</u> sixteen
              A   B

    was the <u>cheapest</u> made item in the <u>entire</u> trade fair.   Ⓐ Ⓑ Ⓒ Ⓓ
             C   D

36. Dr. Jones, who had been in practice in <u>the town of</u> Williamson for thirty odd
                                           A

    years, never <u>objected for</u> his <u>patients'</u> calling <u>at night</u>.   Ⓐ Ⓑ Ⓒ Ⓓ
                 B   C   D

37. <u>In spite of</u> Nell's <u>original</u> intention to buy the dress, she <u>changed her mind</u>
        A   B   C

    because of <u>the price was high</u>.   Ⓐ Ⓑ Ⓒ Ⓓ
               D

38. Kate was in the conference room <u>discussing</u> plans with <u>the other</u> committee
                                    A   B

    members when the chairman <u>had called</u> to say <u>he'd be</u> late. Ⓐ Ⓑ Ⓒ Ⓓ
                                C   D

39. The oldest contestant in the <u>hundred-yard</u> dash surprised <u>us</u> spectators <u>by run-</u>
                                A   B

    <u>ning</u> faster than <u>everyone</u> in the race.   Ⓐ Ⓑ Ⓒ Ⓓ
      C   D

40. <u>During</u> the Industrial Revolution, industry was <u>taken out of</u> the home; people
        A   B

    moved to cities <u>where</u> <u>had been built</u> many factories. Ⓐ Ⓑ Ⓒ Ⓓ
                   C   D

SUPPLEMENT

CONTRACTIONS

Notice that the contractions below are used in more than one type of verb structure.

he's; she's; it's *equals* he is; she is; it is
    He's an excellent student. *He is* an excellent student.
he's; she's; it's *equals* he has; she has; it has
    It's rained for several days. *It has rained* for several days.
I'd; you'd; he'd; she'd; we'd; you'd; they'd *equals* I had; you had; she had; we had; you had; they had
    They said *they'd met* earlier.   They said *they had met* earlier.
I'd; you'd; he'd; she'd; we'd; you'd; they'd *equals* I would; you would; she would; we would; you would; they would
    She'd drive if she had a license. *She would drive* if she had a license.

IRREGULAR VERBS

The principal parts of commonly used irregular verbs are listed alphabetically below. Practice these verbs by making up sentences. For practical purposes, you may begin your sentences with *sometimes, yesterday,* and *several times.*

Example: Sometimes I write to my friend.
               Yesterday I wrote to my friend.
               Several times I have written to my friend.
Example: Sometimes I catch some fish.
               Yesterday I caught some fish.
               Several times I have caught some fish.

Present	Past	Past Participle
am, are, is	was, were	been
beat	beat	beat(en)
become	became	become
begin	began	begun
bend	bent	bent
bet	bet	bet

180

bite	bit	bitten
bleed	bled	bled
blow	blew	blown
break	broke	broken
breed	bred	bred
bring	brought	brought
build	built	built
burst	burst	burst
buy	bought	bought
catch	caught	caught
choose	chose	chosen
come	came	come
cost	cost	cost
creep	crept	crept
cut	cut	cut
deal	dealt	dealt
dig	dug	dug
do	did	done
draw	drew	drawn
drink	drank	drunk
drive	drove	driven
eat	ate	eaten
fall	fell	fallen
feed	fed	fed
feel	felt	felt
fight	fought	fought
find	found	found
fit	fit(ted)	fit(ted)
flee	fled	fled
fly	flew	flown
forget	forgot	forgot(ten)
forgive	forgave	forgiven
freeze	froze	frozen
get	got	got(ten)
give	gave	given
go	went	gone
grind	ground	ground
grow	grew	grown
hang (a coat, a picture, etc.)	hung	hung
hang (a person)	hanged	hanged
have	had	had
hear	heard	heard
hide	hid	hidden
hit	hit	hit
hold	held	held
hurt	hurt	hurt
keep	kept	kept
know	knew	known
lay	laid	laid
lead	led	led
leap	leaped (leapt)	leaped (leapt)
leave	left	left
lend	lent	lent
let	let	let
lie	lay	lain
lie (tell an untruth)	lied	lied
lose	lost	lost
make	made	made
mean	meant	meant
meet	met	met
pay	paid	paid
put	put	put

quit	quit	quit
read	read	read
ride	rode	ridden
ring	rang	rung
rise	rose	risen
say	said	said
see	saw	seen
seek	sought	sought
sell	sold	sold
send	sent	sent
set	set	set
shake	shook	shaken
shine (shoes, etc.)	shined	shined
shine (the sun)	shone	shone
shoot	shot	shot
shut	shut	shut
sing	sang	sung
sink	sank	sunk
sit	sat	sat
sleep	slept	slept
slide	slid	slid
speak	spoke	spoken
spend	spent	spent
spin	spun	spun
split	split	split
spread	spread	spread
spring	sprang	sprung
stand	stood	stood
steal	stole	stolen
stick	stuck	stuck
strike	struck	struck
swear	swore	sworn
sweep	swept	swept
swim	swam	swum
swing	swung	swung
take	took	taken
teach	taught	taught
tear	tore	torn
think	thought	thought
understand	understood	understood
wake	woke	woken
weave	wove	woven
wed	wed	wed
win	won	won

IDIOMS, TWO-WORD VERBS, AND EXPRESSIONS

Idioms, two-word verbs, and expressions constitute a large part of both spoken and written English, so it is necessary to understand them. Two-word verbs (verb plus preposition) that may not be separated, are marked N.S.

About to, on the verge . . . almost ready to do something
of   He was about to leave when the telephone rang.

Above all . . .	of the greatest importance
	We were told to drive carefully but, above all, not to exceed the speed limit.
All of a sudden . . .	suddenly
	All of a sudden he left the room.
As a matter of fact; . . .	in truth
in fact	She is very intelligent; as a matter of fact, she has written three textbooks.
As long as . . .	since, because, in that
	As long as you are here, why not stay for dinner?
As usual . . .	occurring most of the time
	Peter was late for school, as usual.
Ask out . . .	invite to go somewhere (a date)
	Oleg asked Clara out last night.
At hand . . .	near, of priority
	First, resolve the business at hand.
At least . . .	in the minimum
	He didn't pass the test but at least he tried.
At times; . . .	occasionally
from time to time	At times Yousef helps his father.
Be hard on . . .	treat someone or something harshly
	When she failed, she was hard on herself.
Be over . . .	be finished, be through
	What time is the movie over?
Bear in mind; . . .	remember; not forget
keep in mind	You must bear in mind that you have only one hour to complete the test.
Blow up . . .	become very angry
	When he saw the broken window, he blew up!
Blow up . . .	fill with air
	He blew up the balloon for the small child.
Break down . . .	cease to function
	His car broke down and it had to be towed to a garage.
Break out . . .	erupt
	The fire broke out in the factory yesterday.
Bring up . . .	raise a child
	That little girl is well-behaved; her parents have brought her up very well.
Bring up . . .	raise (a subject)
	In our discussion he brought up the subject of holistic medicine.
By heart . . .	(learn) by memorizing
	He learned to play the piece by heart.
By the way . . .	incidentally
	By the way, have you sold your car yet?
Call back . . .	return a telephone call
	She said that she would call us back later.
Call off . . .	cancel
	The game was called off because of rain.
N.S. Call on . . .	visit
	Some friends called on us last night.
Call up . . .	telephone
	Before he left, he called up all his friends.

	Calm down . . .	become quiet, tranquil
		The policeman tried to calm the mother down.
	Can tell by . . .	can comprehend, know instinctively
		I could tell by the expression on his face that he was unhappy.
N.S.	Can't stand; . . .	won't or can't tolerate
	can't bear; put up with	I can't stand that loud noise.
		She won't put up with rudeness.
N.S.	Not care for . . .	dislike, not desire
		He didn't care for the dress she was wearing.
		I don't care for any coffee right now.
	Catch cold . . .	contract a cold
		Dress warmly so that you don't catch a cold.
N.S.	Catch on . . .	understand
		She didn't catch on to the joke that he told her.
N.S.	Catch up with . . .	reach the same level as others after being behind
		She hurried to catch up with her friend.
	Change one's mind . . .	decide against
		He changed his mind about going and stayed home.
	Cheer up . . .	raise one's spirits
		She cheered up her sick friend.
N.S.	Come across; . . .	meet or find something or someone unexpectedly
	run across	While I was cleaning my closet, I came across some old paintings.
	Come to . . .	revive, become conscious
		After she fainted, it took her five minutes to come to.
	Come true . . .	actually occur
		Her wish finally came true.
N.S.	Count on . . .	depend on, rely on
		One can always count on Fernando to help.
	Cut back . . .	reduce the amount
		The doctor told him to cut back on his activities.
	Cut down . . .	reduce the amount
		She had to cut down on her calorie intake.
	Cut off . . .	terminate, suddenly disconnect
		I will have to call her again; the telephone operator cut us off.
N.S.	Cut out . . .	quit, stop
		He finally cut out smoking.
N.S.	Deal with . . .	control or handle (a matter)
		Each of us must deal with daily problems.
	Do exercise . . .	exercise
	Do a favor . . .	do a small task for someone
		My friend asked me to do a favor for her.
	Do housework; . . .	be involved in work
	do homework;	
	do a job; do research	
	Do one good . . .	be beneficial for one
		The doctor told him that a vacation would do him good.
	Do over . . .	repeat, do again
		If you've made a lot of errors, do the composition over.
	Draw up . . .	prepare (a contract)
		After the contract had been drawn up, he signed it.
	Drop a line . . .	write a letter
		Drop me a line and let me know how you are.

	Drop off . . .	leave (someone or something) at a designated place by car or foot
		I dropped off the package on the way to school.
	Drop out . . .	quit (school)
		Mike was sorry that he had dropped out of school.
	Eat out . . .	eat at a restaurant
		We usually eat out once a week.
N.S.	Feel like . . .	be inclined, have the desire
		I feel like going swimming.
N.S.	Feel sorry for; . . .	have compassion toward
	take pity on	I feel sorry for children who are abused by parents.
	Figure out . . .	calculate, understand
		He couldn't figure out what she meant.
	Fill out . . .	complete (a written form)
		Please fill out the application.
N.S.	Find fault with . . .	criticize
		He always finds fault with her cooking.
N.S.	Find out . . .	obtain information
		She has found out the name of the school.
	For good . . .	permanently
		They plan to live in the United States for good.
	Fringe benefit . . .	advantages besides salary
		One of the fringe benefits of that union is medical coverage.
	Get along . . .	progress
		She's getting along in school just fine.
N.S.	Get along with . . .	be friendly with, not fight
		Are you getting along with your roommate?
	Get back . . .	return
		What time did you get back from the dance?
	Get down from . . .	descend
		She told her son to get down from the tree.
	Get in touch with . . .	make contact, communicate with
		He got in touch with me by telephone.
	Get lost . . .	be unable to find the way, lose direction
		When he drove to Lake Arrowhead, he got lost.
	Get one's way . . .	be allowed to do what one wishes
		That child is spoiled because he always gets his way.
N.S.	Get out of . . .	avoid work, or trouble, or problems
		She got out of washing the dishes by saying that she had a headache.
	Get out of . . .	leave an institution; leave a car
		He got out of jail last week!
		She got out of the car at the shopping center.
N.S.	Get over . . .	recover from grief or illness
		She finally got over her aunt's death.
	Get ready . . .	prepare for an event
		How long did it take you to get ready for the party?
N.S.	Get rid of . . .	discard, throw away
		He finally got rid of the old newspapers.
N.S.	Get through . . .	finish
		What time did you get through with your work?
	Get up . . .	arise, get out of bed
		They get up at seven o'clock every morning.

	Give away . . .	give, rather than sell, a possession
		The children gave away some of their toys.
	Give back . . .	return (something)
		He gave the book back when he was through.
N.S.	Give in . . .	relinquish one's position or "stand" to another person
		I wanted to go to the mountains but my husband wanted to go to the beach, so I gave in.
	Give someone a ring . . .	telephone someone
		I'll give you a ring next week.
	Give up . . .	surrender
		They gave up their idea of buying a house because it was too expensive.
	Go around . . .	be sufficient
		We had enough food to go around.
	Go away . . .	leave for a time
		He went away last Saturday and he won't be back until next week.
	Go to bed . . .	retire
		She goes to bed at 11:00 P.M.
	Go without saying . . .	be so obvious that it does not need explanation
		It goes without saying that if one spends all of his money, one will not have any in an emergency.
	Good for one . . .	beneficial for one
		The change of climate was good for him; he felt much better.
N.S.	Grow out of . . .	no longer fit; (reference is to children); outgrow.
		The child grew out of his clothing, so his parents had to buy him more.
	Hand in; . . .	give over to someone, give
	pass in	The teacher asked her students to hand in their papers.
	Hang up . . .	put the phone in its place; put clothing on a hanger
		After talking to her friend, Mary hung up the phone.
		As soon as she entered the house, she hung her coat up.
	Hard of hearing . . .	partially deaf
		You will have to speak more loudly because he's hard of hearing.
	Hard to imagine; . . .	difficult to accept as being true
	hard to believe	It was hard to believe that the girl was only twelve; she looked eighteen.
	Have in mind . . .	be thinking about (a plan)
		What type of shoes do you have in mind to buy?
	Have trouble; . . .	used in describing circumstances
	have difficulty; have a	She had trouble understanding him.
	problem; have fun;	They were having a good time when I saw them.
	have a good time	
N.S.	Hear from . . .	have communication
		Have you heard from your friend?
N.S.	Hear of . . .	be familiar with
		Have you ever heard of Paul Muni?
	Hold off . . .	delay, restrain oneself
		Since it was still early, he held off going.
	Hold still . . .	remain motionless
		The photographer told them to hold still while he took their picture.
	How come . . .	why?
		How come you are late?

N.S.	In charge of . . .	responsible for
		Marita is in charge of decorations for the dance next Friday.
	It's time . . .	to be timely for a particular action or decision
		It's time you decided what career to choose.
	In the meanwhile; . . .	refers to an action during the time of another action, such as *while*
	in the meantime	He listened to a nightly radio drama; in the meantime he heard the news.
	In the red . . .	in debt
		For the first two years, the business was in the red.
	In the way . . .	being an obstacle
		Every time he tries to take his sister's pictures, his little brother gets in the way.
	Inside out . . .	in reversed position
		She didn't notice that her sweater was inside out.
	It doesn't matter . . .	it is of no consequence; "it's okay"
		It doesn't matter whether you hand in your paper tomorrow or the next day.
	It takes time; . . .	refers to that which is required
	it takes courage, etc. . . .	It takes time to develop proficiency.
	It takes an hour, etc. . . .	It takes courage to do what one fears.
		It takes an hour to get downtown.
N.S.	Keep an eye on . . .	guard, watch over
		You had better keep an eye on your purse when you go shopping.
	Keep away . . .	maintain some distance
		Keep away from that fire!
N.S.	Keep in touch . . .	continue communicating, make contact
		After you return, please keep in touch with us.
	Keep off . . .	not walk on a particular surface
		That sign says to keep off the grass.
	Keep out . . .	not enter
		They were told to keep out of the storage room.
	Keep on, keep up, . . .	continue
	keep going	You are doing good work. Keep it up!
		He kept playing the radio while his roommate tried to study.
	Keep one company . . .	be a companion to someone
		She doesn't like to eat alone so her friend sometimes keeps her company.
	Keep someone waiting . . .	delay someone
		His girlfriend kept him waiting for a whole hour.
N.S.	Keep track of . . .	keep a record of
		You should keep track of your expenses.
	Lay off . . .	dismiss from a job
		During the depression, many workers were laid off.
	Leave out . . .	omit, delete
		answer all the questions; don't leave anything out.
	Let down . . .	disappointed
		When he called off the date, Mary felt very let down.
	Let go of . . .	release, set free
		The mountain climber was told not to let go of the rope.
		After questioning the boys, the police let them go.

	Let (someone) know . . .	inform (someone) I called him to let him know that I would be late.
	Let up . . .	ease, be less strong After she had taken the medicine, the pain let up.
	Like nothing better . . .	prefer one thing to all other things My friend likes nothing better than to listen to classical music.
	Little by little . . .	gradually His health is improving little by little.
N.S.	Look around . . .	examine one's surroundings While he was waiting for her, he looked around.
N.S.	Look down on . . .	show disrespect to People are equal; one shouldn't look down on others.
	Look forward to . . .	anticipate with pleasure I look forward to seeing you again.
N.S.	Look into . . .	investigate He promised to look into the matter as soon as possible.
N.S.	Look like; . . . sound like; smell like; feel like; taste like	resemble She looks like her mother.
N.S.	Look out; . . . watch out	be careful Here comes a car. Look out! Watch out!
	Look over . . .	examine, study Before you sign a contract, look it over carefully.
	Look up . . .	find information in a book If you don't know the meaning of a word, look it up.
	Lose one's balance . . .	lose equilibrium After drinking so much beer, he lost his balance.
	Made by hand . . .	not manufactured The lace on her collar was made by hand.
	Make a bed . . .	also: make peace; make friends; make a mistake; make a wish; make an effort; make a loan; make a deposit; make a decision; make an announcement; make arrangements; make a deal; make progress
	Make a face . . .	distort one's features The child did not like the food and she made a face.
	Make a living; . . . earn a living	earn money to live on She made a living by selling weavings.
	Make believe . . .	pretend The child made believe that she was a bird.
	Make ends meet . . .	be able to provide necessities of life In a depression, it is difficult for some people to make ends meet.
N.S.	Make fun of . . .	joke about (something or someone) He made fun of her new hat.
	Make (meals) . . .	prepare (meals) Sydney used to make breakfasts on Sunday mornings.
	Make sure . . .	confirm, be certain Make sure that you lock the door of your car.
	Make up . . .	invent, create The boy made up a story about a planet.
N.S.	Make up . . .	reconcile after an argument The couple had quarreled but later they made up.

Make up . . .	apply cosmetics
	The actress made up her face expertly.
Make up one's mind . . .	decide
	She couldn't make up her mind which dress to buy.
Mean a lot . . .	be important (to one)
	He called often because he knew it meant a lot to her.
Mix up . . .	confuse
	The students were mixed up about the instructions.
Must be . . .	assume to be true (in present time)
	She isn't at school; she must be sick.
Must have been . . .	assume to be true (in past time)
	He wasn't home when I called; he must have gone somewhere.
Named after . . .	given the same name as
	The child was named after his grandfather.
Never mind . . .	don't concern yourself with
	Never mind taking me home; I'll take the bus.
No business doing something . . .	refers to an action of poor judgment
	He was an intelligent man; Ron had no business telling him what to do.
No use . . .	pointless, of no value
	Apparently she isn't coming, so there's no use waiting.
None of one's business . . .	refers to personal matters that should not be of interest or concern to someone else
	She didn't think the problem was any of their business. (She thought it was none of their business.)
On a diet . . .	required to eat special food for health or for weight loss
	She doesn't eat desserts; she's on a diet.
On the verge of . . .	be about to happen or do
	The miner was on the verge of discovering gold when the cave collapsed.
Once in a while . . .	occasionally
	Once in a while he does the cooking.
One by one; . . . one at a time	singly, individually
	He interviewed the applicants one by one.
Out of business . . .	no longer doing business
	That store didn't make a profit for its owners so they went out of business.
Out of date . . .	old style
	Some people use slang that is out of date.
Out of gas . . .	having no more gas
	We had better stop at a gas station before we run out of gas.
Out of one's mind . . .	insane
	The noise was so terrible; the poor man thought that he would go out of his mind.
Out of order . . .	not functioning properly
	That telephone doesn't work; it's out of order.
Out of sight . . .	not visible
	I can't see the airplane any longer; it's out of sight.
Out of touch . . .	not in contact or communication
	We haven't spoken or written to each other in a long time; we have been out of touch.

	Out of town . . .	in another city or town
		My husband won't be home until Friday; he's out of town.
	Out of work . . .	without employment
		He's collecting unemployment insurance because he's out of work.
	Over and over . . .	repeatedly
		You may have to do the exercises over and over before you get them correct.
N.S.	Pass away . . .	die
		Her grandfather passed away a year ago.
	Pass out . . .	faint, lose consciousness
		When she got the bad news, she passed out.
	Pick out . . .	select, choose
		Have you picked out your furniture yet?
	Put away . . .	put things in their proper place
		Will you ask the children to put away their toys?
	Put off . . .	postpone, delay
		Tom put off his dental appointment until next month.
	Put on . . .	add (weight), add (clothing)
		She asked him if he had put on weight.
		He put his coat on and said good-bye.
	Put out . . .	extinguish (a fire)
		The firefighters quickly put out the fire.
	Put out . . .	set outside
		Did you put the bottles out for the milkman?
	Put together . . .	assemble
		Can you put this puzzle together?
	Read over . . .	to read from beginning to end; to get information from reading material
		Before signing, you'd better read it over.
	Run away . . .	flee; escape
		The horse has run away and must be captured.
	Run out of . . .	have no more remaining
		Tricia couldn't bake cookies this morning because she had run out of sugar.
	See . . .	understand
		I saw that it was futile to explain.
N.S.	Send for . . .	ask (a specialist) to come in times of need
		When the pipe began to leak, she sent for a plumber.
		When the baby got sick, she sent for the doctor.
	Show up . . .	appear
		John hasn't shown up in class for three days.
	Shut off . . .	stop the flow of (gas, water, electricity)
		If you don't pay your bill, the gas company may shut off the gas.
	Stand out . . .	to be prominent
		He was unusually bright and therefore he stood out in the class.
	Stay up . . .	not go to bed
		I have a bad habit of staying up until midnight.
	Take a chance . . .	risk
		Although we didn't have tickets, we took a chance that we would be admitted.
	Take advantage of . . .	use the opportunity for
		The museum movies are free; we should take advantage of them.

Take advantage of . . .	abuse a kindness
	She takes advantage of her neighbor by borrowing things too often.
N.S. Take after . . .	resemble, look like
	Who do you take after, your mother or father?
Take . . . (an amount of time)	use a particular amount of time for an action
	It took her two hours to get ready for the party.
Take apart . . .	disassemble, separate the parts
	The repairman took the clock apart.
Take care of . . .	watch over, be responsible for
	She took good care of her children.
Take down . . .	remove from a high place
	Will you take down that painting?
Take down . . .	write (write down on paper)
	The teacher asked us to take down some information.
Take hold of . . .	grasp
	If you are frightened, take hold of my hand.
Take off . . .	remove (clothing)
	Since it was a warm day, Jan took off his jacket.
Take off . . .	depart (referring to) an airplane
	The plane took off at exactly 6:15 A.M.
Take one's time . . .	not hurry, not rush
	It's early; take your time getting ready.
Take out . . .	escort someone somewhere
	The young man took the girl out to dinner.
N.S. Take over . . .	assume responsibility
	The teacher asked the student to take over the class.
Take pains . . .	be very careful with, be particular
	Mrs. Beuhel took great pains with her sewing.
Take part in . . .	participate in
	Helene didn't want to take part in the demonstration.
Take place . . .	occur, happen
	The festival will take place on Sunday.
Take responsibility . . .	assume responsibility
	The children took responsibility for feeding their dog.
Take something for granted . . .	not appreciate, expect continuance
	Some people take their friends for granted.
Take time off . . .	obtain free time from work
	She took time off to do some shopping.
Take turns . . .	alternate
	Pedro and Thomas took turns driving to San Francisco.
Talk over . . .	discuss
	Before deciding, she talked it over with a friend.
Tear down . . .	demolish
	The building was torn down to make room for the new museum.
Tell apart . . .	distinguish between or differentiate
	The twins look so much alike, it's difficult to tell them apart.
These days; today; . . . nowadays	currently; present passage of time
	Everything is costly these days.
Think over . . .	consider carefully
	Before we bought the house, we thought it over carefully.
Throw away . . .	discard, get rid of
	Please throw away all the old newspapers.

N.S. Throw up . . .   regurgitate
                                          After eating the spoiled food, the dog threw up.

     Tired out . . .   fatigued, exhausted
                                          She was tired out from cleaning windows all day.

     Try on . . .   put on to test the fit, size, and/or appearance
                                          She tried on a beautiful fur coat.

     Try out . . .   test
                                          Before I bought my car, I tried it out.

     Turn back . . .   return to original place
                                          Since the road was in poor condition, they decided to turn back.

     Turn down . . .   reject, refuse
                                          Nina turned down Bob's offer of marriage.
                                          She was turned down by the college at which she had applied.

     Turn off . . .   stop (radio, stove, TV, records, lights)
                                          He finally turned off the lights.

     Turn on . . .   start (radio, stove, television, lights, motor,
                                          washing machine, etc.)
                                          When the dishes were placed in the dishwasher, she turned it on.

     Upside down . . .   reverse position, "bottom is up"
                                          We noticed that the painting had been hung upside down.

N.S. Wait on . . .   serve
                                          A waitress named Prudence waited on us.

N.S. Wait up for . . .   not go to bed while waiting for someone
                                          Miriam always waits up for her children.

     Wake up . . .   awaken, open one's eyes after sleeping
                                          What time do you wake up in the morning?

     What is it like? . . .   asking for a description
     What was he like? . . .   What was your childhood like?
     What has it been like?   What is it like to be a twin?
     (etc.). . .   What did he look like?
                                          What has it been like to live in a foreign country?

     Why not? . . .   Why don't you?; Why shouldn't I? etc.
                                          Why not stay for dinner?

     Without question . . .   for certain, unquestionably
                                          Without question he is the best tennis player in the city.

     Worn out . . .   threadbare from long use; exhausted
                                          The old carpet was worn out.
                                          By the end of the day, she was worn out.

COMMON ERRORS IN WORD USAGE

Often words are combined with other words incorrectly. The student of English must be careful to avoid incorrect word combinations.

Listed below are combinations that are *not* correct. Pay special attention to the correct combination of words.

(incorrect):   (reason . . . because)   (The reason he's late is because his car broke down.)
                                            xxxxxxxxxx
CORRECT: reason . . . that   The *reason* he's late is *that* his car broke down.
(incorrect):   (different than)   (He is different than the other boys.)
                                                          xxxxxxx

CORRECT: different from   He is *different from* the other boys.
(incorrect):   (being as)   (Being as he was a little boy, he became restless during the long
                     speech.)
CORRECT: being   *Being* a little boy, he became restless during the long speech.
(incorrect):   (despite of)   (Maureen went swimming despite of her cold.)
CORRECT: in spite of   Maureen went swimming *in spite of* her cold.
             despite   Maureen went swimming *despite* her cold.
(incorrect):   (near to)   (The nurse put the flowers near to the bed.)
CORRECT: near   The nurse put the flowers *near* the bed.
             next to   The nurse put the flowers *next to* the bed.
(incorrect):   (off of)   (The boy fell off of the roof.)
CORRECT: off   The boy fell *off* the roof.
(incorrect):   (could of)   (He would of come if he had felt better.)
             (might of)
             (must of)   (He must of been ill last night.)
             (should of)
             (would of)   (She should of done her homework yesterday.)
CORRECT: could have   He *should have* come if he had felt better.
             might have   He *must have* been busy last night.
             must have   She *should have* done her homework yesterday.
             should have
             would have
(incorrect):   (equally as good)   (Those vegetables are equally as good as the vegetables in the
                     other store.)
CORRECT: equally good   The vegetables in the two stores are *equally good.*
             as good as   Those vegetables are *as good as* the vegetables in the other stores.
(incorrect):   (kind of a)   (I don't know what kind of a material it is.)
             (sort of a)
             (type of a)
CORRECT: kind of   I don't know what *kind of* material it is.
             sort of
             type of
(incorrect):   (at about)   (He arrived at about five o'clock.)
CORRECT: about   He arrived *about* five o'clock.
(incorrect):   (because . . . why)   (Because he was out of town is why he was absent.)
CORRECT: because   He was absent *because* he was out of town.
(incorrect):   (win him)   (George won him in the chess game.)
CORRECT: beat him   George *beat him* in the chess game.
             win   George *won* the chess game.
(incorrect):   (a half a)   (He ate a half a grapefruit.)
CORRECT: a half   He ate *a half* grapefruit.
             half a   He ate *half a* grapefruit.
(incorrect):   (these kind)   (I like these kind of candy.)
CORRECT: this kind   I like *this kind* of candy.
             these kinds   I like *these kinds* of candies.
(incorrect):   (out loud)   (He read the article out loud this morning.)

CORRECT:	aloud	He read the article *aloud* this morning.
(incorrect):	(prefer than)	(She prefers rice than potatoes.)
CORRECT:	prefer to	She *prefers* rice *to* potatoes.
(incorrect):	(seldom ever)	(He seldom ever plays golf.)
CORRECT:	seldom	He *seldom* plays golf.
	hardly ever	He *hardly ever* plays golf.
(incorrect):	(superior than)	(His painting skill is superior than the others.)
CORRECT:	superior to	His painting skill is *superior to* the others.
(incorrect):	(be sure and)	(He told us to be sure and be there on time.)
	(try and)	(He told us to try and be there on time.)
CORRECT:	be sure to	He told us to *be sure to* be there on time.
	try to	He told us to *try to* be there on time.
(incorrect):	(in between)	(He sat in between the two girls.)
CORRECT:	between	He sat *between* the two girls.
(incorrect):	(in back of)	(The gymnasium is in back of the school.)
CORRECT:	back of	The gymnasium is *back of* the school.
	behind	The gymnasium is *behind* the school.
(incorrect):	(outside of)	(They made the dog sleep outside of the house.)
CORRECT:	outside	They made the dog sleep *outside* the house.
(incorrect):	(kind a)	(It's kind a cold today.)
CORRECT:	somewhat	It's *somewhat* cold today.
(incorrect):	(feel badly)	(She feels badly that she can't go to the dance.)
CORRECT:	feel bad	She *feels bad* that she can't go to the dance.
(incorrect):	(both . . . as well as)	(Both Syd as well as Phil are intelligent.)
CORRECT:	both . . . and	*Both* Syd *and* Phil are intelligent.
(incorrect):	(most all)	(He answered most all of the questions correctly.)
CORRECT:	almost all	He answered *almost all* of the questions correctly.
(incorrect):	(leave, meaning "permit")	(The boy sometimes leaves his dog sleep on his bed.)
CORRECT:	(let)	The boy sometimes *lets* his dog sleep on his bed.
(incorrect):	(many of people)	(Many of people shop here.)
CORRECT:	many of the people	*Many of the people* shop here.
	many people	*Many people* shop here.
	many of them	*Many of them* shop here.

Below is a list of commonly misused words. Be sure to spell and to use each of the following words correctly. Check the meaning of each word (or group of words).

hung—hanged, real—very, desert—dessert, counsel—council—consul, sight—site—cite, to—two—too, weather—whether, some—somewhat, sure—certainly, proceed—precede, alright—all right, most—almost, continually—continuously, like—alike, advice—advise, when—whenever, what—whatever, who—whoever, altogether—all together, like—alike, around—about, beside—besides, besides—next to, already—all ready, between—among, farther—further, quite—quiet, it's—its, who's—whose, you're—your, defined—definition, beauty—beautiful, later—latter, lose—loose, percent-percentage, principle—principal, there—their—they're, accept—except, maybe—may be, formally—formerly, aggravate—annoy, awfully—very, good—well, former—first, latter—last, healthy—healthful, leave—let, imply—infer, in—into, somewhat—quite, learn—teach, likely—liable, locate—settle—move, respectfully—respectively, terribly—very, way—ways, interesting—interested, conscious—conscience, win—beat, relieve—relief, capital—capitol, corps—corpse, dual—duel, forth—fourth, passed—past, prophesy—prophecy, better—had better, statue—stature—statute, so—so that, so—very, considerable—considerate, suspect—suspicion, too—very, course—coarse, kind of—somewhat, sort of—somewhat, another—other—the other—others, bad—badly, less—lesser, specially—especially, live—alive, negligent—negligible, able—enable

The student is sometimes confused about the following words. The words marked wrong are *not* in the English language.

(wrong):   (carefulness)
xxxxxxxxxxxxxx

RIGHT: care

(wrong):   (anywheres)
xxxxxxxxxxxxxx

RIGHT: anywhere

(wrong):   (suspicioned)
xxxxxxxxxxxxxx

RIGHT: suspected

(wrong):   (irregardless)

RIGHT: regardless

(wrong):   (somewheres)
xxxxxxxxxxxxxxxx

RIGHT: somewhere

(wrong):   (complected)
xxxxxxxxxxxxxx

RIGHT: complexioned

(wrong):   (suppose to)
xxxxxxxxxxxxxx

RIGHT: be supposed to

(wrong):   (hisself)
xxxxxxxxx

RIGHT: himself

(wrong):   (theirselves)
xxxxxxxxxxxxxx

RIGHT: themselves

(wrong):   (sometime)
xxxxxxxxxxxxx

RIGHT: sometimes
          some time

ANSWERS TO TESTS

(The Pretest answers are given with the answers to the other full-length simulated TOEFL tests.)

A single answer to a question is not always the only possible answer. You will notice, therefore, that in a number of instances alternate answers have been provided.

SECTION I
Exercise I. 1.
1. doesn't have; takes
2. has; likes
3. is preparing
4. seldom/rarely; is writing
5. must be snowing
6. can hardly; is blowing; is getting

7. are; usually plans
8. should be; playing
9. is; thirteen, *or* thirteen years old, *or* thirteen years of age; appears
10. doesn't know how; has

Exercise I. 3.
1. have been taking/have taken
2. has been offering/has offered
3. has seen
4. hasn't eaten
5. has just received

6. have been growing/have grown
7. have visited
8. Have you registered
9. have been expressing/have expressed
10. has been; has never forgotten

Mixed Exercise 1: Part A
(Mixed Exercises include questions pertaining to material from the first page of the book to the page to which the student has progressed. The structure and the reference to the explanation is given after each answer.)
1. C   Present perfect
2. D   Present tense
3. B   Present continuous

4. B   Modals in present time
5. A   Present perfect
6. C   Present perfect
7. D   Present tense
8. A   Present continuous
9. C   Modals in present time
10. B   Present perfect

Mixed Exercise 1: Part B
1. have just gone. Present perfect
2. A   is being. Present continuous
3. D   was. Past tense in the *since* clause with present perfect
4. B   look. Subject-verb agree.
5. D   are seldom. Negative frequency adverbs

6. A   is making. Present continuous
7. C   negotiating. Modal continuous in present time
8. C   is preparing. Present continuous
9. C   sometimes isn't. Frequency adverbs with negative contractions
10. C   have agreed. Present perfect, completed action

Exercise I. 5.
1. delivered; was entertaining
2. was walking; saw
3. were watching; came over
4. didn't hear; was in the engine room checking.
5. heard; investigated

6. was turning; came
7. was demonstrating; tripped; fell
8. could not play; had to work
9. were moving; started
10. was doing; ordered

Exercise I. 7.
1. had gone
2. had been competing
3. had mixed

4. had been
5. had been going on
6. had been cleaning

196

Exercise I. 8.

1. had been raining
2. hasn't been working
3. lost; stopped
4. had been accruing

5. was watching
6. had violated
7. had developed

Exercise I. 10.

2. I should have done my homework, but. . . .
3. I must have left my book. . . .
4. He was going to sing last night, but. . . .
5. He may have been sleeping.
6. I could have gone to the rock concert last week, but. . . .

7. I wasn't going to watch the horror film, but. . . .
8. She would have returned the books yesterday, but. . . .
9. He shouldn't have driven fast/He shouldn't have been driving fast. . . .
10. The child must have been (afraid).

Mixed Exercise 2: Part A

1. C   Past modals
2. B   Past perfect
3. B   Past continuous
4. A   Present perfect
5. C   Past tense

6. A   Present modals
7. D   Present perfect
8. B   Present tense
9. D   Past tense
10. C   Past perfect continuous

Mixed Exercise 2: Part B

1. B   be talking. Present modals
2. B   has had. Present perfect
3. C   doesn't. Subject-verb agree.
4. A   would certainly have kept. Past modals
5. D   used to. Used to, past tense

6. B   had barely. Negative frequency adverbs
7. A   was. Past for deceased
8. A   for 3 weeks. *For* and *since*, present perfect
9. C   were wearing. Past continuous
10. B   had been. Past perfect with reporting verbs

Exercise I. 14.

1. will be watching; gets
2. goes; will be working
3. will be preparing

4. drives; will be flying
5. will you be doing; attends
6. won't still be conferring

Exercise I. 16.

1. will have redecorated
2. will have replaced
3. will have been

4. will have been talking
5. will have been discussing
6. have built

Exercise I. 18.

Completion of sentences should include the following tenses:

1. Present continuous
2. Present perfect
3. Past tense
4. Past continuous
5. Future/future expression
6. Past Modal and Expression of intention
7. Present perfect/present perfect continuous
8. Future continuous
9. Future perfect/future perfect continuous
10. Present tense

11. Past perfect continuous
12. Past perfect modal expressing probability
13. Past perfect
14. Future continuous expression
15. Past perfect modal or past expression expressing intention
16. Present modal expressing possibility
17. Past tense
18. Future continuous/continuous modal/future
19. Present perfect
20. Future/future continuous; present tense

Mixed Exercise 3: Part A

1. C   Past continuous
2. B   Present perfect continuous
3. B   Future perfect
4. A   Past perfect
5. D   Present, time clause with conditional future possible

6. C   Present continuous
7. C   Future perfect continuous
8. B   Present continuous
9. A   Present continuous
10. D   Past expression of intention

Mixed Exercise 3: Part B

1. B   found. Past with past continuous
2. C   would like. *Would* with like for specific occasions
3. B   has never forgotten. Present perfect
4. B   had already returned. Past perfect
5. A   ruled. Past tense
6. A   speaks. Present tense in time clause with future clause

7. A   for seven months. Present perfect *for* and *since*
8. B   should have borrowed. Past modal
9. B   live. Subject-verb agree.
10. D   could. Negative frequency adverbs

SECTION II

Exercise II. 1.

2. The foreign heads of state have just been welcomed by the mayor.
3. Yesterday the mail wasn't delivered until 5:00 P.M.

4. The new textbook will be published next May.
5. The noise is being caused by a cement mixer.

6. By dawn tomorrow the forest fire will have been extinguished.
7. The cooperation of students is needed in order to have a successful program.
8. As soon as the ambulance arrived, the wounded man was driven to the hospital.

Exercise II. 3.
2. is having/is getting; done/cut/set/washed/etc.
3. have; made/remodeled/altered/etc.
4. has just had; stolen
5. will have/hope to have/expect to have; paid (paid off)

Mixed Exercise 4: Part A
1. B   Present perfect
2. C   Past passive
3. A   Past tense
4. C   Future perfect
5. D   Causative passive

Mixed Exercise 4: Part B
1. B   likes. Present tense
2. D   were being tested. Past continuous passive
3. C   will have had. Future perfect
4. D   is used to it. *Be used to*
5. A   will be performed. Future passive

SECTION III
Exercise III. 1.
2. Was the concert attended by the majority of the student body?
3. Has she decided to take a course in shorthand before she applies for a job?

Exercise III. 2.
2. Who has won this year's debating contest?
   What kind of contest has Katsumi won?
3. Whose cat was found yesterday by Jack, a next-door neighbor?
   Who found Zobi's cat yesterday?

Exercise III. 4.
1. didn't it
2. has he
3. don't they

Exercise III. 5.
(Sample answers are given.)
1. He; so do I
2. They; we weren't either

Mixed Exercise 5: Part A
1. A   Past perfect continuous
2. D   Causative passive
3. C   Past modals
4. B   Future perfect
5. D   Future passive

Mixed Exercise 5: Part B
1. B   may be. Modal
2. D   neither did Lien/Lien didn't either. Tag ending
3. C   was able to win. When achieving a goal, use *was able* not *could*.
4. D   belonged. Past tense
5. D   be cut down. Past passive

SECTION IV
Exercise IV. 1.
1. was sleeping
2. had been
3. hadn't crossed
4. would hike

9. The washing machine can't be installed until the tenant moves in.
10. An old building was being torn down as we drove by.

6. have had it/have gotten it dry-cleaned/washed
7. had; corrected/rewritten
8. have/get; repaired/fixed/cleaned

6. A   Future continuous
7. B   Past tense
8. C   Frequency adverbs in present tense
9. D   Future passive
10. A   Causative passive

6. D   has never eaten. Present perfect
7. B   should have given. Past perfect modal
8. D   prepared. Past tense
9. B   preparing. Present continuous
10. A   threaten. Active voice

4. Are they going to go for a long walk if they finish their work early?
5. Was the candidate being careful, when he gave his speech, not to offend any political group?

4. Why should Karen have lent her bicycle to George?
   To whom should Karen have lent her bicycle?
5. At which hotel will Mr. and Mrs. Perry be staying?
   How long will Mr. and Mrs. Perry be staying at the Logan Hotel?

4. won't she
5. weren't they

3. She; but he isn't
4. The show; neither will the film
5. We; they did too

6. B   Tag endings
7. A   Formation of questions
8. C   Formation of questions
9. B   Past perfect
10. D   Tag endings

6. B   is meeting. Present continuous
7. A   has the annual meeting . . . been postponed. Formation of questions
8. B   decided. Present perfect
9. C   was being loaded. Past passive
10. B   is notified. Present time clause with future

5. didn't have; left
6. had been promoted
7. were
8. was saved/could have been saved

9. were watching (are watching)

Exercise IV. 2.

(Answers in an informal style are added in the parentheses when the statement is assumed to be currently true.)

1. I told them that Betty was an excellent student. (I told them that Betty is an excellent student.)
2. She said that she was going (was going to go) on a business trip next week. (She said that she is going on a business trip next week.)

Exercise IV. 4.

2. is soon. was soon
3. will help. would help
4. would the politician. the politician would
5. divorced. had divorced
6. had to. has to

SECTION V

Exercise V. 1.

1. had remembered/had remembered to
2. hadn't repaired; would be/might be/could be
3. remodel
4. were
5. hadn't been changed
6. would have cooked/might have cooked/could have cooked; had had

Exercise V. 2.

1. *was*. were
2. *would visit*. would have visited
3. *stops*. would stop/stopped
4. *returned*. return

Mixed Exercise 6: Part A

1. B   Past passive
2. C   Conditional unreal past
3. D   Past continuous
4. A   Past form with past reporting verb
5. D   Continuous modal in present time expressing probability

Mixed Exercise 6: Part B

1. C   found. Past tense
2. B   had broken. Past perfect with reporting verb
3. A   would like. *Would* in polite form
4. D   were. *As if*, unreal present
5. A   had better. Modal

SECTION VI

Exercise VI. 1.

(Wherever necessary a "sample object" has been included.)

1. us to come
2. not to move
3. to compete
4. him to use
5. to pass
6. to obtain
7. to be repaired
8. didn't mean to
9. to change
10. to have been chosen
11. Jane to apply

Exercise VI. 2.

1. working
2. being picked up
3. to be; talking
4. not turning on

10. had

3. He wanted to know if you were planning to take a speech course. (He wanted to know if you are planning to take a speech course.)
4. We thought that Paul hadn't eaten breakfast yet.
5. Joe wondered how long she had been married.

7. will she. she will
8. do I like. if I liked/whether I liked/whether or not I liked
9. can't answer. couldn't answer; he's. he was
10. has just awakened. had just awakened

7. were; could get/might get/would get
8. may/might/could
9. received
10. had been made

5. *was*. were
6. *would be*. will be
7. *weren't discovered*. hadn't been discovered
8. *was*. were

6. C   Present continuous
7. D   Conditional passive past unreal
8. B   Nominative clause with reporting verb
9. D   Tag endings
10. A   Past perfect

6. C   had been. Conditional unreal past
7. C   would have to. Past form with past reporting verb
8. A   had been built. Past perfect passive
9. A   omit *us*. Past reporting verb
10. B   would never have. Past perfect modal

12. not to have won
13. to have
14. to set
15. not to touch
16. to give
17. to practice
18. the teacher to give you/to be given
19. to register
20. to speak
21. to make
22. to go
23. to find; to have been taken

5. taking; to get
6. to communicate
7. questioning; using/having used
8. to have been found; hunting

9. not to risk; having had/having; losing
10. being carried
11. their reducing/their having reduced
12. laughing

Exercise VI. 4.
1. rehearsing
2. not being able
3. going
4. didn't hand in
5. look it over
6. major
7. be
8. to spread

Mixed Exercise 7: Part A
1. C   Perfect infinitive
2. A   Tag endings
3. D   Past tense with past reporting verb
4. A   Possessive with gerund
5. D   Infinitive
6. A   *Would,* Past tense

Mixed Exercise 7: Part B
1. C   is elected. Present tense in conditional clause with future
2. C   to finish. Infinitive
3. B   did he tell you. Formation of questions
4. B   were to be inspected. Future passive
5. B   his working. Gerund with possessive

SECTION VII

Exercise VII. 1.
1. the
2. no article
3. the
4. no article
5. no article
6. the; an
7. the

Exercise VII. 2.
1. *three-minutes egg.* a three-minute egg
2. *a third time.* the third time
3. *University of Colorado.* the University of Colorado
4. *the raw fish.* raw fish
5. *a honorable man.* an honorable man
6. *the page thirty-four.* page thirty-four
7. *the telephone.* a telephone
8. *has largest animal.* has the largest animal
9. *the fish or the chicken.* fish or chicken
10. *security system.* a security system
11. *two childs.* two children
12. *One of hospitals.* One of the hospitals
13. *the Fred's restaurant.* Fred's restaurant
14. *the cotton.* cotton
15. *a house.* the house; *tree.* trees; *the glass.* a glass

Exercise VII. 5.
1. to bring
2. laid
3. was raised
4. hung up
5. her boyfriend
6. is used

Exercise VII. 6.
See Irregular Verbs in the Supplement for Correct Answers.

13. your speaking; writing
14. to purchase
15. to go; (to) work; arranging
16. our visiting; to discuss

9. open; to find
10. his having received; to hear
11. my playing the piano
12. having; breathing; trying; to remain
13. being carried
14. to have been running
15. to watch; surf

7. D   Present tense in conditional clause with future possible
8. C   Proposal clause
9. B   Present perfect passive
10. A   Present tense

6. B   composing. Present continuous
7. B   omit should. Proposal clause
8. D   to be. Infinitive
9. D   to become. Infinitive
10. C   become familiar. Proposal

8. the
9. no article
10. the; the; the
11. a
12. no article; the
13. a; the
14. a

16. *one luggage.* one piece of luggage
17. *typewriter's keys.* typewriter keys
18. *Pacific Ocean.* The Pacific Ocean; *west coast.* the west coast
19. *the lettuce, the apples, the fish.* lettuce, apples, and fish
20. *the chess.* chess
21. *Peace-keeping force.* The peace-keeping force
22. *an information.* information
23. *city of Venice.* the city of Venice
24. *only one.* the only one; *statistic class.* the statistics class
25. *in the past times.* in past times; *in the present times.* in present times

7. is lying
8. lend
9. came; began
10. took over the responsibility
11. laid

Exercise VII. 7.
 1. regularly
 2. frightened
 3. originally
 4. carefully
 5. the most interesting
 6. as eloquently as
 7. a little
 8. any other
 9. fewer
10. useless
11. the same as

12. beautifully
13. such a crowded a place
14. worse and worse
15. a greater amount of
16. happily
17. suddenly
18. the more strongly
19. fundamentally
20. a very
21. the younger

Exercise VII. 8.
1. *the greater*. the greatest
2. *anyone*. anyone else
3. *most all*. almost all; *bad damaged*. badly damaged
4. *quick*. quickly
5. *as*. than
6. *good or accurate*. well or accurately
7. *conclusive decided*. conclusively decided
8. *high poisonous*. highly poisonous; *real dangerous*. very dangerous
9. *yet*. anymore

10. *illegal shipped*. illegally shipped
11. *loudly ringing*. loud ringing
12. *twice more than*. twice as many imported cars this year as
13. *original*. originally
14. *so many*. as many; *like*. as
15. *near enough heavy*. nearly heavy enough
16. *too much*. very much
17. *much interests*. many interests; *primary*. primarily
18. *most all*. almost all; *sort of*. somewhat/rather

Exercise VII. 9.
1. he/he does
2. ours
3. herself/it
4. he/he had
5. him
6. hers; his; his/hers
7. whose
8. him; me
9. himself

10. those
11. that/the one
12. you; him
13. those/the ones
14. those
15. those/whoever
16. which/that
17. in which/where
18. in whose

Exercise VII. 10.
 1. *me*. I/I am
 2. *than yesterday*. the one/that yesterday
 3. *not her*. not she
 4. *where*. that
 5. *him*. his
 6. *which*. in which
 7. *whom*. who
 8. *where*. in which
 9. *them*. they
10. *Who*. Whom (formal)

11. *them*. those; *us*. we
12. *whomever*. whoever
13. *themselves*. them
14. *which*. that
15. *them*. those
16. *which*. whose
17. *about*. Omit the second *about*
18. *which*. whose
19. *This here kind*. These kinds
20. *whose*. for whose

Exercise VII. 11.
 1. at
 2. on
 3. on
 4. of
 5. on
 6. to
 7. at
 8. to
 9. to
10. on; on

11. with
12. for
13. to
14. for
15. from
16. by
17. with
18. with
19. of
20. of

Exercise VII. 12.

approve of	affected by	similar to	take a chance on
recover from	grateful for	suitable for	compete with
subscribe to	sympathize with	critical of	angered by
authority on	complain about	involved in	skillful in
enthusiastic about	different from		

Exercise VII. 13.
1. has been dedicated to
2. was pleased with
3. are affected by
4. will be committed to
5. have been opposed to

6. were disturbed by
7. is composed of
8. was blamed for
9. has been married to
10. were involved in

Exercise VII. 14.
1. *on*. at
2. *with*. to
3. *in the*. at
4. *for*. of
5. *by*. from
6. *at*. from
7. *in*. on
8. *with*. of
9. *with*. of
10. *for*. of
11. *for*. in
12. *to*. with
13. *about*. to
14. *for*. to
15. *about*. to
16. *to swim*. in swimming
17. *for*. of
18. *with*. in
19. *than*. from
20. *from*. about

21. *with*. to
22. *from*. of
23. *for*. like
24. *into*. with
25. *by*. with
26. *on*. with
27. *of*. for
28. *from*. for
29. *with*. to
30. *for*. with
31. *from*. by; *for*. to
32. *about*. with
33. *for*. of
34. *to produce*. from producing
35. *about*. of
36. *in*. to
37. *for*. in
38. *of*. from
39. *against*. from
40. *in spite*. in spite of

Mixed Exercise 8: Part A
1. C   Possessive pronoun
2. D   Verb word
3. B   Adjectives
4. B   Gerund with possessive
5. A   Prepositions
6. A   Verbs
7. D   Gerunds
8. D   Demonstrative pronouns
9. C   Verbs
10. D   Adverbs
11. B   Articles
12. B   Present perfect
13. A   Object pronoun

14. B   Irregular verbs
15. D   Articles
16. A   Comparative adjectives
17. C   Infinitives
18. A   Present perfect
19. D   Adjectives of equality
20. B   Two-word verbs
21. D   Adverbs
22. A   Indirect object
23. C   Nouns, present continuous passive
24. C   Prepositions
25. A   Verbs, adjective past participles

Mixed Exercise 8: Part B
1. A   me. Object pronoun
2. B   luggage. Nouns
3. B   like that of other animals. Demonstrative pronouns
4. B   washed. Causative passive
5. B   an educated man. Articles
6. C   all the other composers. Comparative of indefinite pronouns
7. A   who. Relative pronouns
8. B   by. Prepositions
9. D   pencil. Nouns
10. D   very. Adverbs
11. A   played/had played. Past perfect
12. A   whose. Possessive pronoun
13. C   himself. Reflexive pronoun
14. A   explained/explained to us. Reporting verb
15. B   has lain. Verbs
16. B   better. Comparative adjectives
17. A   excited. Adjectives
18. A   It's. Contractions

19. C   the most poorly. Adverbs with past participles
20. A   about two sisters who meet.
21. B   be. Proposal clause
22. A   who. Relative pronoun
23. C   more quickly. Adverbs
24. A   had been equipped. Past perfect
25. D   three-mile. Nouns as adjectives
26. C   primarily. Adverbs
27. B   typewriter. Possessive nouns
28. D   on. Prepositions
29. C   as well as. Adverbs
30. D   what she should do. Nominative clause
31. A   to get. Infinitive
32. A   in whose care. Relative pronouns with prepositions
33. D   we/we did. Subject pronouns
34. A   those. Demonstrative pronouns
35. A   them. Object pronoun
36. A   active. Suffixes, nouns and adjectives

SECTION VIII
Exercise VIII. 1.
1. (Jack) think. thinks
2. (a percentage) are given. is given
3. (Mary)
4. (One) have decided, has decided; (people) expresses. express
5. (effects)
6. (Rice) were served. was served
7. (chance) were. was
8. (Terry;) only one who
9. (comments)
10. (every painting) have been donated. has been donated
Exercise VIII. 2.
1. (anyone) their. his (or her)
2. (one) your. his or her
3. (Every) boy and girl his, his and her
4. no clear antecedent which. This experience
5. (Neither) they. she
6. (you) one. you
7. (many) a their. his or her
8. they. people
9. (Members) its. their
10. no clear antecedent them. the socks
Exercise VIII. 5.
(Sample conjunctions are given.)
1. She went to bed early; however, she didn't sleep well.
2. Rosa likes to read poetry; moreover, she sometimes writes her own poetry.
3. She eats only low-calorie food because she wants to remain slim.
4. Lincoln had been a successful lawyer before he became president.
5. Dr. Jenner developed a vaccine for smallpox; consequently, many people were saved.
6. I didn't carry an umbrella; as a result, I got wet.
7. Some think that he is unfriendly; on the contrary, he likes people very much.
8. Since Leo arose at 6:00 A.M., he hasn't eaten anything.
9. It's rude to keep people waiting unnecessarily; furthermore, it's a waste of valuable time.
10. We'd better hurry or else we'll miss the train.
11. While he was lecturing about the mysteries of the mind, he dropped his notes.
Exercise VIII. 7.
1. prepared prepares; left leaves
2. throws threw; runs ran; scores scored
3. tells, told; went had gone; gave gives
4. bought buy; were are
Exercise VIII. 8.
(Answers should be similar to those given below.)
2. To estimate the success of such a project, the accountant used a computer.
3. Roger, stopped for speeding, was given a ticket.
4. Drinking (or: while drinking) a cup of coffee, Tom spilled it on his homework.
5. Bill, being in a hurry, took the route through the desert.
6. The table, having been made (or: made) from cherry wood, was, I thought, beautiful.
7. Considering many items, the importer tried to find one that would sell well.
8. Liao, having reported his dog lost, is searching the city streets for him.

11. (deal;) (they)
12. (Most jewelry pieces) has been sold. have been sold
13. (To visit zoos) are, is
14. (people; income) exceed. exceeds
15. (price) have decreased. has decreased; (prices) has increased. have increased
16. (Learning) have interested. has interested
17. (Whoever) are finished. is finished
18. (ornithologists; a number) is. are
19. (Neither)
20. (Many) a have regretted. has regretted; (they)

11. (Somebody)
12. (Nobody) they. he or she
13. (Each) their, his and her
14. (rat) his. its
15. (you) you're. your
16. (assistants)
17. (mind) he. Mr. Patel
18. (dog)
19. (president) their. his
20. (she) himself. herself

12. Doctors state that exercise is beneficial; nevertheless, one should not overdo it.
13. Ingredients must be listed on food products so that people will be able to buy wisely.
14. Inasmuch as programs showing violence may be harmful to children, many parents want such programs removed from television.
15. She won't enroll next fall unless she can get a college loan.
16. Mark is a marvelous potter; as a matter of fact, many of his pieces have been shown in the Frank Lloyd Wright exhibition house.
17. The bay has become contaminated with chemicals; thus it isn't safe to eat the fish from the bay.
18. Although he slept eleven hours last night, he is still tired.

5. is afraid was afraid; has had
6. would be able will be able; used uses
7. would be featured will be featured; is a guide will be a guide; explain, will explain; learn will have learned

9. Ed believes his invention, having been considerably improved, (or: considerably improved) will be a success.
10. Before taking the test, the students were given instructions.
11. To earn extra money, Peggy had to work overtime.
12. Viewed from afar, the rock formations looked like buildings.
13. The medical advice which the clinic offered was appreciated by the patients.
14. The new airport installations were, of course, of great interest to Mr. Sjoberg, a retired pilot.

Exercise VIII. 9.

2. Formed from plants thousands of years ago, coal has been an important source of energy for the United States.
3. Rushing to find gold in 1848, people neglected their farms, families, and businesses.
4. Having read many books on raising children, Mel thought he was an expert.
5. The novel, after having been (or: after being) promoted by the publisher, sold widely.
6. Being a geologist, Sima has great knowledge of glacier movement.

7. The two men, having agreed on the price of the car, shook hands.
8. The Constitution, written after the American states had won their independence, is considered to be a remarkable historical document.
9. Being a carpenter, Carl knows how to repair his own roof.
10. An analyst for the aerospace industry, Miss Reuter will show charts demonstrating recent advances.

Exercise VIII. 10.

1. . . . file folders, and stationery.
2. . . . but she likes (she does like) raw clams.
3. . . . and then have some lunch.
4. . . . and get advice when needed.
5. . . . and Gloria was riding behind him.
6. . . . but also insulting.
7. . . . and (had) written.
8. . . . and walking.
9. . . . but he can't write it.
10. . . . dental and medical expenses.
11. . . . and to provide jobs.

12. . . . and because of having to take care of
13. . . . and prepare a program suitable for everyone.
14. . . . not to interfere with nor to worry about
15. . . . and how to determine
16. . . . is neither moderate
17. . . . but everyone can.
18. . . . both attractive and successful.
19. . . . and compose music.
20. . . . and dangerous.
21. . . . and because the prosecutors
22. . . . better than it cuts.

Exercise VIII. 11.

1. Arches, used architecturally, are both strong and beautiful.
2. An arbitrator not only listens to both sides in an argument, but also helps people come to an agreement.
3. A neutral substance is neither acidic nor alkaline.
4. Arnold will both attend graduate school and teach a class.

5. The company promised either to repair the product or to send a replacement.
6. He not only didn't receive compensation but also didn't receive any acknowledgment.
7. The play was not only excellent but also beautifully performed.

Exercise VIII. 12.

1. The senator from Iowa has announced plans to run for office again in the next election.
2. Doctor Park told us that he enjoyed ballet more than symphony music.
3. The machine may not, despite efforts to correct it, ever be without defects.
4. Not only were the streets full of holes, but also the street lights didn't work.
5. Some prints were available. Others were shown without frames.
6. Having carefully followed the procedure, Victor was disappointed when the experiment failed.
7. We noticed a woman about twenty years old sitting at the typewriter.
8. John is worried about all of the questions he will have to answer when he is at a job interview tomorrow.
9. Mr. Naro received a telegram yesterday while he was teaching.
10. Everyone enjoys the beauty of the national parks. Park guests can learn about the great variety of flora and fauna by going on guided walks with the rangers.
11. Activities will be planned for both young and mature adults.

12. When the rate for loans was lowered, an improved economy was expected.
13. Melvin spent the evening reading, listening to a new record, and reviewing the notes of his speech.
14. Gaston invited the woman who was wearing a white dress to dance with him.
15. Finally someone provided a logical solution to the problem.
16. Unable to find his way home, he used the North Star to guide him.
17. It was wonderful to see all of my friends again.
18. When he learned of his dog's death, he grew depressed.
19. After assisting in the administration of training programs, Mrs. DiCarlo was appointed as chief of staff.
20. Limericks used to be popular but they are rarely written anymore. (or: rarely are they written anymore.)
21. Before Luba signed her name, she studied the petition carefully.
22. Even though there are laws to protect consumers, there is a lack of enforcement.

Exercise VIII. 13.

(Sample answers are given.)

1. Declaring that the water levels were low after a long absence of rain, experts warned people to use less water; otherwise a serious situation could develop.
2. With three ships and a number of sailors, Columbus left Spain in 1492 to find the new route to India. Many of the

sailors on the ships, however, became frightened when there were no other ships in view, and wanted to turn back.
3. Released from jail recently, Joe can't get a job because perspective employers can see Joe's jail rec-

ord. Joe, feeling that this practice is unfair and that his jail record should be sealed, is suing the city.
4. Although the Namib Desert in Africa looks lifeless because of almost no rain, it has a number of unusual plants and animals which scientists like to study. According to scientists occasional fog that rolls in from the ocean provides the desert with moisture.

ANSWERS TO SIMULATED TOEFL TESTS

The structure and the reference to the explanation is given after each answer.

Pretest

1. D *Used to* and *would* in past tense
2. B Types of clauses and sentences. *Like* as preposition
3. D Nouns
4. C Reporting verbs
5. A Proposal clauses
6. B Past continuous
7. D Using participles and phrases
8. A Past modal
9. C Demonstrative pronouns; adjectives of equality
10. D Parallel structure
11. A Past tense with past perfect
12. B Using participles and phrases
13. A Direct speech
14. B Variation of endings
15. C Conjunctions
16. B his or her. Pronoun-antecedent agreement
17. D any other artist. Comparative of indefinite adjectives and pronouns
18. B animal. Nouns
19. A traffic. Nouns
20. A The article stated. Independent and dependent clauses

21. B were. Subject–verb agreement
22. B but also. Parallel structure
23. B usually. Adverbs
24. D thoughtfully. Parallel structure
25. A by which. Relative pronouns
26. B omit *but.* Conjunctions
27. C omit *they.* Rules of written expression
28. A built. Causative Passive
29. A whose. Relative pronouns
30. D to have been destroyed. Infinitives
31. D larger. Comparative adjectives
32. B hitting. Gerunds
33. C lying. Verbs
34. C us. Nonreflexive pronouns; Reflexive pronouns
35. B who leaped. Relative pronouns
36. C researchers say unemployment (etc.). Using participles
37. B that. *Reason* with "*that* clause" in Common Errors
38. C their. Gerund with possessive
39. A hadn't died. Conditional, past unreal
40. C from. Prepositions

Test 1.

1. C Prepositions
2. D Demonstrative pronouns
3. B Parallel structure
4. C Adverbs
5. A Proposal form
6. D Types of clauses and sentences
7. A Using participles
8. C Future perfect
9. B Tag endings
10. B Gerund construction as subject
11. D Adjectives with countable and uncountable nouns
12. B Hyphenated adjectives
13. C As if as though. Conditional present-unreal
14. D Double comparative adjectives
15. B Using participles
16. B had been. Past perfect
17. C forms. Parallel structure
18. D and. Special parallel structure
19. B privately. Adverbs
20. D can be either. Special parallel structure
21. A to. Infinitives

22. C want. Exception to present continuous
23. D economics. Nouns
24. B was getting. Establishing viewpoint
25. C had been declining. Past perfect continuous
26. D practiced/were practicing. Reporting verb
27. B are running. Subject–verb agreement
28. A hadn't. Conditional past unreal
29. A realistically. Adverbs
30. D as if. As if, conditional possible
31. B a few. Adjectives
32. A We. Subject pronouns
33. D is often discussed. Types of clauses and sentences
34. C to name. Infinitives after verbs
35. D the present. Articles
36. A was. Subject–verb agreement
37. D their. Pronoun–antecedent agreement
38. D give. Verbal forms compared
39. C so that. Conjunctions
40. D them. Pronoun–antecedent agreement

Test 2.

1. C Parallel structure
2. C Parallel structure
3. B Infinitives
4. B Literary variation in sentence order
5. D Types of sentences and clauses

6. A Infinitives
7. D Using participles; Types of clauses and sentences
8. B Types of clauses and sentences; Using participles
9. B Indirect speech
10. A Present continuous

11. B   Present perfect
12. D   Gerunds; Basic rules- avoid wordiness
13. A   Adverbs
14. A   Idioms and expressions
15. C   Verbs followed by indirect objects
16. A   nor. Neither-nor, Parallel structure
17. A   that. Nonrelative pronoun
18. D   to rise. Verbs
19. B   could cause. Conditional present-pretend
20. D   from 1937. Prepositions
21. D   purchased and sold. Passive
22. D   further. Adverbs
23. A   omit in November. Basic rules
24. B   heavily. Adverbs
25. C   has been. Present perfect

Test 3.
1. B   Verbals-comparing
2. A   Articles
3. A   Present perfect; Passive or active voice
4. D   Prepositions followed by gerunds
5. D   Types of clauses and sentences
6. B   Reporting verbs
7. A   Parallel structure
8. A   Basic rules-be direct; Modal in present time
9. B   Proposal clause
10. C   Demonstrative pronouns
11. D   Adjective and adverb with countable and uncountable nouns
12. B   Basic rules, double negative
13. B   Perfect gerund -gerund with possessive
14. C   Types of clauses and sentences
15. C   Time and conditional clauses with future
16. A   increasingly adverb
17. C   omit "additional." Basic rules-avoid repetition
18. C   less. Adjectives with countable and uncountable nouns
19. B   health. Noun and adjective suffixes, Basic rules-correct part of speech
20. A   Having sung. Using participles

Test 4.
1. B   Basic rules-active voice preferred; Parallel structure
2. C   Conjunctions-punctuation
3. D   Causative passive; Using participles
4. A   Relative pronouns; Passive
5. A   Relative pronouns
6. C   Parallel structure
7. B   Infinitives
8. D   Reporting verbs
9. C   Adjectives-forms of measure
10. B   Verbals, inifinitives
11. C   *Before* and *After* with past tense
12. D   Using participles-after time words
13. C   Basic rules-avoid slang
14. A   Prepositions
15. D   Basic rules-avoid double negatives; Adverbs-*anymore* and *yet*
16. B   half a year. Supplement-common errors
17. C   than. Comparative adjectives and adverbs
18. B   Mary. Nouns-possessive
19. D   He's usually available. Types of sentences-avoid run-on sentences
20. C   were. Subject–verb agreement

26. B   have been domesticated. Subject-verb agreement
27. C   number. Adverbs
28. C   making. Gerunds
29. A   Contradicting. Using participles
30. C   was going. Subject–verb agreement
31. A   take place. Tense consistency
32. B   whose. Relative pronoun
33. A   primarily. Adverbs
34. B   harvest. Verb word
35. A   to the police. Reporting verbs
36. B   omit *but.* Conjunctions
37. B   had chosen. Past perfect
38. C   omit *more.* Comparative adjectives
39. B   let. Verbs
40. B   from which. Relative pronoun with preposition

21. A   offices. Countable nouns
22. B   its. Pronoun–antecedent agreement
23. B   had given. Past perfect; Parallel structure
24. D   will be played. Passive voice
25. C   the worst. Comparative adjectives and adverbs
26. B   useless. Adjectives
27. B   interested. Adjectives and participles
28. C   running. Gerunds
29. A   sometimes wants. Position of frequency adverbs in present tense
30. C   who. Relative pronouns
31. C   one (*or:* he or she). Pronoun-antecedent agreement
32. B   didn't require. *Would rather,* nonproposal form
33. C   as. Prepositions
34. B   knew how to. *Know how to* in modals and expressions
35. B   has voted. Subject–verb agreement
36. D   as. Equality in adjectives and adverbs
37. D   wanted to. Infinitives in short response
38. A   travel. Establish point of view-tense consistency
39. A   impatient. Adjective with linking verb
40. B   had been. Past perfect

21. A   those. Demonstrative pronouns
22. B   address. Verbals, causative
23. C   she. Subject pronoun
24. A   realizing. Using participles
25. B   played. Past tense; Active voice
26. B   omit *from.* Relative pronoun
27. B   more than enough. Adverbs
28. D   an interesting cover. Parallel structure
29. C   prepared. Causative passive
30. C   were. Subject–verb agreement
31. A   That. Nouns-*pair*
32. C   as much as. Comparison of equality and inequality, adverbs
33. A   Considering. Types of sentences; Using participles
34. A   As carefully as. Comparative in adverbs
35. C   the most cheaply. Adverbs
36. B   objected to. Prepositions
37. D   the high price. Conjunctions, because
38. C   called. Past tense
39. D   everyone else. Comparative of adjectives and pronouns
40. D   many factories had been built. Types of clauses, sentence order

Index

*The letters *ae.* stand for *avoid errors.* Many points in the text appear under the heading of *avoid errors.*

**The letter *n.* stands for *note.* Many points in the text are emphasized after the word *note.*